D1049133

From the Ground Up

Essays on Grassroots and Workplace Democracy by C. George Benello

With Commentaries by Harry Boyte, Steve Chase,
Walda Katz-Fishman, Jane Mansbridge,
and Chuck Turner

Foreword by Dimitri Roussopoulos

Edited by Len Krimerman, Frank Lindenfeld,
Carol Korty, and Julian Benello

South End Press
Boston, Massachusetts

Cover design by Sheila Walsh
Text design and production by Steve Chase
Printed in the U.S.A.
First edition, first printing

Library of Congress Cataloging-in-Publication Data

Benello, C. George
    From the ground up: essays on grassroots and workplace democracy/by C. George Benello; with commentaries by Harry Boyte...[*et al.*]; forward by Dimitri Roussopoulos; edited by Len Krimerman...[*et al.*].— 1st ed.
    p. cm.
    Includes bibliographical references and index.
    ISBN 0-89608-390-X (cloth): $30.00. ISBN 0-89608-389-6 (paper): $12.00
    1. Political participation—United States. 2. Community power— United States. 3. Management—United States—Employee participation. 4. Libertarianism—United States. I. Boyte, Harry Chatten, 1945-   . II. Krimerman, Len. III. Title.
    JK1764.B44 1992   91-28535
    323'.042'0973—dc20   CIP

South End Press, 116 Saint Botolph Street, Boston, MA 02115
    98 97 96 95 94 93 92   1 2 3 4 5 6 7 8 9

Table of Contents

Part V: Commentaries

Part VI: Editors' Afterword

A Mind Like A Furnace

Dimitri Roussopoulos

George Benello must be remembered, first and foremost, as an anarchist. Erudite and widely read in the anarchist tradition, he was drawn above all to anarchism because this philosophy was most useful regarding the key questions: how should society and its economy be organized; how should human beings live together?

George and I were teaching at Goddard College in the mid-1960s when we first met. We were drawn together like magnets. I recognized in him what I sought for myself—a balance between critical social theorizing and the application of theoretical insights in practice. Hence, our many intellectual discussions were connected to concrete projects that cried out to be organized from alpha to omega. George had a wonderfully synthetic mind: he would quickly zero-in on the essence of another writer's contribution to the clarification of a question and then meld this with yet another writer's insights. The end result was an up-to-date overview of the latest literature on the topic being investigated. His restless personality was crowned with a mind that can best be characterized as a furnace, connected to this or that motor depending on his interest at the time. This furnace had to be constantly fed with sources of energy, large or small, rough or smooth. He had a rare intellectual quality which made an exchange exciting. Whenever I would tear apart one of his ideas, in the heat of such an exchange (as perhaps only an Italian and Greek could partake), George would simply put the new pieces together and work through the thought again. This rare quality was generous, patient, and completely without an egoistic center. Once an idea was reshaped, I would rush it into print.

This was the time (late 1960s) when the "New Left" was going through a decisive period of self-redirection. George and I went to work trying to influence the next decade's theory and practice on the pivotal question of organization. Together we edited *The Case for Participatory Democracy: Some Prospects for a Radical Society* (published in paperback by Vintage). The contributors were George Woodcock, Rosabeth Moss Kanter, Murray Bookchin, Gerry Hunnius, Colin Ward, and many others.

This effort attempted to introduce the anarchist tradition into the debates about the future of social movements arising in industrial societies. The anthology included two of George's early essays. It was well received and must have contributed to the shape of social protest in the 1970s.

In the spring of 1967, George joined the editorial board of *Our Generation,* a magazine I founded in the mid-1960s and which is still being published in Montreal, Canada. Shortly after joining the magazine, he moved to Montreal and his presence there led to a period of close and fertile collaboration. George and I helped the journal undertake the publication of numerous articles and reviews about anarchism in its many diverse forms. By the fall of that year, we published George's classic essay, "Wasteland Culture: New Political Sociology." (See Part I below.) This essay was very widely discussed, and its influence on restructuring social life and on the whole emerging strategy for social change was significant. In our Spring 1968 issue, we published responses to George's essay by a variety of New Left activists in Canada and the United States, as well as by some well known anarchists. "Wasteland Culture" was subsequently republished in several books on political sociology.

George's anarchist approach also made him one of the most incisive critics of Marxism. His contributions here updated the anarchist critique of Marxism by focusing on such weak flanks as the Marxist account of the psychology of power, the organizational problem, and the theory of human nature. These were all exposed in his essay, (reprinted in Part II) "The Conflicting Traditions of Anarchism and Marxism."

In subsequent years, after George returned to the United States, a country and culture which he understood well and about which he offered some of his most compelling criticism, our collaboration waned.

However, in the early 1980s, when I circulated the idea of founding a network of anarchist writers, researchers, and teachers, George was one of the eager enthusiasts. Helping to found *Anarchos Institute* in Montreal in the spring of 1982, he remained committed to the idea and loyal to its objectives throughout its varied phases. Through *Anarchos*, both of us sponsored and helped organize the well attended international Venice gathering of some 3,000 anarchists interacting with the theme of Orwell's *1984*.

George and I were proud of our history as anarchists, inquisitive about the world, conscious of its problems, open to doubts and challenges. This pride was strong enough to accept revisions, yet modest enough to consider the real issues faced by men and women in today's world. Our common conviction was that society must be changed: specifically, that domination and hierarchy in all their forms must be abolished.

This anarchist conviction is shared, in great measure, by new movements of protest and resistance which have arisen during the past three decades throughout the industrial world. These movements are concerned with such diverse issues as the international military buildup, ecology, the status of women, students, and youth, the poor and unemployed, gay rights, the homeless, racial and ethnic discrimination, imperialist interventions by super-power blocs, and the deterioration of our cities and consequent loss of community. In all, they have involved many millions of people.

Common to most of these movements is a fundamental opposition to domination and exploitation. Their dynamism has opened up new regions of both theory and practice, questioning and transforming previous notions of radical social change, including those of Marxism. But as yet, they have given rise to no prevailing counter-theory of power and structural change—and here is where the present volume can prove to be of great use. For George's major contribution was to construct and to test in practice just such a counter-theory. This is the anarchist theory of grassroots empowerment and local self-reliance, with its emphasis on face-to-face democratic decision-making throughout *all* social institutions: in the family, the workplace, community and global politics. This theory is the thread which runs from his early analysis of the "wasteland culture" (Part I) through his more theoretical accounts of social organization and transformation (Part II), to his practical writings concerning the road to democracy at work (Part III), and his final Green-leaning essays on sustainable and decentralized strategies for making global peace more attainable.

Any realistic analysis must include the possibility of near total failure in attempts made to change society so that the planet may survive. However, given its present contradictions, the current world system of nation states and patriarchal institutions may well collapse just when it seems most stable. In the chaotic scramble that would follow, new social directions may become possible. Such a situation would hold promise for those who, like George Benello, believe in self-management based on local initiative, direct democracy in all spheres of life, and a libertarian commonwealth. A new sensibility, with many affinities to anarchism and self-management, has been percolating over the last three turbulent decades. *From the Ground Up* has much to offer to this sensibility and to all of those who seek a realistic and grassroots alternative to the established power structures and their disempowering assumptions.

Notes On A Practical Utopian

The Editors

To those of us who put together this commemorative anthology of C. George Benello's essays, George was more than a political visionary. We knew him as a modern Renaissance man. Indeed, George was an artist, inventor, sports enthusiast, entrepreneur, navigator, peace activist, philosopher, writer, educator, and administrator. He studied at a Japanese Zen monastery, recorded Japanese music, and exhibited a one person show of his Sumi ink paintings in Tokyo. He produced programs for listener-sponsored radio station KPFA in the San Francisco Bay area on topics as diverse as Japanese music and peace issues. He loved sailing and was a keen tennis player. He invented a lightweight three-wheel car, the Arrow. He traveled widely and spoke Italian, French, Japanese, and Polish. He was also a dear friend, mate, and father.

George is perhaps best known, however, as a visionary thinker whose writings powerfully influenced the New Left of the 1960s, the workplace democracy movement of the 1970s, and the budding Green movement in the 1980s. His previous publications include two books he co-edited, *The Case for Participatory Democracy* (1971), and *Readings in Humanist Sociology* (1985). His articles and essays, the best of which are reprinted in this anthology, appeared earlier in such movement journals as *New University Thought, Manas, Anarchy, Liberation, Peace News, Humanity and Society, Changing Work, Black Rose,* and *Our Generation.*

George, however, was an organizer as well as a theorist. Above all, he believed in putting his ideas to the test of practical implementation. In 1962, for example, George was part of a crew that sailed into a South

Pacific nuclear test zone to protest the testing of atomic weapons. He served as the New England coordinator of Turn Toward Peace, was a member of the Executive Committee of the War Resisters League, and served on the advisory board of the New England Committee for Non-Violent Action. He was particularly influential in the development of the movement for workplace democracy in the United States. He served as Executive Director of the short-lived Federation for Economic Democracy, which gave birth to two major technical assistance organizations: the Boston-based Industrial Cooperative Association and PACE, the Philadelphia Association for Cooperative Enterprise.

George was also an educator and publisher. During 1965-1969 he was Director of Adult Education and Professor of Sociology at Goddard College in Plainfield, Vermont. Some years later he was Coordinator of the Five College Project on Economic Participation and Self-Management and Adjunct Professor in the School of Social Science at Hampshire College in Amherst, Massachusetts. George also helped to further nurture radical social thought and activism by serving on the editorial board of *Our Generation* and of *Current*. He was a founder and contributing editor of *Changing Work* magazine. He was also an active participant in the Association for Humanist Sociology and a founding member of the *Anarchos Institute*, which organized anarchist conferences.

Surveying all of it, George's life, work, and thought exhibit an unusual and comprehensive consistency. He was a philosopher, educator, and an activist who wrote about and practically promoted the implementation of his concerns for peace, social justice, local self-reliance, and economic democracy. He served as an inspiration to many organizers active today in the social movements which have emerged in North America and elsewhere over the last thirty years.

The Contours of Benello's Social Thought

One connecting thread that runs through George's work is his libertarian decentralist perspective: a concern with the negative effects of over-centralized power and a vision of a participatory, democratic alternative to big government and big business. As Dimitri Roussopoulos points out in his preface to this book, George wrote within the anarchist tradition of such thinkers as Pierre Proudhon, Peter Kropotkin, Lewis Mumford, Emma Goldman, Paul Goodman, and Murray Bookchin.

For George, anarchism meant resolute opposition to big government, corporate capitalism, and state militarism all of which he saw as interconnected forms of hierarchical and undemocratic power. Indeed, as can be seen in this book, he was a fierce and insightful critic of the hierarchical, authoritarian model of organization that is pervasive throughout our culture.

Yet, anarchism meant more than critique to George. It also meant a vision for political decentralization, economic democracy, and psychological development. While he never fully elaborated or systematized his visionary ideas, George's anarchist outlook led him to a utopian vision of a society no longer dominated by either giant corporations or the state. Underlying his thought is the need to decentralize the state into small-scale, semi-autonomous units, federated through various political mechanisms. He believed strongly in localism, and in political decentralization based on participatory democracy. This, in fact, was part of his prescription for the revitalization of American cities destroyed by the combined onslaught of de-industrialization and neo-conservative policies directed against the poor.

The other key thread in George's writings is his concern with means: how best to achieve the utopian goals of political decentralization and economic democracy. Unlike those anarchists and Marxist revolutionaries who espouse a strategy of armed struggle against centralized institutions, George rejected political violence because of his deeply felt sense that the means we use in our struggles for change crucially influence the outcome of our struggles. Yet, for all of his cautions about "revolutionism," he did not turn to the reformist strategies of conventional liberals and progressives as an alternative. As an anarchist, George was very critical of conventional national politics. While not ruling out electoral strategies completely, he de-emphasized them in favor of a participatory politics of direct action, political education, and alternative institution building.

Arguably, George focused his most creative energies on developing a practical strategy for building models and precursors of the new society in the here and now. He believed the existence of working models of alternative institutions joined into interconnected networks could help convince people of the desirability of fundamental social change, provide an ongoing "school" for learning the skills of participatory democracy, and meet peoples' immediate needs that are currently neglected or distorted by corporations and the State.

In particular, George believed that promoting the spread of democratic organization to the workplace was one of the best ways to focus our organizing efforts because so much of our culture and society is dominated by the influence of the giant hierarchical corporations. George frequently pointed to the Mondragon cooperative network in the Basque region of Spain because it exemplified a thriving model of workplace democracy in practice.

The major emphasis of his work at the time of his death was actively promoting the formation of technical assistance groups that would encourage and help ensure the success of newly formed democratic workplaces. He believed that, when organized into networks similar to the cooperatives associated with the Workers Bank in the Basque area of Spain, the spread of participatory democratic organizations would have a large ripple effect. The existence of functioning models of alternatives would demonstrate that democracy at work is possible, even profitable, and feels better to most workers than top-down models. This, he felt, would go a long way towards enticing people away from hierarchical corporations as more and more jobs become available in self-managed industries. On the practical level it would also make more possible the emergence of self-reliant, semi-autonomous local communities. Such communities would be based on an involved, empowered local citizenry, and would embody the principles of social justice, economic equality, ecological sustainability, and peace. In this way, George thought it would be possible to reconstruct our society into a decentralized, participatory democratic one, working from the ground up.

George was not a productivist, however, focused only on the workplace. Indeed, he had many exciting, yet practically realizable, proposals for mobilizing entire communities around a program of renewal. His proposals include such daring ideas as promoting local self-reliance by using local currency, declaring nuclear free zones, and encouraging local import substitution and energy production. As the essays in this book attest, George Benello was a practical utopian and holistic visionary.

How This Book Is Organized

George had long intended to publish an edited collection of his best political essays on grassroots and workplace democracy. He was kept from doing this, however, because he was too busy with the practical implementation of his ideas. We have chosen to complete this project of George's in order to make his perspective and wisdom available for a younger and wider audience within today's social movements for peace, justice, and ecological sanity.

The articles included in this collection were, of course, written at various times in George's life over a span of twenty-five years and each one was originally intended to stand alone. Readers thus may well find it rewarding to begin with any essay or section of the book that most interests them. We have, however, tried to identify the developmental logic of the essays and combine them in such a way as to draw out the full implications of George's thought. Instead of organizing George's writings chronologically, we have organized these essays around four major themes: 1) the decentralism needed for any viable politics of the future; 2) an exploration of the different theories of community empowerment; 3) practical ideas on how to bring democracy into the workplace; and 4) some key strategic proposals for returning democratic power to our local communities.

To further explore the relevance of these ideas for social movements in the 1990s, we have invited a number of contemporary thinkers and activists who worked with George—or were influenced by his work—to critically comment on the essays that appear in the first four sections of the book. Section five thus includes commentary pieces by Jane Mansbridge, Walda Katz-Fishman, Chuck Turner, Steve Chase, and Harry Boyte who critically assess George's ideas from a variety of vantage points. (The commentaries of both Turner and Boyte are based on interviews conducted by Len Krimerman.)

These people add a variety of important perspectives to the book. Jane Mansbridge, a social theorist at Northwestern University, has written extensively about issues relating to organizations, power, and democracy. Walda Katz-Fishman, who teaches sociology at Howard University, was co-editor with George of *Readings in Humanist Sociology*, and worked with him in the Association for Humanist Sociology. Chuck Turner is an African-American community activist and educator who worked closely with George in the Industrial Cooperative Association. Steve Chase, a co-founder of the Green Committees of Correspondence and the Left Green Network, most recently edited the influencial *Defending the Earth: A Dialogue Between Murray Bookchin and Dave Foreman*. Harry Boyte, author of numerous books on grassroots democracy, is Director of Project Public Life at the University of Minnesota's Hubert H. Humphrey Institute of Public Affairs and is a key theorist of the new populist citizen movements. Following the commentaries is an editors' afterword which assesses their arguments and offers a response to them based on an analysis of George's unique contributions to decentralist thought.

In an effort to preserve the historical integrity of George's writings, we have updated the language of his essays with a very light hand. We have, however, sometimes added passages and even entire sections from essays not chosen for publication to the essays published here. We have done this whenever it helped clarify or deepen George's perspective for the reader. For those who would like to know the source of these additions, bibliographic information appears at the end of each chapter. The years the essays were originally written have also been included after the title of each chapter. In lieu of extensive foot notes, we have included a complete bibliography of George's writings, works cited in his essays, and some relevent works which have appeared since his death.

Acknowledgements

There are many people who helped make this book possible. After George's sudden and untimely death in 1987, several friends decided to prepare this commemorative anthology. George's son Julian, who was then in his mid-20s, was in the middle of helping with this project when he was killed in the 1988 explosion of Pan Am flight 103 over Lockerbie, Scotland. This volume is dedicated to both George and Julian Benello. In particular, we gratefully acknowledge Julian Benello's help in the initial stages of assembling this anthology of his father's work.

We also wish to thank the many friends of *Changing Work* whose efforts enabled that magazine to publish its Winter 1988 Benello memorial issue; some of the articles from that publication are reprinted here. Editorial and production workers for that issue, in addition to the editors of this book, were Frank Adams, John Brightly, Severyn Bruyn, Anthony Esposito, Denis Filipetti, David and Eva Gil, Peter Kardas, Nancy Kellerman, Clara Kozol, and Lin Nelson. The word processing for publication of the present manuscript was provided by Gisele Tobin at Diversified Computer Services and Bill Montrose volunteered his able proofreading skills.

Thanks are especially due to Dimitri Roussopoulos, Jane Mansbridge, Walda Katz Fishman, Chuck Turner, Steve Chase, and Harry Boyte for their essays and interviews which are included in this volume. Their work has added much to the vitality and timeliness of the book. But above all, we want to send out our very deep appreciation and admiration to Steve Chase, our editor *extraordinaire* at South End Press. Steve was strongly supportive when this project needed support and constructively critical when the manuscript demanded it. In virtually every way, our book has been touched by, and is the better for, his sharp editorial skills and sound political vision—from design to substance, from wording to organization. Finally, it seems more than fitting that these essays on grassroots and workplace democracy be published by a worker-managed collective that embodies so many of George's ideas.

Part I

The Need to Decentralize

Chapter 1

We Are Caught in a Wasteland Culture (1967)

> I sat upon the shore fishing with the arid plain behind me.
> Shall I at least set my lands in order?
> —T. S. Eliot, "The Wasteland"

A People-Killing Culture

We live in a people-killing culture, and, if we use the term culture in its anthropological sense, there is good basis for saying that primitive South Sea Island cultures are considerably more advanced than our own machine-dominated society. What is implied is that there are certain psychological and ecological universals—laws which define the conditions under which human growth and self-realization can take place, no matter what the level of technology. The material conditions of culture may change and evolve, but the basic conditions under which the primacy of the person can be affirmed do not. We live in a society today in which both the scale and structure of human organization represent forces powerfully opposed to the possibility of human growth and freedom. But the sheer momentum of the organizational and technological apparatus makes for acceptance, and so we content ourselves with attempts at internal adjustment while the juggernaut rolls on.

The majority of approaches to socio-cultural criticism focus either on alienation as the primary characteristic of advanced industrial societies or on domination and exploitation, if the emphasis is economic rather than psychosocial. The first, however, is primarily a psychological category and fails to show how different sectors of society exhibit more or less of it. Moreover, it describes a condition but not its psychosocial and structural causes. The second category too easily leads to a devil theory or leaves us with a view of human nature and social structure that sees domination and exploitation as innate. Basing itself either on psychoanalytic or Christian versions of original sin, the second approach is a dogma of liberals and "realistic" politicians alike which effectively blocks significant change. Both conditions exist as powerful forces in society. The problem first of all is to see them not as metaphysically ordained—with the Absurd as the root cause of all alienation or Human Evil as the root cause of exploitation—but rather as conditions deeply rooted in a particular, albeit pervasive, dynamic. The problem secondly is to understand the dynamic in which both alienation and exploitation exist as interactive and related features.

The Ontong Javanese call a person poor not when s/he is lacking in material goods, but when s/he lacks the requisite of shared living. When one lacks family, working partners, or intimate friends, one is then considered poor. The notion here is of psychic deprivation. We shall use the term *loss of affectivity* to signify this and understand affectivity to mean something like libido or Eros, recalling such psychoanalytic studies of civilization as *Life Against Death* by Norman O. Brown, and *Eros and Civilization* by Herbert Marcuse. Affectivity is the energy available to carry on the purposes of the individual in society. It inheres in social institutions and is generated through personal interaction under the conditions of stability, trust, and belief in the possibilities of collaboration for common purpose.

Psychic Scarcity and the Loss of Wholeness

The Wasteland Culture is described poetically by T. S. Eliot in "The Wasteland," "The Hollow Men," and in other poems of that period. To switch to an economic metaphor, we live in an economy of *psychic scarcity*, wherein there is a net lowering of affectivity throughout the culture. The face-to-face associations which Robert Nisbet, George Homans, Charles H. Cooley, and the cultural anthropologists speak of as constituting the nuclear structure of society, its basic building blocks, have lost their functional relevance, being dissociated from the big organizations which are the locus of politics and power. Thus, to continue the economic metaphor, the primary associations which when healthy are the producer centers of affectivity have been displaced within the social structure and what results is an economy of psychic scarcity.

When large organizations utilize human energy resources, they are drained away from the other spheres of family, local community, church, leisure and cultural activities. We must modify this by noting that it is the spheres indicated that produce energy in the form of affectivity. If other spheres existed which restored the balance, we would then at least have equilibrium. But the large organizations, as we shall see, are sterile, and their huge physical productivity is at the expense of the creation of a psychic surplus.

Not simply riches, but psychic rewards inhere at the top of a narrow pyramid. Thus people flee from the barren base of the wasteland culture and scramble up the various status hierarchies to where the psychic plenty is. The success ethic is thus a structural product of the wasteland culture. The vertically organized, high-rise society characterized by big organizations with their status hierarchies becomes fundamentally power-ridden, since only through power can the elements of psychic plenty be achieved. As a result the contemporary ideology of organization—for this is what we have in its full-fledged glory, and this is what must be changed—glorifies the *status quo* in all its anti-human splendor. As Paul Goodman put it in *People or Personnel*, people are personnel, to be fitted to the purposes of the organization. Moreover, in the pyramid organization is coterminous with compulsion; where compulsion does not exist, organization is impossible, and where compulsion is unnecessary, organization is also not required.

The wasteland culture thus constitutes a power-ridden system. The important purposes of the society are carried out by large organizations which are densely organized at the top into interlocking directorates. The members of the directorate see each other at work and at play, as community figures or as business or political leaders. They operate the committees, boards of trustees, cabinets, and other forms of face-to-face associations which are the inevitable forms in which decision-making takes place. The lives of the members of these groups are rendered meaningful, and their effectiveness is heightened, through the graded relevance and integration of the fundamental spheres of work, leisure, public, and private life.

As we go down the vertically organized ladder of these establish-ments, we find that the density of intensive structure soon gives way to a machine form of organizing. Work is specialized, and jobs are narrowly defined according to a set of procedures. As a result there is little chance for an integration of purposes and functions within the work, and less chance still for an overall integration of work with the other spheres of living.

It is the corporation, moreover, which determines prices, profits, the where and how of production, and how resources of the land will be allocated. In short, it determines to a basic degree the environment we live in. The public sector is not driven by profits but uses the same hierarchical model of organization as the corporation, and is likewise an inefficient system, in terms of productivity and use of personnel. The rigidity, hierarchy, and rewards of this system discourage innovation and involvement in work.

The real reasons for the present structure are discernible though hidden. The organizations are power-ridden, and thus the purpose of the system is not efficiency as such, but *efficiency of control.* We live in a society in which power is to a high degree co-ordinated, not in a terrorist political fashion but rather in a manipulative, economic-techno-logical fashion. In a society dominated by machine production, the machine becomes the most effective instrument for political control within the society. Exploitation goes on behind a facade of bureaucratic administration wherein power is concealed, distant, and highly ration-alized.

Communities are built to fit into the demands of the highway system which in turn is determined by the demands of Detroit rather than of rationality; foreign policy is determined by the stages in the develop-ment of weapons systems and in the meanwhile the landscape degen-erates into urban chaos. In its external effects, the organizational style has destroyed the integrity of the nuclear units of the society. A number of studies, summarized in Maurice Stein's *Eclipse of Community,* docu-ment this erosion, as does Homans' study of the history of Hilltown, a New England community. As the big organizations have drawn off life and energies from the communities where people live, a wasteland culture has emerged.

It is the big organizations which socialize and determine values now, rather than the communities where people live, with their structure of local organizations—town meeting, church, grange, and so forth. The result is manipulative, power-ridden people. The split between the administrator and the professional is exacerbated and built in, and the wasteland culture is institutionalized in big organizations through inequitable distribution of the scarce values of prestige and power, which cluster disproportionately at the top. While professionals derive satisfaction predominantly from their work, administrators derive satisfaction from the control of people within the organizational apparatus. In short, they are politicians, but authoritarian ones. They are the Riesman's "other-directed" people, attuned to personal nuances, molding themselves in the image of those above them. They believe in authority figures and are submissive to them, while in turn deriving satisfaction from the exercise of authority over those beneath themselves. They are conventional and unquestioning, and also hostile and aggressive, but tend to displace their hostility onto those inferior to themselves, or onto outgroups. They downgrade emotions, which they view as a sign of softness.

There is a circular reinforcement between the conditions of affective deprivation in the family which produces the power-centered, manipulative personality and the authoritarian, power-ridden organization of society. The society trains and socializes children to want what the society can provide, creating personality types oriented to the values that are prevalent. But the origins of the power orientation in affective deprivation should show us that psychosocially it is the high rise, power-ridden *structure* of society that must be changed, not simply the exploiters who inhabit the top. If people happily join in the scramble up the status ladder to power, it is not universal human nature that drives them, but rather a fundamental reaction to an environment of psychic scarcity.

The fragmentation of the spheres of work and leisure, family and public life, destroys what Keniston has called the deep psychic need for wholeness. Growth and realization involve a central process of dynamic unification. Affectivity can expand from narcissism to broader involvement only when the basic spheres of life are objectively interrelated.

The Organization Is The Problem

We are still tied to a liberal-progressive tradition which holds that, if we but liberate humanity from its chains of exploitation, it will simply fall into Utopia. We seem to share the Marxist belief that to look too closely at the shape of the good society is utopian, which means unrealistic. But as Martin Buber pointed out, it is the faith in revolution as solving all problems that is naive, not the effort to create paradigms of the future. Without the outlines of the desired society already in evidence, revolution becomes simply the replacement of one set of elites with others. The all-important element that was reintroduced into politics by the New Left is Utopian vision. If the Great Depression of the thirties is symptomatic of what the Communist vision spoke to, the rapidly growing alienation of the wasteland culture of the sixties was equally symptomatic of the need for a new vision. The old vision spoke to the visible facts of exploitation in its crudest form: millions out of work and an economy that was crumbling. The contradictions in the system were obvious and its failure was basic: it simply failed to work. But the requirements of the new vision are different. It is not that the system fails to work, for it works all too well, and in the process grinds up human beings. Domination and exploitation have retreated behind the smooth facade of administration, and thus the problem is to give resistance a proper object. But if it is the basic organization style and structure that is the problem, then the objective must be to create a different style and structure.

The basic problem is the problem of organization. Organization is power, which is what politics is about. All organization is ultimately political, and so the problem is to counter organized power with organization, but with a different *kind* of organization and a different *kind* of power. Both institutional change and attitude change are needed. The answer lies in a changed infra-structure where human association is a matter of face-to-face groups living and working together. Both the heart as well as the organizational form are involved.

The problem is to develop an approach to change which takes into account both social structure and human nature. One-sided approaches to change do rebound into something worse than before: the French Revolution led to the Reign of Terror; the Russian Revolution led to Stalinism and the purges.

The decentralists—Paul Goodman, Lewis Mumford, Ralph Borsodi, Erich Fromm, and others—have argued for a fundamentally altered approach to the problem of organization. But to speak of decentralizing skews the perspective slightly. What is needed is a change in organizational form. Organization is power only for those sectors of the organization which are involved in face-to-face communication—as at the top—where decision-making in its full dimensions takes place: proposing, planning, deciding, and testing. The need is to spread this form throughout the entire organizational structure. Given the structure, the functions must follow.

Egalitarian and Group-Based Organization

What would be the structure and values of egalitarian organization? It is based on groups, rather than the individual as the nuclear unit. People are not simply socialized in primary association; their basic identity is inseparable from those primary groups. Where the present organizational style creates a mass of personnel fixed in special pigeonholes and a status hierarchy with an elite in control at the top, the alternate style would create groups which communicate both vertically and horizontally through a system of delegates whose power is limited by the groups they represent. Structure and function interrelate, and thus the values that flow from such a structure would be in accord with it. Since decision, control, and power are distributed throughout the organization, the dichotomy between the professional, job-oriented and the status, administration-oriented would disappear; authority would not be dissociated from function. Economic reward, presently tied to a system of status hierarchy so as to reinforce it, would give way to a more egalitarian system of rewards. With power distributed throughout the organization, there would be no scrambling for status positions, where the power is. This in turn would reinforce the work orientation, since evaluation of achievement would be based on how well the job is done, not on ability at inter-office or inter-organizational politics. Authority would be rational, since based on professional capacity.

The psychological effect on the individual would be to increase both freedom and involvement, rather than one at the expense of the other. Where work based on financial reward reinforces self-seeking individualism and encourages a passive orientation toward authority, work based on functional incentives reinforces responsibility, co-operativeness, and involvement. With self-fulfillment through pride in work—Veblen's instinct of craftsmanship—and from joint endeavor, many of the conflicts between free enterprise and overall planning on the macro-economic level will be lessened. The worker as producer would not be dissociated from the worker as consumer, or the worker as community member, and thus the project of integrating work more fully with the other spheres of living will become possible. This would occur as the "needs" of the productive enterprise become identified with the needs of all its members, since its members after all form the society.

Strategy of Change: Offering a Counter-Community

If we can agree that the primary problem in advanced industrial society is the problem of organization and how it works, then we have already taken a large step toward determining how to go about changing it. The quickest way is also the shortest way. At the heart of the present ideology of organization is an image which is strongly dystopian, wherein human possibility is seen as confined totally within the vast economic-technical structures set off against it. This one-dimensionality, as Herbert Marcuse calls it, serves to define a pervasive ethos which tends to limit thought as well as action. Change must strike at the heart of this, and for this to happen, it is not enough to agitate and lecture. People must experience the implications of a different ideology. Thus rather than seeking to tinker with existing organizations, since it is the structure and ideology which must be changed, it is better to build from scratch.

At the top of the present organizational structures, there is a degree of community. But on the other levels the pseudo-community that prevails palls when confronted with the real thing. Thus any organization that seeks seriously to work for change must be capable of offering a vision of an empowering counter-community. The pervasiveness of the reigning ideology gives it a specious power: its basic failure to satisfy and be functional is masked from view because there is nothing else on the horizon. People do not opt out in general because there is nowhere to go. Those at the top have their community and power, but for the rest, the wasteland culture is fundamentally repressive. But people have grown cynical; having invested energy in the present system with minimal rewards, they are not about to listen to mere promises. Thus there is the need to create alternative structures.

Attitudes, and thus beliefs, are formed and also changed at the level where people interact directly with one another—in cells, chapters, or groups. There is now arising, in fact, a sort of movement toward therapeutic communities where people join together in such face-to-face groups to benefit from mutual openness, honesty, and an ethic of mutual aid. Such openness and self-disclosure is essential for human growth. Three levels are involved in the process of change. Groups must be created which function as therapeutic communities, where members are expected to live, not merely talk about, the values of openness, honesty, co-operation, deriving from a less dystopian view of human nature, based on the primacy of the person. But for this to happen the vision must be made clear: the goal is a society organized in such a fashion that the basic activities of living are carried out through organizations whose style and structure mirror the values sought for. But again, just as within the groups, the objective is to live the values, so the broad social objectives must be demonstrated, not preached. The movement for change must seek to mobilize the resources that can actually create the alternative structures of work, education, community living, communication, that are seen as representing the values of openness, psychological freedom, and participation.

Traditionally the project of intensive organization into cells, chapters, and other forms of face-to-face groups has been the prerogative of conservative groups or of totalitarian regimes. The Birch Society on the far right, mimicking the secret cell organization of the Communist Party during the days of the International, used it. But the early Christian Church also used it during the period of communistic Christianity, before the time that it developed its own organizational hierarchy of bishops. The church also used public or group confession, another feature which parallels the psychology of openness adhered to by modern therapeutic communities.

In Japan, a similarly patterned organization, the Soka Gakkai, or Value Creating Academy, has a political arm (Komeito, the Clean Government Party) which is the third largest political party in Japan today. It too has a cell structure involving a maximum of ten households and derives from a neo-Buddhist tradition which in its own way effectively combines the Yogi and the Commissar, by explicitly preaching that both social change and individual change are necessary.

The Soka Gakkai sees society as decadent and competitive, and explicitly demands a new morality of its members: cooperation, mutual involvement, responsibility for one another. What results is an organization that is the envy of the unions, the political parties and the churches, with a [1967] membership close to ten million, one-tenth the population of Japan, and with an unparalleled commitment from its members, exemplified in proselytizing fervor and fund-raising capacity. Members of a cell receive financial assistance when required and come to feel great solidarity with their group. Community is fostered by all manner of singing groups, discussion groups, dance groups, and cultural groups.

As the movement develops and enlists members and the resources of money and human skills, it must seek to achieve take-off: the stage where it can begin to build significant paradigms that challenge the style and structure of existing institutions. At this stage there will develop a powerful reinforcing process which should give great impetus to the movement. There will be a process of mutual reinforcement and interaction between the three basic levels described above where change is taking place: *first*, the level of changed human relationships wherein openness, honesty, and cooperation take the place of manipulation, dishonesty, and selfishness. The direct existential satisfaction derived from groups acting as therapeutic communities will become evident and will thus clarify the meaning of goals and programs. *Second*, as resources become available for the creation of definite projects, concrete and definite achievements will give embodiment and meaning to both the group experience and the goals. *Third*, because the vision is a total one, rather than centered on specific issues and problems, projects of many sorts will reinforce the vision: co-operative schools, day care centers, community unions, newspapers, radio, and later producer enterprise. As the projects grow, the organization will gain associational density: associations of schools, mass media, community projects, and so forth.

Wholeness in living is in fact a product of the objective interaction and interpenetration of the basic spheres of human existence. When one is lucky enough to be able to realize in one's personal behavior values which are also exemplified in one's daily work and for which there exists an articulated vision embracing all of social life, then one can be said to be living wholly.

Is This a Totalitarian Movement?

The objection is raised by those imbued with a liberal ideology that such a movement is totalitarian. By virtue of its own extensive organization, its overall goals, its capacity to call forth commitment, it can create true believers. The answer to this must be given on four levels. First, for the individual, the process that should take place is precisely the freeing from authoritarianism and the recognition of the importance of personal participation. Second, if we are speaking of the totalitarianism of the group, evidence indicates that groups which are democratic in structure must confront the deep-seated authority problems of their members and that this is one of the dominant features of group process. When, with capable assistance, they do so effectively, what emerges is group leadership.

Third, if we are speaking of the totalitarianism of the organization, the answer is that its goal is not, like the Birch Society, to infiltrate and take over existing structures, but to create its own. A major task will be to develop a truly democratic structure for the organization or organizations seeking to achieve change. Fourth, if we turn to the idea framework, there is nothing totalitarian in having an ideology of organization, since we have one already. It all depends on which ideology. Opponents of participatory democracy argue that it is totalitarian because it requires the participation of everyone, thus denying the freedom of non-participation. Not so; although where there are group tasks, then group participation in managing the task will be expected, since a theory of participation must be based on the primacy of groups as the nuclear decision-making units.

The nuclear units of the new organization must show by their operation that the ideology they are committed to is one which asserts the primacy of the person. Given this, the initiation of the process of integration on the primary level can begin: the demonstration that there can be an integration rather than an inevitable conflict between working together in a primary association and asserting the primacy of the person. The dialectic of this process is a continuing one, wherein the group as it accepts new members confronts its own problems as well and grows toward solidarity.

The primary stage in the growth toward solidarity is a cathartic one, wherein frustrations which have had no outlet and have been repressed and de-repressed, are raised to the level of consciousness. Group members must be encouraged to speak out, releasing pent up frustrations and bitterness. An historical example of the successful use of this method is the Chinese "speak bitterness" groups used at the beginning of the Revolution to enable farmers and other oppressed to give vent to their bitterness and frustrations against the landlords, war lords, and others who exploited them. People who have achieved no compensatory method of dealing with alienation, such as opting out, internalize their condition and see it as something for which they are to blame. They see their loneliness as a result of their own failings and thus to their loneliness is added guilt. But when neighbors are organized into groups and experience small successes in changing the conditions of their neighborhood, the sense of powerlessness and loneliness gives way to solidarity and a sense that something can be done.

It is significant that in both the Soka Gakkai and the Birch Society there was no charismatic figure who molded their followers into a loyal mass, in the fashion of Castro or Mao. Solidarity is achieved through ideology and structure, which in both cases speak to existential need. The identification of theory and practice, of working for values that are also lived, creates a level of commitment which a single-issue organization can never match. The investment in such organizations is worth the effort, because the psychic returns are great; and this is so precisely because a high level of commitment is made possible, in fact required, thus defeating the alienation of the wasteland culture.

Some object that imparting an ideology is manipulative and its proponents seek only to free people psychologically. As if training people to be more adjusted within the framework of a system that grinds up individuals to suit its profit-making ends is not itself an advanced stage of manipulation! The present ideology masks itself as a non-ideology and as the only rational way to carry on the project of technological advance. The imperative is to question this thesis at its roots by posing to it an alternative organizational view. This alternative would affirm and maintain the primacy and integrity of the person through the objective integration of life and work. For this, what is needed is insight into the many ways in which the present pattern of working and living together affects us so as to make us mistrustful, leery of open mutuality, and apathetic toward the possibility of having any real effect.

An Ecosystem Paradigm

In a one-dimensional society, pervaded by its monolithic assumptions, the importance of paradigms is great. There is an extensive literature of criticism dealing with alienation, fragmentation, exploitation and other variants, but people see no other way. They either ascribe their problems mentally to a conspiratorial group behind the scenes—as with the Birch Society and elements of the Left—or simply shrug their shoulders fatalistically, ascribe conditions to the determinism of the *weltgeist* or technology and try to make out. But for new models to represent serious structural change, they must be significant alternatives to existing institutions, capable of equalling or surpassing them in quality of output.

What must be created is a set of organizations which taken together are mutually interdependent and thus form an ecosystem. The ecosystem then can provide the major environment for each organization considered separately and reinforce rather than destroy the variant style and structure. Such an ecosystem in particular would have to incorporate banks, so that the traditional systems of control would not be enforced as a result of external financial dependency.

The problem is not how to influence politics but how to *be* politics—thus not how to get into power but how to transform and humanize it. The thrust of the analysis is thus toward the intensive view of the democratic project. The civil rights movement, at first preoccupied with the extensive project of bringing in the still disenfranchised, later turned toward intensive projects with its Poor People's Corporations, its Freedom Labor Union, and its co-operatives. But where the issue is the quality of life itself, it is not simply the many injustices of the present power-ridden system which can serve as the motive for change, but rather the experience, as it is created, of a life made meaningful through institutions which truly serve. In the historical development of such a movement, the nuclear structure comes first. But as it grows, confrontations will inevitably occur, and with them a new form of political power will develop. At this time the necessity of maintaining the essentially para-political goals of the movement must be balanced with the political struggle to maintain itself and grow. But by then what is being defended is not simply a set of discrete political goals, but a way of life.

The objective then is a society which is fully democratized. This means a society both densely and intensively organized in an integrative fashion wherein the basic activities of life interrelate. Such interrelatedness is inevitable when the center of concern changes from the efficiency of the organization in pursuing its particular objectives to the primacy of the person as the locus for the objective interrelation of human purposes. The central image of this process is people working in face-to-face relations with their fellows in order to bring the uniqueness of their own perspective to the business of solving common problems and achieving common goals. Expertise and technology are then the servant, not the master of such groups, since, where the primacy of the person is affirmed, there is no formula that can define the substance of the common good. Particular groups, associations, and communities must work out particular solutions and a particular destiny in accord with a style and culture that evolve uniquely. In 1918 Mary Parker Follett wrote that democracy has not yet been tried. It has still not been tried.

At present the centralist and power-oriented ideology grows unchecked, and in the upper reaches of the warfare state coalesces into smoothly meshed elites, patriotically cooperating to make the world safe for "democracy." With this comes the pyramiding of inequities of income and of power, so that while the rich grow richer and more powerful, those at the base drop out into increasing poverty. And underneath the base, things begin to crumble: the long hot summers multiply, crime rates reach new highs. There is no lack of symptoms that evidence a breakdown. But breakdown does not give assurance of reform. Thus the movement for change must rely primarily on the validity of its own vision and the congruence of its structure with that vision if it is to benefit from the breakdown. It can then draw off energy and resources from the present system, as it becomes increasingly a fundamental and mutually exclusive alternative to it. As it develops a critical mass allowing it autonomy in major ways it can renounce the present system, creating its own fundamental institutions of law and government, and at this stage it will have passed from paradigms into politics.

What is being affirmed is the organic or systematic quality of the present social structure which, with all its defects and even contradictions, is still based on a powerful, albeit neurotic and destructive, power dynamic. To effect significant change nothing less than a different dynamic and motive system must be created, and so the requirement of building anew is an imperative one—thus the need to precede politics with paradigms and to avoid the old trap of getting into power. In the end, it is a philosophy of the person and of human possibility that is in question. But the expression of this philosophy must confront the organized power of dehumanization that has grown so tremendously in this century and created the wasteland culture we see around us. For this, it is not enough to be on the right side, committed to the right philosophy. One must act.

From Our Generation, *Vol. 5, No. 2, Fall 1967.*

Chapter 2

Genuine Peace
Requires Real Democracy
(1964)

Powerlessness and the War System

Those of us who are actively concerned with the question of how to achieve peace on this planet are now coming more and more to confront the question of how our society inhibits the healthy urges which could serve to release us from the psychological and ideological rigidities of the war system. More broadly, the issue is whether, given its present organization, contemporary society is able to achieve or maintain peace. Up to now, most of the organizations involved in the quest for peace have focused on the steps to be taken in the international sphere, while having no agreed upon analysis of the domestic scene. Thus, in this country's peace movement, there has been a good deal of effort to influence the elites, along with little fundamental criticism of the role they play in the social structure.

Since peace involves the positive process of replacing violence by other means of settling conflict, and because this in turn requires the development of understandings between the Communist world and the West, it can be argued that some sort of institutional change is necessary. For if insurgency is satisfied with specific reform goals, and does not seek to transform the institutional structure of society by getting at its centralized make-up, the war system will probably not go away. This is really what we should mean by decentralizing: making institutions serve human ends again by getting humans to be responsible at every level within them. Thus, instead of the repetitive and usually symbolic peace marches and Polaris climbings that have characterized the direct action part of the peace movement to date, an effort should be mounted in every area of public life to decentralize and democratize it. Otherwise we are left with the possibility of future missile silo sitters, carrying out whatever orders new technologies can issue.

The thesis of *Community and Power,* an important work by Robert A. Nisbet, is that society is organized today in such a way that the primary modes of association—family, village, church group, guild, or economic unit—no longer are functionally related to the bureaucratic elites which actually perform the major functions within society. These primary groups are no longer recognized as functionally significant—economically, legally, or politically—even though they are the subject of much compensatory eulogy. It is rather the individual who is functionally related directly to the elites and to the State. The primary modes of association, where basic behavioral patterns, values, and attitudes, are formed and where responsibility operates as a result of face-to-face confrontation, are thus dysfunctional, and the bureaucratic modes of organization do not relate to them. Although not everybody is subject to any single bureaucratic barony, the experience of powerlessness arises from the fact that the primary modes of association, where the individual has decision-making power, are themselves powerless.

This analysis would not be complete without the recognition that it is the State that has been the cause of the powerlessness of the primary group, at least as much as has the development of technology. Thomas Hobbes, as well as the present apologists for countervailing power, define freedom negatively—as freedom *from* the associations which have traditionally mediated between the individual and the State. *Positive freedom* would find its locus in the primary modes of association where behavioral patterns are formed, values are created, and personal responsibility based on personal confrontation can develop. Thus Hannah Arendt, seeking an antidote for totalitarianism, has gone back to the town meeting and similar forms of communal decision-making as examples of a genuinely effective participatory process.

In the contemporary democratic state, the popular vote is seen by many as the locus of political decision-making. It is the vote, however, which best exemplifies the failure of the modern political process: the single, isolated act in which each individual allows his or her opinion to be added to the sum total and tallied in a fashion that is purely quantitative. Only the mystique of a General Will could justify this as genuine participation in government. Economically, this mystique is replaced by the mystique of the market place; and so in both areas we find the faith that the aggregate of individual wills, acting out of self interest, will mystically turn into the General Will, and the common good.

Confronting Disempowerment, Recapturing Potency

In short, our society today displays a peculiar situation: the externals are fine, a car in every kitchen, the whole bit. But the extensive literature on anomie and alienation indicates the existence of basic malaise. Statistics on divorce, delinquency, homicide, drugs, alcoholism, suicide... all verify this. The etiology of this situation revolves around the loss of individual potency and freedom as a result of existence in a centralist bureaucratized society. Basic human and spiritual impulses find no mode of social expression. The primary group has lost its functional meaning and relevance to the remote economic, political and social units. My own outrage about this condition is primarily a moral one over the tremendous human wastage and frustration created by our society in its dedication to ends that offer short term efficiency, but are in the long term anti-human and destructive of the higher potentialities of life.

And here is where the challenge lies: the challenge of building a society which in its psychological economy can afford peace, because frustration with it need not be displaced and because people are enough themselves so they need not project their drives and guilt onto a scapegoat. The danger here is that to tinker with all that is repressed can easily lead to the creation of objects onto which to displace hostility, and of a threatening Enemy onto which can be projected the aggressive drives and figures of one's unconscious. But the counter to this does exist: to give people back a sense of potency through practical proposals in which they involve themselves directly, so that the energy released by appealing to the discontent is used creatively.

Insurgency, by focusing on the unmet needs that are a product of our fossilized society, can lead us back to a sense of potency if it can manage to strengthen individual participation through primary groups directly involved in the political process. Tactically, the agenda for action should not start with the military elites, although the pacifists usually do.

Rather, the recapturing of potency will in itself serve as an antidote to the projective mechanism which locates the cause of our difficulties in the activities of Communism. The other way to potency is war. As Nisbet says, "The power of war to create a sense of moral meaning is one of the most frightening aspects of the twentieth century."

The peace movement in this country has largely failed to confront the centralized and disempowering way our society actually operates. It has seen its purpose mainly in terms of an attempt to Speak Truth to Power (the name of an American Friends Service Committee pamphlet published in the early 1960s which had an important influence on pacifist thought, mostly for the better). Aside from a small group of personal witness pacifists who spoke truth directly but nevertheless failed to do any more than that, the peace movement can be divided into two categories: those who attempted to work directly with the elites, mostly within the government by lobbying, advice, seminars, and the like, and those who sought to build grassroots support for peace ideas.

The liberal-rational, Speak Truth to Power assumptions of the peace movement fail to confront the realities of the present in two crucial ways, therefore. First, in speaking truth to the power of the elites, in terms of an approach through enlightened self-interest, they fail to appreciate the extent to which the elites are committed to the mythology of the war system. They do not want nuclear destruction, but their assumptions have worked so far, have not proved fatal, and have been hugely profitable to a large segment of industry. And it is only within the boundaries of the profit system that the corporate elites would have any space to move. So long as profits are tied to defense production, speaking truth to the elites involved is not likely to get very far. The Administration is a much better bet since patronage today mainly means handing out defense contracts, rather than jobs in government, which is one reason why Congress is little help. But the Administration, rightly or wrongly, has seen itself as a prisoner of these myths, even when it does not share them.

However, the attempt to build grassroots support has never gathered much strength. Why? Because the foreign policy questions posed by the peace groups, even though they involve the basic question of survival, in no way tie in to the existential condition of people in our society. The remoteness of technology allows communities to go on with their daily activities with no sharp awareness that 4,000 miles away, but within fifteen minutes of delivery, a nuclear warhead stands ready, at the press of a button, to obliterate them all. The war system intensifies the general malaise which is part of the existential condition within our society. But the ties are not obvious ones, and so while it intensifies the sickness, it also provides a scapegoat, and in so doing a national sense of pseudo-purpose, as a substitute for the deficiencies at home.

Fortunately, facts are on the side of the peace movement, and many of those who exercise power are cognizant of the facts. Thus we may avoid nuclear war, but if we do so, it will not be to the credit of the peace movement to date. Moreover, the institution of war will still be with us. As long as our sense of powerlessness continues, along with its counterpart, projection, and so long as our centralized society is dominated by the core bureaucracy of the State, organization for war will continue because it meets basic needs that are inherent in the organization of our society.

Combining Insurgency and Organization

To counter the power of the present elites on the one hand and the alienation of the citizen and worker on the other, a combination of organization and insurgency must create new centers of power based on new models of decision-making, where human beings confront each other directly and responsibly. Insurgency will be necessary at the point that these new groupings seek to be more than simply one more voluntary organization and claim their say within the whole. From this can arise a new set of priorities based on a new kind of moral commitment, sufficient to defuse the war system. But the answer to our initial question, Is this society capable of achieving peace? is that without a change in its centralist elitist structure, it is not.

From Changing Work, *No. 7, Winter 1988. The essay was originally written in 1964.*

Chapter 3

Participatory Democracy and the Dilemma of Change (1969)

The 1966 founding document of Students for a Democratic Society—the Port Huron Statement—spoke of participatory democracy as the basis for the organization of society:

> As a social system we seek the establishment of individual participation, governed by two central aims: that the individual share in those social decisions determining the quality and the direction of his life; that society be organized to encourage independence in men [sic] and provide the media for their participation.

The original intuition of the New Left, which saw a society of participation as the goal and sought ways to work toward such a society, was correct, in my view. The trouble is that the intuition lacked any adequate articulation in terms of an analysis of the social order and of how to change it. This is understandable in view of the fact that the only systematic theory which has combined analysis and a theory of change in terms at all acceptable to the New Left has been Marxism. The anarchist and decentralist analyses of people like Paul Goodman and Lewis Mumford and some of the English and European anarchists have no built-in theory of change, and in fact anarchism itself has always been ambivalent on the subject of change: some anarchists have been revolutionists, while others have opted for various schemes for building libertarian institutions into existing societies.

In the work of C. Wright Mills the rise of elites is contrasted with the early American democracy of small town and rural countryside where town meeting and the system of geographic representation were not undercut by the existence of corporate and other organized forms of power which are national and even multi-national in their scope. But his analysis, in the tradition of Max Weber and Vilfredo Pareto, focuses on the nature of the elites themselves, rather than on the organizational forms which gave rise to them. Consequently, this tends to reinforce the moralism of the traditional populist approach to change, which has been influential on the Left: get rid of the elites, and the people will naturally find the most suitable forms of self-government. The assumption here is that it is not individual members of the elite but a ruling class which constitutes the problem, and when this is replaced with a different class with different values, the problem will be solved.

Beyond Elites: The Organizational Imperative

The difficulty with this approach is that it ignores the extent to which individuals are shaped by the institutions in which they operate. The value of the anarchist analysis, when applied to organizations, is that it is fully conscious of the extent to which organizations shape even those who purport to control them. It is useful to see this in terms of the kinds of structures imposed by the organizational imperative. Faced with a given task requiring group effort, obviously the nature of the task imposes its demands on the form of human organization. However, far too much in the way of technological necessity is ordinarily attributed to the task itself. It is possible, as experiments in England have shown, to assemble a car from the ground up by a single group of workers and to do this as efficiently as by conventional methods, thus eliminating the assembly line. What has become increasingly evident as a result of such experimentation is that it is not efficiency which dictates the organizational forms of industry so much as *efficiency of control*. Given a system where, from the start, power is concentrated among a few, much of the centralization of control and specialization of function that exists results from the desire to maintain the system of control and has nothing to do with efficiency. Some studies indicate, in fact, that increasingly the new technology requires decentralization, not concentration.

The fundamental feature of the organizational imperative can be expressed as follows: in the short run it is more efficient to have an elitist structure, dominated by an educated and knowledgeable minority. From this perspective the difficult task of developing a participatory structure, and then educating people into using it, is time-consuming and inefficient. It is only in the long run that the values embodied in full participation (which assures work that is non-alienating, by virtue of the degree of control that the worker has over the nature and product of his or her work) pay off in efficiency.

There are several problems which arise when organizing for participation. The most basic one is that it is always easier to organize in an elitist fashion; this organizational form is simpler than democratic participation, requiring less educational effort and permitting policy to be decided in a simple way by a few. Anyone who has gone through the agonies of broad scale democratic debate is aware of these facts, even taking into account that often the agonies are caused more by the failure to structure the decision process adequately than by anything inherent in the process itself. Effective decision-making requires small groups which meet regularly and which maintain effective channels of communication with each other. At the Standard Auto Works in England, for a period production was entirely under workers' control; the lesson to be learned from their experience was that primary importance lay in the careful organization of the work groups and in the communication between them. It may be easier to organize in elitist fashion, but the psycho-social costs extend far beyond the productive operation. And as modern management research indicates, in the long run alienation produces inefficiency.

Another problem in the initial organizing for participation is that given a society in which inequalities of class and status are built in, organizations that are formed within such a context will mirror these inequities. The organizational imperatives of industrialism have made organization more intensive and its form more crushing than ever before. As Robert Nisbet has pointed out, our present organizational forms are closer to an armed corps or a garrison than to anything else. Thirdly, the process of organizing a productive enterprise initially requires a high level of entrepreneurial skills involving capital accumulation, market research, technological planning, and human organizing. Subsequently, the enterprise can be operated by workers possessing essentially machine-tending and operating skills. This too builds in a class division which is inegalitarian and anti-democratic. Moreover, the power of the machine multiplies vastly the impact of the production organization on the environment. For this reason such organization is very powerful and its authoritarian aspects are reinforced.

I have indicated the seeming naturalness of the evolution of private power, especially in its corporate and productive form. In many ways this evolution took the path of least resistance toward an industrialized, technological society. It suggests that the basic organizational form—here the corporation—is of fundamental importance in determining the social order and its values. But, most important, it indicates that the problem is a systemic one, not to be attributed to the set of elites which arose with the maturing of the system as a whole, *but rather to the basic organizational form of the system.* Not only is the corporation the prime locus of power, with its capacity to allocate resources, determine productive priorities, delineate the shape of cities and determine where people will work. It is also the model for the other major organizational forms throughout the society: the universities, even the church hierarchies, the professional associations, the unions. Some of these organizations are formally elective, some not. But even where the electoral choice also represents a significant policy choice, there is no continuity of participation by the rank and file, and hence it is easy to argue that they could not participate, simply because they are not trained to. Hence the myth of participation, without the substance, perpetuates itself.

It is possible now to clarify the essential differences in social analysis and social philosophy between the revolutionists and those who advocate that society must be restructured from the ground up, not the top down. The revolutionists see the basic problem as that of getting rid of the elites—a class whose power is so great as to be qualitatively different from that of other groups. It is true that power is exercised disproportionately at the top, but the question is, is getting rid of the elites going to solve the problem?

It is important here to recognize that within the managerial elites, the organizational relationships are still coercive. They are imbued with the organizational ideology, co-opted so as to ensure they identify with the values and beliefs of their peers, and bribed by exorbitant rewards.

But above all, theirs is the exclusive prerogative to exercise power within the organization, and through this they are corrupted to its purposes. The power, however, is not a free power capable of serving humane and universal ends; it is power to seek the pre-established ends of the organization, and from this derives the paradox that the rulers of such organizations have great power but little freedom.

A system of quantitative and monetary reward substitutes for modes of organization that could achieve complete and free association of people in their tasks. Work is thus degraded, and the free play of human spontaneity, ingenuity, and imagination is denied. It is apparent that class conflict creates the need for power-ridden and coercive organizations, which produce a controlling group that identifies primarily with organizational objectives. Yet this does not explain fully the impact of such organizations on their members. As the enterprise evolves from one person rule to government by managers on behalf of ownership groups that often remain uninvolved, even management takes on many of the characteristics of hired hands. Ultimately the objectives of the enterprise—a stable market, steady growth, an adequate return to the investor—do not derive from any controlling group at all, but rather from the general socio-economic environment of which the enterprise is a part. This environment dictates the general objectives. The salient fact is, thus, that at no level, even the top, is the full play of human purpose given scope. Those who rule the vast industrial baronies are not free to turn their productive powers to objectives that extend beyond the criteria imposed by cost accounting. Hence, basic social needs go begging, since their fulfillment is insufficiently profitable, while what is produced is often socially useless or even destructive.

The Philosophy of a Participatory Society

Every socio-political system involves a philosophy of human nature. Where the system is coercive and authoritarian, the philosophy is usually dualistic, seeing humans as evil and prone to disobedience. Contemporary philosophies have tended to be dystopian and reductionist, seeing the world as absurd, and people as ruled either by biology or by iron laws of history. One of the major requirements for a society made up of self-administered institutions which are fully participatory is a view of humanity that extends beyond a dualistic and need-centered psychology. When motivation is reduced to biological drives, it is impossible to understand the role of responsible participation. Psychological research indicates, however, that the opportunity to participate in key decisions affecting one's life is a prerequisite of mental health, and the problem is to fit this within a suitable psychological context. Third force psychology provides such a context, since it posits a set of motives beyond deficiency needs and having to do with the urge toward self-actualization.

Self-actualization can occur when the basic needs—the biological drives, the security needs, the ego's need for recognition—have been met. Persons are then free to actualize their potentialities, and this requires that they be able to identify with larger values that transcend themselves, and participate significantly in the areas of work and public life that affect their own existence. It also requires that the basic areas of life—work and leisure, private life and public life—be capable of significant integration. This basic viewpoint can be described as the affirmation of the primacy of the person. Respect for human potentiality and growth under conditions of freedom requires that organizations be seen as tools for the realization of human purposes rather than instruments for the manipulation of human material viewed as personnel. This dictates a policy of total opposition to the current widespread depersonalization imposed by the size, structure, and mindless goals of existing organizations.

It requires that work be re-defined so as to be made meaningful, by allowing everyone involved a say in what is produced, how it is produced, and how income from production is used. The fetishism of commodities, leading to the worship of the gross national product, must give way to a respect for the conditions under which human growth and realization are possible. In community life it requires that local units be the locus of decision-making regarding the significant aspects of the physical and social environment, and that such units have a say in the control of productive enterprises within their province.

The organizational imperative remains: the more extensive the organization, the greater the danger of top-down control, and the more skillful the organizational design must be to avoid this. Hence, far from the populist vision that, once the elite is removed from power, the social order will naturally become democratic, precisely the reverse is true. The path of least resistance always leads back to elitism; the fundamental problem is how to organize for extensive participation within a context imposed by the technology of extensive organization. The New Left, in talking of participatory democracy, has had an invaluable insight. But for understandable reasons having to do with the magnitude of the problem and the paucity of its own resources, it has been unable to translate the insight into a strategy for achieving change.

Building Free Association

At present the typical bureaucracy, whether public or private, is highly organized at the top, but only at the top. Here small committees rule, and decision-making is continuous and constant. As one goes down the hierarchy, group decision-making soon gives way to a machine style of organizing wherein orders flow down from the top and information flows up from the bottom. But the paradigms of complete decision-making are the small face-to-face groups that rule the corporate and bureaucratic worlds: the boards, trustee committees, executive councils and so forth which meet regularly to plan, propose, execute and dispose. The problem thus becomes specific: to design organizations which meet the technological requirements while at the same time embodying the full decision process throughout the organization. Rather than being group-oriented only at the top, organizations must embody group structure throughout their own structure so that the one is coterminous with the other.

Such free association involves a voluntary enlistment of members who freely identify with the goals of the organization. For this to happen they must identify themselves as part of the free organization, voluntarily committed to its goals, personally involved with its members. When such identification exists, there is no need for status hierarchies and inordinate prestige for leadership. In the kibbutzim, where everybody is involved and community exists, people qualified for management must be sought out and asked to take the job, since no special status goes with the position. Contrary to the popular myths, the divorce of power from function, which is at the heart of coercive organizations, reduces efficiency. Where workers' control operates, for example, on the work floor, floor management is taken over by workers, and management overhead is significantly reduced. In general, free associations, such as free universities, free radio, off-off Broadway theater, do a better job for their members and for society than the commercial enterprises, and they do it more cheaply. People are motivated by the job itself, not by extrinsic considerations such as status and prestige, and energy is directed to the task at hand.

In those cases where this has been attempted (e.g., in the Mondragon Cooperatives for example) the result has been higher productivity and, understandably, far higher worker morale. The myth that organizational efficiency requires an authoritarian structure is thus laid to rest. Efficiency is not the problem, but organizational design is. It is true that there is little hope that those now in control of the corporate baronies will be swayed by such arguments, since the pay-offs deriving from the existing system vastly favor them. But it is also true that doing away with the existing elites will not solve the problem. Workers, and certainly their union bosses, have an extensive stake in the system as it is and a faith in the ideology of hard work for upward mobility into the bourgeoisie. Job specialization is part of the general apparatus of control, and for the worker with a fragmented and worm's eye view of the whole, the thought of greater responsibility through participation cannot be attractive.

The question is, if one forsakes revolutionism, how can one achieve change within the context of an advanced industrial society? It should be apparent from what I have said that the problem of participation is a root organization problem for a society deeply involved in technological advance. Its adequate solution depends upon the question of how power and wealth are distributed throughout the society, for it makes no sense to speak of participation without applying it to the disposition of the capital surplus which comes from production. Moreover, resistance to what would be involved, namely a change in the organizational structure, would come not only from the top, but from all those within the present institutional orders whose main security comes from doing what they know how to do. The ritualized conformism of the bureaucrat is a necessary by-product of the bureaucratic hierarchies and helps maintain the system of control.

Faced with the prevailing mythology regarding efficiency, only the actual creation of participatory institutions that work can adequately prove that they are viable. And, while it makes sense to start with simpler institutions rather than the productive enterprises, sooner or later such a movement for change must confront the workplace. A movement seeking to organize from the ground up to achieve full participation will have the greatest impact when it creates effective productive organizations, since it is here that social organization confronts most fully the existing technology. The productive enterprise is the core institution in an advanced industrial society, and hence, if it can be self-administering and participatory, it takes the ground out from under the supporters of the present authoritarian system.

When asked what it was after, Students for a Democratic Society answered that it was merely trying to put into practice what it preached. When people do this in such a way as to humanize the existing technology, rather than renounce it, then the strategy of change operates maximally within social and cultural realities. Moreover, both the pragmatic and the ideological objections to basic structural change are met: the organizations are built, shown to work, and the objection that change must be wrought through the accepted channels is bypassed. Rather than resorting to the tweedledum and tweedledee of electoral politics—which can come once the movement has built a sufficient base—structural change is introduced, but introduced specifically for the purpose of democratizing the society. This in no way discounts the importance of resistance to unjust laws, unjust wars, and oppressive policies. But it adds to it another dimension which relates directly to the structural causes of the injustice: the runaway economy which gives rise to, in fact requires, the military-industrial complex; the inability to integrate social purpose into the productive process which gives rise to slums and ghettoes; the resulting social and urban chaos which gives rise to riots and violence. The development of a movement dedicated to the building of self-administering, free institutions is immensely difficult, requiring the collection and coordination of extensive resources. But it is both the most absent and most needed ingredient in a movement for social change.

From Priscilla Long (ed.), The New Left, *1969. This version also incorporates several paragraphs from "Organization, Conflict and Free Association" in Benello and Roussopoulos eds.),* The Case for Participatory Democracy, *1971.*

Part II

Theories of
Community Empowerment

Chapter 4

Rethinking Democracy
(1981)

Complementary Issues, Seldom Explored

Though focusing on different but complementary issues—the unitary democracy of small groups and the scale of social units—Jane Mansbridge's *Beyond Adversary Democracy,* and Kirkpatrick Sale's *Human Scale* represent areas seldom explored yet of signal importance in constructing a good society. Mansbridge's book studies the democratic process, as found in New England town meetings and in alternative work organizations, and finds it a complex mixture of coordinate and conflicting interests. Decision making processes, she says, must vary within the same organization to take account of the degree of coordination or conflict. Sale's book explores the impact of scale on organizations and communities and makes a powerful argument for inherent limits, for human scale and for decentralism.

Mansbridge takes as her central task the analysis of adversary democracy, which she points out is remarkably similar to laissez faire economics; she contrasts this with unitary democracy, which is practiced in small groups and small communities. Unitary democracy is based on consensus, face-to-face contact, common interests, and equal respect. Adversary democracy is based on majority rule, secret ballot, equal protection of opposing interests. Her argument is that small groups can practice unitary democracy, and often do, although even here there are times when adversary methods must be used, since interests at times conflict. Large groupings must rely on adversary methods, although unitary elements at times can be introduced.

Her book contains two case studies, one of a New England town meeting and the other of a counseling and crisis center. One of the best things about the book is the way Mansbridge is able to make sense of her information so that it sheds light on basic issues of equality, power, and participation. As a result, the discussion of these issues, and of the place for unitary and adversarial methods of decision-making, is grounded in a wealth of close observation, giving unusual cogency to her conclusions. However, she accepts the inevitability of large organizational systems, especially the state, and hence posits that the present representative system of adversarial democracy is unavoidable. Kirkpatrick Sale's virtue is that he stands this argument on its head, arguing that since nation states necessarily entail adversarial relations—both agree on this point—they should be abolished.

Sale's position can of course be accused of being "utopian" and impractical. In response, he quotes Leszek Kolakowski: "It may well be that the impossible at a given moment can become possible only by being stated at a time when it is impossible." Sale's advocacy of a return to human scale allows him to both look at how societies built on a human scale have worked throughout history and to consider how a contemporary society would look if we actually did remain true to the limits of human scale. In the process, Sale gives us more than he promises. To fully make the argument for the sort of decentralist, ecological and participatory society he envisions, he must move beyond questions of scale (decentralism alone can leave us with local oligarchies) to deal with questions of organization, and thus discusses at length workplace democracy and community control.

Toward a Science of Social Ecology

Both books, taking different approaches, represent contributions to the emerging science of social ecology, a science which explores the fitness or compatibility of social settings with the broader natural environment and their capacity to contribute to human growth and freedom. One cannot read these books without wanting to put them together and then move on to grasp more of what collectively the two books imply. I believe the direction of such research would be as follows: first, it would be based on the recognition that the basic unit of society is the group, not the individual. At present, groups and organizations exist, but they are not formally recognized as power wielding or politically potent. Thus we have the anomaly of "private" corporations with the scope and the resources of nation-states. Formal recognition of functional groups was proposed by the Guild Socialists (see Follett's *The New State*): the conventional argument against it is that formal recognition would bring even more power. But what if corporations were themselves democratized? Formal recognition would then entail enfranchisement, but also functional control by affected groups—local, regional, and national.

Beginning with such an analysis, a set of propositions emerge about how a human scale, decentralist democracy can be constructed. The first has already been suggested: functional groups which carry out the basic purposes of society, involving work, education, culture, and community, should constitute the basic societal units. This mirrors the Yugoslav idea of dissolving the political into the social: a functional democracy will not create a second, remote and massive governmental entity side-by-side with the existing network of institutions at the base. Rather, it will serve as the linkage and coordinating system for existing institutions. A second proposition having to do with the nature of the organization's base would be: no decentralizing—or enfranchisement—without full democracy at the base. This will minimize local oligarchies, classism, racism, sexism, and other forms of inequality; it also implies criteria of equity for enfranchisement. A third proposition is the decentralist maxim: decentralize all functions to their lowest possible level, leaving only enough power for upper level organizations to perform necessary coordination. The fourth proposition would be the participation maxim: all those affected must have a say in the decision-making process. Here, as anyone who has been involved in participatory organizations knows full well, the trick is to create a system with sufficient delegation of authority and internal differentiation so that not everyone is involved in all decisions all the time.

Still another important proposition: democratic decision making requires face-to-face groups. It is a dialogic process involving proposing, discussing, agreeing, implementing, and evaluating. Here we begin to see the nature of the changes needed. For a decentralist democracy to work the scale must be such that close and full human interaction exists throughout. Sale discusses this at length, and several "magic numbers" emerge: face-to-face groups operate best at the level of 7 to 10, with an outer limit of 20. Task organizations operate effectively with outer limits of 400 to 500. Communities operate effectively on the level of 5,000 to 10,000, up to perhaps 40,000. In all this, the face-to-face group is of primordial significance, for it is here that the process of political and cultural socialization takes place, replacing possessive individualism with a capacity to integrate individual needs into collective social purposes.

All of this implies that for participatory, or base-empowering democracy to work, the political must become the psychosocial: attitudes and a consciousness which facilitate group integration, decision-making and social purpose must be developed. Thus the political must become the personal. This takes us into difficult areas, conditioned as we are by liberal-individualist culture. The fear of organization is omnipresent, and the notion that groups can contribute to, rather than detract from, freedom is not familiar. What needs to be seen and felt is that there is positive freedom within the group. If the group is experienced as a friend, not an enemy, cooperative activities which enhance life are developed, responding to both the functional necessity for joint action in many areas and to the human need for primary groups. A further proposition then: participatory groups form the basic defense against the threat to freedom which occurs when institutions lose their capacity to respond to human needs. Another proposition clarifies this: since organization is power, if power is to remain responsive to the base, the base must be more organized than any upper level units. Otherwise, power will inevitably emerge somewhere else to dominate the base.

A commonwealth based on democracy at the base through functional group organization would be characterized by a delegate system, not the present representative system. Delegates would be governed by a mandate formally expressed through group decisions. Representatives cannot really represent a mass of disconnected individuals, as Sale points out, for there is nothing more tangible than opinion polls, or at best referenda, to go on. A functional democracy would also possess upper level organizational linkages based on the delegate system in which the concerns and needs of basic institutions were carried upward to regional levels. Yugoslavia is probably the best example we have of such a functional system, but it is not based on the necessary decentralism into self-sufficient communities at the base, and the dissolution of the political into the social is offset by the existence of a self-perpetuating bureaucratic elite, described by Djilas. Nevertheless, it can tell us much.

One moral to be derived from the functional approach—for the reasons indicated we should be concentrating not on either representative or consensual democracy, but on functional democracy—is that freedom must not only be defended; it must first be created. Sale's book is of great value because it presents the argument for human scale which leads to radical decentralism. It needs to be supplemented by a work—not yet written—which fleshes out the sort of functional perspective suggested above. Also, Sale's book does not really tell us why we have the sort of hypertrophy in every sector of society that we encounter all around us. We are thus left to assume that giantism is a product of some sort of social oversight. Its causes are nowhere explored, and this, despite his references to Lewis Mumford, who has given us an excellent analysis of the reasons for the periodic appearance through history of what he termed the Megamachine.

Moving Beyond Theory

Given the fact that all liberal thought, and unfortunately a lot of socialist and progressive thought, turns to the State to cure us of our ills, Sale's book is of great value, in its analysis of the inherent dysfunctionality of size and of the State as a large-scale mass organization. As he points out, crime rates rise in close correlation with the growth of urbanization. Mass violence grows in proportion to the number and size of nation-states. It is true that in an armored world, those without armor may seem to be either heroes or fools. But just as there are those who opt out of the rat race in favor of simplicity and ecological soundness, so opting out of the national rat races may be more possible than we think.

We are at a time historically where the matters discussed by Sale and Mansbridge may suddenly move out of the realm of theory. If the economic crisis that many predict actually occurs, we will be faced with the need—and also the opportunity—to engage in basic social reconstruction. A crash would create vast openings for basic types of change, available to the right as well as the left. If at that time a democratic decentralist movement were able to present a coherent vision of an ecologically sound and democratic future, it could have an impact.

At present, the existing alternative visions are partial and are polluted by statist and centralist assumptions regarding how society should be reorganized. Both Sale's and Mansbridge's books point us in a different direction, focusing on critical problems inherent in both the scale and political structure of the present system. Sale rejects that system to argue for an alternative which lies clearly outside the existing definitions of social reality. By pushing the logic of democratic decentralism beyond what exists, he invites us to examine a set of issues which have usually been totally ignored. Issues of human scale have only very recently been raised by writers like Leopold Kohr and E.F. Schumacher. Propositions about scale are for the most part evidential and historical, and there is as yet little theory. Moreover, the study of scale is intimately linked to the study of structures appropriate to different levels of scale— as Sale himself recognizes, by including a section on workplace democracy.

The study of social and political alternatives of which both books constitute examples, is subject to two kinds of criticisms. The first is the realpolitik objection which views politics as the art of the possible and goes on to define the possible in terms of the existent. There is little point in debating this position, except to comment that it represents a failure of social imagination, if not also a failure of nerve. The second criticism, made by many though not all Marxists, is that the problem is not how to think out and develop the new social forms, since they will arise spontaneously, once the old have been torn down. It is true that visions alone, no matter how scientific, will not make for change. But neither will strategy without vision. The value of these books is that they suggest that there is a lot we do not know and have not begun to think about and that things are not as simple as they seem. Moreover, they point us in potentially fertile directions, towards a theory of genuinely democratic— decentralized and human scale—alternatives to outworn and oversized representative institutions.

From Our Generation, *Vol. 15, No. 2, Summer 1981.*

Chapter 5

The Conflicting Traditions
of Anarchism and Marxism
(1974)

A Point of Agreement

Extensive division of labor is the central feature of modern industrial and post-industrial society. It is evident within major institutions, and even more clearly so within those organizations, corporations and state-owned firms that are the main manifestations of production and technological advance.

For Marxism, the division of labor arises out of the interplay between humanity and nature. Originally society is perceived by Marxists as communal. But at the point that a surplus is created, it is appropriated by those who maintain a commanding position within society. Out of this emerges the class structure of all subsequent societies, manifested in its purest and most heightened form, since people are shorn of the traditional relations of mutual obligation and shared values under capitalism. The division of labor is thus responsible both for the specialization of work into narrow job categories and for the separation of the worker from control over the means of production. The result of this is alienation, both from control over the process of production, and from the products as well. The only solution to this, for Marxism, is to abolish the division of labor and reintegrate human beings both with the tools of their labor and the fruits of their labor. Here Marx took a resolutely utopian stand, refusing to admit that the division of labor was essential to either technological advance or industrial productivity. This stand was congruent with Marx's view, expressed in his early writings, that not only class divisions, but also the divisions of town and country should be abolished, and it represents a basic principle of utopian thought, which has always sought to reintegrate humanity in such a way that all members of the society could share holistically in the major areas of social life.

The anarchist tradition, although it is far less unified on many points than Marxism, shares with it the belief that the division of labor must be abolished to create a liberatory society. If anything, it is clearer than Marxism in its stress that, not only must the division of labor be abolished, but that the division between work and community life, and between manual and intellectual work, must also be abolished. The Chinese have espoused this goal, but it is worth remembering that Mao Tse-tung had once been an anarchist himself. Anarchism parts company with Marxism most clearly in perceiving the necessity of building integrated social forms as the precondition of a successful revolution, conceived of as a fundamental social transformation. For while anarchism shared with Marxism its utopian view of the goal—an egalitarian and libertarian society in which self-determination extended into the forms of daily life, dispensing with all forms of coercion and authoritarian power—on the question of strategy anarchism parts company with Marxist thought.

Is Class the Only Form of Domination?

Marx conceived of class struggle as the basic social fact, seeing divisions of class as the result of a process of social evolution involving the creation of a productive surplus. Because Marx defined class in terms of the relations of production, Marxism has tended to restrict its class analysis to the capitalist model, wherein class is defined in terms of ownership of the means of production. Anarchism, however, has focused on the question of human organization in a much more general way, seeking to understand the psychosocial mechanisms from which domination and power relationships derive. It sees class as based on the control of the means of production as a particular case of a more general form of class division. Hence anarchist thought is more easily able to comprehend within the realm of its theory the existence of "New Classes" based on Communist Party elites; the monopolization of the means of production and of capital are only one form of power. The authoritarian state, which in addition to controlling capital possesses a monopoly on its other instrumentalities as well—its bureaucracies, its means of violence, its ideological control—has far more powerful means at its disposal. To call fascist dictatorships or the U.S.S.R. "state capitalist" is to emphasize state domination as such; this must be understood on its own terms, not as manifested exclusively through capital and its control.

Marxism, however, reifies class conflict as an historical universal: "The history of all past societies has consisted in the development of class antagonisms... One fact is common to all past ages, viz., the exploitation of part of society by the other." This formulation fails in two ways. It fails to account for the continued existence throughout history of bureaucratic forms which combine domination with a capacity to subdue antagonism by a system of rewards and status and by a rationalization of domination through the use of rules which mystify and conceal it. Second, it fails to recognize the extent to which primitive societies vary widely in their manifestation of a whole pattern of traits which tend toward the formation of a coherent gestalt or system. Some societies are egalitarian, co-operative, pacifistic, and relatively permissive; at the other end of the spectrum, other societies are riddled by social divisions and hierarchy which are property-oriented, competitive and aggressive. Both forms seem to be equally stable and enduring.

It is true that recent Marxism has taken cognizance of bureaucracy as a phenomenon occurring within socialism as well as capitalism. Also, it has combined its class analysis with a psychoanalytic theory of authoritarianism which explains the power orientation in terms very similar to those used by contemporary anarchists such as Alex Comfort and Paul Goodman. Nevertheless, the focus on the psychosocial origins of domination and hence of class has never been reconciled with the macroanalysis of class found in early Marxist thought and in Marx himself. Marxists cannot have it both ways: either class is perceived as a product of a historical dialectic, which of itself leads progressively to higher stages of human development into the stage in which class itself is transcended in the classless society, or class is to be understood as the particular product of a fundamental and continuing psychosocial dynamic which occurs under given conditions throughout human history, the overcoming of which constitutes the central radical project.

How Much Can We Rely on History?

The strategic implications of this difference in perspective are profound: in the case of the Marxist view of the process of historical development, capitalism must be accepted as a necessary stage, since only through the ultimate clarification of class divisions through the dominance of the economic forms of organization over all others can the internal contradictions of class itself be made to give way. This constitutes a reliance on historical forces which in its modern form is expressed by a reliance on technological advance to create the conditions for the abolition of class. Involved in this debate is the question of the role of scarcity in leading to a state of liberation. For Marxism, it is the evolution of the technology of production, out of which a surplus is created, that creates both classes and class society and at the same time the continuing dynamic whereby class itself can be transcended.

The reading of human history as inherently progressive, following the Darwinian ideas of evolution, is in fact the major basis for distinguishing anarchist thought from Marxism. In the main anarchists have refused to grant that history is revelatory of any *geist* or inherent dynamism which can be relied on to create the good society. Refusing to rely on history to do its job for them, anarchists seek where possible to build the future into the present by creating the nuclei of the good society within the existing situation. As a consequence, anarchists have tended to rely more on pre-industrial and pre-capitalist social forms out of which to build the libertarian values required by a good society.

Engels saw factory structure which imbued the workers with authoritarianism and hierarchy as the necessary basis capable of giving discipline to a workers' movement; the anarchists, in quite opposite fashion, saw the necessity of building a movement on those who were least imbued with such forms of consciousness. The anarchist focus on the psychosocial aspects of the problems of organization is central; for anarchism, theory must confront this central fact of authoritarian organization, whether economically exploitative or political, whether class-determined or bureaucratic, and build an alternative to it. Authoritarian structure itself is the central problem.

Such an approach has strategic significance today, within the context of the debate on whether Marxian categories have been superceded or are still relevant. Marxist methodology still dictates the search for the "objective contradictions" within the capitalist system which will lead to the possibility of class division and struggle. But with the continuing extension of the areas of bureaucratized organization characteristic of the modern welfare-warfare state, the major contradiction has less and less to do with relation to the means of production and more and more to do with the official ideology of freedom vs. the highly oppressive and authoritarian living and work environment. Whether as urban resident, welfare recipient, hospital patient, white-collar worker or blue-collar worker, today's citizen confronts at every turn large and authoritarian bureaucracies which process him or her like an IBM card. The central contradiction is precisely the one the anarchists point to: technology has vastly increased the scope of human power, leading to the possibility of human liberation from historic forms of bondage, from disease, and from starvation. It has extended the area of human freedom through communication, transportation and travel, and through the variety of artifacts and products. But it has done this through the construction of a system which is oppressive, bureaucratic, and irrational. The priorities are statist and grandiose: production as such, measured in terms of gross national product, the fielding of huge armies and weapons production, huge and dehumanizing industrial complexes. For the anarchist, the contradiction is that of the power orientation, magnified and abetted through technology, coming into conflict with the full play of human purposes. It is a contradiction which divides one person from another, creating the fundamental division of the dominator and the dominated in many complex forms; more basically, it creates the division within the person himself, thus rendering him both power-crazed and powerless at one and the same time.

The Psychology of Power: the Internal Enemy

The understanding of the psychology of power is a critical element in the anarchist understanding of the exercise of power within organizations. In such organizations the organizational dynamics and psychological dynamics come together. The extent to which people accept the system because they are bedazzled by its size and by the mythology of success and status constitutes a central problem. *The enemy, basically, is within, represented by the internalization of the authoritarian gestalt.* More than theories of alienation, this explains what holds people fast to the system and validates the anarchist understanding that fundamental changes in the behavior patterns—and beyond that in the forms of consciousness—are necessary in order to move toward liberation. The strategic task then becomes one of building the kind of movement which can provide concrete settings for self-determination and liberation from the authoritarian perspective—exactly what the Spanish anarchists were about during the 1930s.

Anarchists have been deficient, however, in applying this understanding of the psychology of power. As often as not, they have failed to develop strategies adequate to their insight about the problem of power within organizations. On the one hand, some anarchists like Michael Bakunin, while espousing the principle of self-determination and escape from authoritarianism, tended to see the revolutionary project as requiring a form of vanguardism involving a leadership by the enlightened, thus resulting of necessity in the creation of a centralist elite. In doing this they have fallen into the trap of Leninism. (Lenin, the supreme strategist of Marxism, saw that the objective contradictions of capitalism were insufficient to lead to revolution. Hence the need to create a revolutionary vanguard for whom the seizing of power was the objective to which all else was subordinate. Morality, humanity, every value was seen as not only subordinate to the revolutionary objective, but in fact as only definable in terms of that objective.) On the other hand, as Murray Bookchin suggests, there are anarchists who tend to reject the problem entailed by trying to create liberatory organizations; they have lapsed instead into cultural and individualist forms which seek liberation outside of the social and political arena.

Understanding the nature of the power system and the psychology of power requires a far broader form of social transformation than a simple mobilizing of the oppressed with the objective of seizing power. Liberatory organization must be created which can both express the psychology of voluntary association free of authoritarianism and at the same time confront and challenge the power system. Only in this way can the revolutionary project result in social transformation. Although this ideal has failed as often as not to be realized in practice, it provides a significant critique of the historical failures of Marxism to transform society. At its worst, Marxism has led to the replacement of early capitalist forms, as in Russia, with a bureaucratic collectivism even more coercive and extensive. In the parliamentary democracies, this strategy has been replaced, as in France and Italy, by the renunciation of revolutionary methods and the acceptance of access to power through parliamentary means. Here and elsewhere, as in Latin America, the Communist parties have tended to become upholders of what in their own terms would be bourgeois parliamentarianism against the various movements espousing guerrilla warfare or extra-parliamentary opposition. Some of these movements are also communist, and many of them Marxist, but the division in strategy can be seen as a product of the failure of capitalist societies to develop the revolutionary conditions which have been predicted as part of their historical development.

At the same time, state socialist countries have been forced to confront the problem of bureaucratic centralism and the emergence of a class system based on the party or the military, and one may argue that this is consonant—certainly from the anarchist perspective—with a flaw in the Marxian analysis of social organization. The Marxists see the need to transform capitalism through a workers' revolution that captures state power and sets up a socialist "dictatorship of the proletariat"; this socialist stage will eventually be followed by a classless communist society. The failure of Marxism, from the anarchist perspective, does not derive from any incompleteness of the revolutionary project, but rather from an inherent flaw in that project itself. The flaw is that it does not pause to analyze the broader organizational question which underlies not simply economic classes but bureaucracy and state power as well.

In contrast, the libertarian ideal of anarchism is unique in locating freedom in the area where the individual and the social meet: in the affinity groups of the Spanish anarchists, in the community associations of the Chilean workers' movement—in short, in face-to-face associations wherein praxis is based on direct experience rather than on the acceptance of a propagated ideology from above. Freedom, to be understood, must be lived for it is only through this experience that authoritarianism can be conquered.

This approach has been given a broad historical dimension in the recent work of Lewis Mumford, in which he traced the periodic emergence of mass totalitarian social forms and the conditions under which this occurs. Mumford diverges critically from Marxism by seeing these forms as originating in certain social, not technologic, conditions; these forms exemplify a certain inherent dynamic and pattern wherein the psychology of power is both expressed and reinforced by mass organization, which Mumford terms the "Megamachine."

For Mumford, it is the appeal of the mythology of power, seen as both power over nature and also as power over other human beings, which causes not simply class divisions, but also the whole system of rationalized domination. This system is concealed by myths of the divine right of kings, and by the appeal to national destiny; it is also concealed by the appeal to technological advance expressed by hierarchy, extensive specialization, bureaucratic regulation, and the division between the dominators and the dominated in the military, industrial and state hierarchies. In this view, just as the basis for positive values rests in man, not history, so the basis for evil, seen in the power orientation, also rests in man, not history. Hence just as human advance is a result of willed and conscious human achievement, so the Megamachine is also neither progressive nor historically determined, but a product of willed and conscious human action, determined by the quest for power.

Such a view explains how imperialism, a product of the inherent expansiveness of the Megamachine, can equally take nationalistic as well as economic forms and affirms that religious, nationalistic and ideological conflicts must be analyzed on their own terms, not as the superstructural manifestations of essentially economic causes. This view is consonant with the tradition of anarchist analysis which sees the state, of whatever ideological persuasion, as inherently warlike and coercive toward its inhabitants or neighbors.

Human Nature

This brings us to the final subject of this essay, the question of human nature. For anarchism this question is primary, since in locating both values and the origins of social evil in human beings rather than history, it is then faced with the problem of explaining how evil can arise not as a product of the historical process, but directly out of human nature. Here, it must be admitted, anarchist theory is weak, as we shall see, since it tends to posit the natural goodness of humans when liberated from the constraints of an unjust society. To the extent that it sees society as the cause of evil, it is left with an asymmetrical and non-dialectical condition in which good comes from individuals but evil comes from society. This avoids the dialectics of how human beings create the social order and in the process create themselves. For, as the Marxists amply remind us, human nature is a mere abstraction outside of its manifestations in society, and hence, if society manifests both human evil as well as good, both must be sought for in the dialectic whereby people create themselves through constructing the social order.

In its theory of human nature, Marxism exhibits two trends of thought, both in the early Marx and in its later Freudo-Marxist manifestations. Marx rejected the *homo duplex* view that has characterized much sociological and psychological thought. This view states that there is an implicit antagonism between humanity and society, expressed on one level in the biological antagonism which Freud saw between the demands of instinct and the demands of socialization and becoming civilized. At another level it can be seen as the area of human freedom and transcendence in which humanity remains only partially determined by its culture and can in turn act back and transform it.

Anarchism in its more simplistic forms has tended to see human beings as naturally good, corrupted by society, and in doing so it has failed to grasp the dilemma of social construction that George Lukacs expressed. Existentialism, in its one-sided emphasis on the absoluteness of human freedom, has also failed to come to terms with the social side of *homo duplex*. But the more sophisticated forms of anarchist thought, that of Paul Goodman and Alex Comfort, among others, have allied themselves with the Left Freudianism of Wilhelm Reich, seeing personal liberation in the psychoanalytic sense of a heightened self-awareness and self-understanding as the necessary concomitant of social liberation. The Freudian Left, even more than Freud, has focused on the problem of repression as the major way in which bourgeois society impinges on the individual. Consequently, they have seen de-repression, either in explicitly sexual terms (as with Reich) or in more generalized libidinal terms (as with Marcuse), as the path toward liberation. But here it can be argued that Marx, with his view of liberation as achieved through the "sensuous human activity" of work, was closer to the truth. This may sound suspiciously like the Marxist moralism that one finds pervasively in the revolutionary societies of Cuba and China, but the response to this is persuasive: erotic de-repression, even if it is expressed more broadly than in sexual terms, is in fact encouraged in contemporary capitalist societies, even though admittedly in distorted form. What is discouraged is not the various privatized forms that the search for the expression of the pleasure principle can take, but rather the opportunity to engage in the productive transformation of the society through control of the reified structures which are the real causes of repression. Such a control would require an integration of affectivity and libido with rationality: the long and difficult job of building a society fit for humanity, on a scale where social purpose could find full play.

What Remains to be Done

Marxism has almost totally failed in its effort to develop a full critique of contemporary industrial society, having for the most part accepted the unholy triumvirate of science, technology and industry as *per se* progressive. Only anarchists such as Paul Goodman and Murray Bookchin, and at an earlier time Peter Kropotkin, have sought to develop such a critique, despite accusations of utopianism. At present, libertarian thought is to be found in various places: among anthropologists such as Jules Henry and Stanley Diamond, who seek to enlighten the present by reference to the communal and co-operative forms of primitive society; among thinkers such as Paulo Freire and Ivan Illich, who seek to de-school society and raise individual consciousness; within the ecology and commune movements, where people seek to restore a more balanced and non-exploitative relationship to nature. In various ways these movements and thinkers are seeking new definitions of the social wherein the human demand for scope and freedom to develop can find its place. The focus here is on the social project itself, and the approach is conditioned by the view that, if the oppressions of class and bureaucratic organization are to be avoided, new social forms are necessary. This leads to the view that to devise strategies for change we must expand the understanding of everyday life, as that point where the social meets the individual.

Thus Henri Lefebvre suggests that in examining everyday life one can find the point of imbalance which can lead to change. A contemporary Marxist thinker, Lefebvre has sought to analyze the concrete conditions of contemporary existence both through the categories of everyday life and through the phenomenon of urbanism in order to be able to come up with a more extensive understanding of the psychosocial conditions of contemporary existence. Here we find a coming together of contemporary Marxist and anarchist thought.

Strategically, the development of an overall social critique must be rooted in the categories of everyday life. For it is here that the comprehensiveness of the critique as an intellectual construct confronts the experience and consciousness of people as a lived experience, comprising more than simply rational understanding.

To expand on Lefebvre, everyday life is where the society interacts in its concrete totality with the individual, while at the same time the individual responds with a consciousness which is in varying degrees both mystified and critical. An abstract social critique in the end must be evaluated by its capacity to shed light on how the social order is reflected in individual consciousness. To do this, such a critique must be capable of enlightening human possibility and human desire as well as concrete ability. It must understand both the warping of human consciousness and needs and also the ways in which the desire for realization and liberation remains. From the libertarian perspective, the desire for freedom is never totally crushed by false consciousness. Unless one accepts the notion of human beings as totally socially determined through socialization and conditioning, one must see self-liberation as the only definitive and lasting form of liberation. As Eugene Debs once said, if somebody can lead people into socialism, somebody else can lead them out again.

Building Workable Alternatives

Present social existence in the West is urbanized and anomic. In the United States more than three-fourths of the people live in cities, largely because the industrial system has sucked them in from rural areas. The system has made the urban centers into megapolitan jungles. It has broken down the integrity of communities and has created ecological problems that defy solution. Despite these ravages, however, a constant remains, even though it is not that of classes in conflict; rather, it is the unchanging human need for concrete and sensuous freedom expressed through interpersonal solidarity and meaningful activity. To speak to such a need requires that the existing organizational style and structure be totally replaced by organizations embodying the principles of free association. Today, the corporate sector of society has become institutionalized in law, in authoritarian attitudes which affect behavior, and in the structure of such supporting institutions as family, schools, universities, foundations, and governments. In the process, a systemic environment has been created, into which authoritarian organizations fit perfectly, while other kinds of organizations are marginal, lack support and the capacity to endure.

To counter the existing system, space must be created for a countersystem—an ecological environment of free institutions, serving mutually as the environment for each other, capable of providing the major cultural reality for individuals in them. The major activities of living must be incorporated—work, communal existence, education, culture, civic life. We can envisage a town or city or a region within a city as embodying free association within a coordinated and linked set of institutions. Such a unit would provide the concrete basis for the exposure of the myths of the existing system. As it developed, it could seek both to expand itself and to practice a politics of confrontation and exposure.

The developing countersystem will require a dialectical linkage with the existing system. Just as it is useless to confront the existing system when an alternative does not exist, so it is useless to build a countersystem which has no bridges to the existing system. If such linkages do not exist, the countersystem will be utopian and irrelevant, developing exotically according to the whims of people who are out of touch with the broader realities that surround them. The countersystem must show itself capable of both humanizing the existing technology and evolving libertarian forms of social structure. As we have seen, the existing system represents the path of least resistance. Restoring the basic links of affectivity and function makes the organization more complex. Hence, building workable alternatives is an essential task. Such alternatives can then seriously challenge the existing system with varieties of confrontation and interaction and can be a significant force for change. It is tempting for revolutionaries to substitute rhetoric for the harder job of restructuring the basic organizational units of the society. Yet such restructuring represents the only route to lasting change.

It is the anarchist argument that liberation must come through reconstruction around the principles of free association and solidarity. This requires a politics of participation that seeks to restructure the institutional units and, from there, work outward to the broader sociopolitical spheres. Only such a politics can confront directly the problem of control, which is also the problem of how power is exercised. Only such a politics can address adequately the social question. The egalitarianism demanded by the socialist vision can only be brought about by solving the problem of participation. When participation is lacking, psychic and material resources cluster in such a fashion as to reinforce the organizational imperative, whether the context be state capitalism or corporate capitalism. A politics of participation requires a respect for the primordial links of solidarity between individuals, which we may define as community. Community in turn thrives only in the context of free and voluntary association.

From Our Generation, *Vol. 10, No. 1, 1974. The last section, "Building Workable Alternatives," is from "Organization, Conflict and Free Association" in Benello and Roussopoulos (eds)* The Case for Participatory Democracy, *1971.*

Chapter 6

The Utopian Urge
(1975)

A Utopian Critique of Social Evil

The crisis of our times is as much one of human consciousness as it is one of social forms. For it is our view of human nature which defines the limits of social possibility, what can exist and what cannot, and hence serves as a context for possible social action.

The utopian urge is part of the perennial human yearning for a better world, for the Promised Land. But until this yearning can link itself to an accurate and specific critique of the causes of social evil, it will remain nothing more than an unformed yearning. To translate the yearning into a critique requires an understanding of the ways in which human consciousness and human nature are oppressed and distorted by the prevailing system. A society generates a set of images which define human nature so as to justify its goals and norms. In the family, school and business office, we are socialized, in part unconsciously, into an acceptance of certain kinds of behavior and certain attitudes towards ourselves and others as basic, i.e. deriving from human nature. To question these kinds of images requires a whole different vision, an affirmation of human nature which can lead to different social forms and different values.

The yearning for a better society is based on the view of human nature that people are innately capable of creating a good society. However, both utopian thought and conventional psychological theories of human nature have, until recently, described human beings as bundles of needs or passions, and as a result, have failed to grasp the importance of human growth and the full scope of human possibility.

The utopian aspect of Marxist thought has tended to be postponed into a vague future implementation, while its anti-utopian elements have become all too obvious. Moreover, utopian thought has had to confront the theories of Freud and the revelation of the destructive potential of the unconscious, as well as the unleashed violence of two world wars.

The "realists" argue that people will only respond to those issues which are obvious and experienced directly: poverty, racism, militarism, unemployment. In so doing, they accept the prevailing ideology that human nature is basically selfish, materialistic and violent. A basic feature of utopian thought is that life should be integrative—involving both intellectual and manual work, that work should be of personal as well as economic value, that the public sphere and the private sphere should be continuous, the rural and the urban should be integrated.

Utopian thought has itself moved toward a greater awareness of the domain of the inward. Indeed, it has been called "eupsychian" rather than utopian to emphasize its preoccupation with psychological phenomena rather than with social forms. With the development of depth psychology and the focus on the unconscious, utopian thought has had to address the problem of human violence, destructiveness, and the irrational part of human nature. Freud believed that human beings are motivated by biological drives such as hunger or sex which reside in the irrational unconscious mind. When these needs are satisfied, we lapse back into quiescence. This has been called the tension-reduction theory of motivation. The thinkers who represent this orientation—Wilhelm Reich, Norman O. Brown, Herbert Marcuse, and other members of the Frankfurt School—address themselves to the whole domain of the irrational in human behavior, and particularly in mass social behavior, which in their view, gave rise to Fascism and the death camps, to overkill and the nuclear calculus of mega-deaths.

The Real Nature of Social Repression

In their earlier writings, the Freudian Left, as some of these thinkers have been called, saw the problem primarily as the repression of basic instincts. Violence and destructiveness were for them the product of the irrational instincts which, when repressed, break out in negative and destructive forms. Hence liberation meant freeing the instincts or libido from the repressive influences of society. Norman O. Brown called for a return to the "primitive polymorphous perverse" that characterizes the generalized sexuality of the infant. Reich, from a different perspective, stressed the perfect orgasm as at least the visible sign that one is saved, while Marcuse spoke of a state where the surplus repression of Eros is lifted. But this singular emphasis on de-repression as the key to a psychologically healthy society, if not to utopia, brings with it some serious problems. The dominance of biologistic and reductionist thinking has diverted attention from the real nature of repression in our society. The real repression is not directed against libidinal gratification. Rather, it comes out of coercive and authoritarian institutions which organize life into "packages" of work and play with increasingly fine detail, infantilizing people into passive consumers. So long as advertising executives give their creative imagination to their Madison Avenue masters, they are perfectly free after hours to visit gay bars, smoke pot and generally mimic the counter-culture. Thus, it is the higher creative functions which are either repressed or exploited by our society, leading to a pervasive feeling of alienation and deprivation.

To combat this feeling of alienation and the loss of rootedness, it is necessary to restore community. But this is a different project than that envisaged by the Freudian Left, whose guiding idea was de-repression. For to liberate us from both the repressive influences of authoritarian families and authoritarian bureaucracies, one must construct alternatives capable of building the positive ties that constitute community. The one-sided emphasis on the de-repression of instinctual energy as the key to our predicament can be viewed as the psychic equivalent of some immature forms of revolutionism that occur on the left. Both wish to tear down repressive structures, believing that a better world will come out of spontaneity; but both fail to grasp the dialectic between freedom and structure. Positive freedom always involves concrete commitments and the building of social forms which can embody the social purposes of a humane society. In our own social experience, freedom too often appears possible only outside of the institutional structures of the society, and hence all structure is seen as oppressive. Attempts to create new social forms—co-ops, communes, collectives, free schools and the like—have often foundered on this dilemma because they see all rules, norms and required commitments as limitations of personal freedom and therefore undesirable.

The problem, therefore, with biological approaches to human motivation, is that they do not do justice to the developmental aspect of human nature, that is, the process whereby instincts themselves can be transformed into conscious and more fully human motivations. Freud recognized this possibility in his concept of sublimation, by which he acknowledged that higher or less biologically immediate motives can grow out of lower or more immediate ones. However, for Freud, civilization is inevitably repressive because people can only be socialized at the cost of taming their unconscious instincts. Thus sublimation does not really alter the basic patterns of sexuality and aggression; underneath our civilized veneer, we remain animals.

Liberation and Psychic Transformation

There is a new psychological movement called Third Force or humanistic psychology which goes beyond the concept of sublimation to recognize that a qualitative change takes place in motivation as it develops. For them, the urge towards artistic creativity, altruistic social action and the desire for knowledge cannot be explained as simply forms of sublimated sexuality or aggression. Genuine psychic transformation is possible, and as the instincts are formed and evolve, a new psychology arises.

From a psychic level oriented to the fulfillment of basic needs—physical needs, but also ego needs for self esteem and recognition—the human evolves to another level. Abraham Maslow has characterized this level as a Being psychology, dominated by the urge toward self-actualization, as opposed to a Need psychology, oriented toward need fulfillment. People, as they evolve, move outward from a state where all action is structured around the satisfaction of personal needs toward a condition where the ego and its needs are themselves transcended by identification with increasingly wider spheres of being and living.

If one accepts the possibility of development through psychic transformation, then human liberation becomes more than simply freeing us from repressive social bonds. Rather, it is the project of constructing a society which encourages human growth through psychic transformation, so that members of society can collectively attain a high level of psychosocial development. To understand what such a society would look like, we must understand more fully what the process of psychic transformation and development entails.

Freud is correct in one respect: psychic transformation involves the kind of struggle and challenge that he saw in the process of becoming civilized. But Freud saw this as a process whereby the basic instincts remained unchanged underneath their sublimations, and hence he saw it as a net loss of psychic energy. Without accepting this view, it is still important to recognize that psychic transformation, like repression, involves a battle with the instincts. In the case of repression, one solves a conflict between instinct or libido and the demands of growth by repressing one side of the conflict. Thus growth is blocked. In order to free the growth process, it is necessary to acknowledge the conflict by recognizing that repression exists. At this point, the problems have only begun, for one must start the process of transforming infantile reactions into those of an adult.

Wholeness and Disciplined Spontaneity

There is a symbolism which illustrates this process. It is a Zen parable in the form of a series of pictures. They show a man wandering through a forest. He comes across a bull. After a struggle, he mounts the bull. He then proceeds to tame it and make it do his will. At a certain point, the bull disappears. Soon after, the man too, disappears. In this parable, one may see the bull as libido, instinctual nature. Humans learns to master this nature, as in the Zen koan, which asks simply, "Who is the master?" With mastery, the instinctual nature disappears, having been fully transformed into human nature. This dialectical process then continues until human nature itself is transformed into a higher state. This may be taken to mean that the process of self-transformation ultimately results in self-transcendence. An analogous form of symbolism found in the West, is the bull fight. But here, the results are bloody, for they involve killing the bull—an idea perhaps more consonant with the Christian dualistic view that instinctual nature is evil and, rather than being mastered, must be done in.

Here we may have recourse to the Oriental doctrine of the Tao, with its Tao or *do*-disciplines seen as basic paths toward enlightenment. They lead to a condition variously termed "no-mind" or "one-pointedness" which can be described as a kind of disciplined spontaneity. In opposition to this, much of western learning leads to a mind burdened by knowledge, especially technical and scientific knowledge, and a psyche which remains unformed. Unlike western learning, the *do*-disciplines involve the full play of human faculties—aesthetic, physical, and intellectual. The learning method used is significant: it is a kind of learning by exhaustion, from doing something again and again. At the points when the task seems impossible, there is often a breakthrough. Psychologically interpreted, this demanding form of learning is necessary in order to break through previous habituations and stereotypic responses to a more informed consciousness. The idea of "no-mind" is precisely one of a highly trained spontaneity, a discipline which is not rationalistic, but penetrates to the core of personality—a trained unconscious, if you will.

If the path to psychic maturity involves transcending Need psychology by identifying with broader social values, then civilization is made fully possible. In other words, people are capable of partaking in the religious and cognitive dimensions of a society without suffering the penalty of inevitable repression. We grow, not by repressing those violent irrational instincts latent within us, but by widening our spheres of commitment and concern to a point where there is a genuine identification of our own good with broader social values for which, critically, we would give our lives. The wider we cast our net, the more we can become what we experience; the broader and higher our ideals, the more scope we have for growing into them. In such a view, society, which can also be seen to manifest a particular stage of development, may itself be transcended as we move beyond the particularistic values of a given culture.

Without the possibility of transforming the biological substratum of human behavior, one is left with the basic dualism illustrated by Freud and the Freudian Left. One may either say, with Freud, that civilization is inevitably repressive, or one may counter with the Freudian Left by saying that Utopia is nothing more than the state of polymorphous, pregenital sexuality. Both views ignore the human desire and capacity to strive for the ideal—the true definition of the utopian impulse.

Utopian thought must come to terms not only with repressed unconscious, internal drives, but also with the reality of externally created social evil. We still must explain how society institutionalizes evil, and particularly, how we have created the dehumanized and power-oriented society we see today. What we must look for then, is how self-reinforcing systems evolve and become institutionalized, serving to socialize subsequent generations born within the system. The potentiality for developing social systems which are either liberating or coercive, from the perspective of the individual, depends on the fact that such systems develop a close correspondence to personality systems. The later studies of the Frankfurt school on the authoritarian personality show that a basic type of social character is involved. Erich Fromm, in *Escape From Freedom*, studied the genesis of the power orientation within the family, an orientation intimately connected with the phenomena of early deprivation. In the words of Abraham Maslow: "To the basically deprived, the world is made up of two kinds of persons: those they can dominate, and those who dominate them." People brought up in an authoritarian family are taught a rigid form of self-control which is congruent with the urge to control others. Emotions are feared, and the periodic and explosive emotional outbursts which such a system engenders then justify the fear. This orientation interacts with authoritarian, power-centered institutions from the family to the larger corporate and state bureaucracies, reinforcing both a basic authoritarian social character and a hierarchical organizational structure.

For those who work within the larger repressive institutions, the process of identification with the internal authority system takes the form of submission to and identification with those in command and domination of those below. Nor are attitudes engendered in work confined to the workplace. Thus the circle completes itself.

The power orientation is thus a personality system, created in part by deprivation, i.e., here possibilities for healthy growth are foreclosed by the rigidities of the system. Where natural forms of face-to-face association have broken down, seeking after power becomes an alternative means to security and a sense of the self. Where natural human functions cannot be fulfilled, power becomes an end in itself, sought after in its own right. From this comes the megalomania which results in an institutional order Lewis Mumford characterized as the "Megamachine"—a mass form of social organization based on coercion and the bribery of external rewards. Such social orders are inherently expansive, since no amount of power can compensate for the loss of natural function and emotion. Hence aggrandizement and the centralization of all vital social, psychic and material resources are basic features of the system. The remaining natural functions and groupings within the social order are eroded in the process, creating a social and psychic wasteland. The resultant environment of psychic deprivation is fertile ground for the continued growth of the power orientation.

Such a system creates a basic division between dominated and dominators. A central feature of such a system is its loss of what we have characterized as the utopian ideal: the loss of personal integrity, expressed as the loss of wholeness within work and living. Such a perspective is central to the libertarian and anarchist traditions, which have refused to accept the fact of human domination wherever it is experienced. Rather than seeing it as a necessary step in human evolution, to be transcended when the final revolution establishes the classless society, they have continuously opposed all forms of domination, whether it be of the state, the industrial system, or the family.

Psychic Growth:
Safeguard Against the Power Orientation

From the psychological perspective developed here, what emerges is that only wholeness, the restoration of individual integrity within social forms which integrate the basic functions of life, can serve as an effective safeguard against the power orientation. But wholeness is a product of psychic growth within a favorable environment, and to seek to impose it from without by some form of pre-established harmony is to fall into the contradiction at the heart of the power orientation. To speak of integration is to speak of a type of wholeness which is openended. For a favorable social environment must be continuously responsive to further modification and transformation, as succeeding generations enter into it and seek to make it their own. Without this feature the link between the social order and the individual need for growth is lost.

If one accepts the transformational view of human nature, one must accept the discipline imposed by consciousness and reason as the necessary prerequisite to development. The answer to our present system, a reified objectivity, is not a regression to pure subjectivity, but rather a reintegration of the two. The oriental *do* disciplines are paradigms in this regard: consciousness and reason, rather than a rigid, abstract, technological rationality, are used to inform impulse. The result is a disciplined spontaneity that is highly trained and totally in touch, while possessed of complete immediacy. Any movement for social change with enduring value must be capable of confronting the basic psychosocial contradiction of contemporary society. It must come up with answers capable of integrating subjectivity and objectivity, the individual and the social. This is the essence of the dialectic of liberation.

Toward Humanist Organization

In summary, humanist (or liberatory) organization must be grounded in the possibility of two kinds of human freedom: freedom from the domination of instincts and human needs on the one hand, and freedom from the domination of reified institutions and their capacity to dominate human consciousness and subjectivity on the other. A theory of psycho-social development which goes beyond instinct theory is necessary for the affirmation of inner freedom; a theory of organizational development which can transcend the various iron laws which equate formal organizations with bureaucracy is necessary for the organizational freedom. It is also necessary to develop a notion of the dialectic of liberation wherein the two types of freedom interact and reinforce each other. Perhaps the most difficult conception here is that of a structure which can evolve through self-organizing and participation, capable of responding continuously to the needs of its members. What is required here is more structure rather than less; humanist organization is more complex, with more horizontal linkages, more decision-making loci, more overlapping sub-structures, and more provisions for modification than hierarchical organization.

As Charles Hampden-Turner has suggested in *Radical Man,* organizational structure is in many ways a reflection of psychological structure; psychological development moves from determination to greater freedom, such that freedom is an end product, not a beginning. If we consider the polar variables of development as expressed for example by Maslow's progression through a needs hierarchy to a Being-psychology, we perceive a similar dialectic of development which takes into account both inner and outer determinations but moves toward greater freedom in both. Freedom is the progressive capacity to master both the inner determinations of biology and early history and the outer determinations of conformism and of socialization to a limited and culture-bound society. Dependency gives way to autonomy, and a consciousness determined by instinctual and social categories transforms into a consciousness aware both of itself and of society.

As previously asserted, these two freedoms are intimately linked. Freedom understood as an end product, rather than a beginning, requires a social context in which growth is promoted rather than hindered—socialization can liberate as well as restrict. And the family, although a crucial early element in such a context, exists only as a subsystem within, and affected by, the larger organizations of the society. Even if family life is growth-promoting, full development can never be attained in a world of repressive and stultifying work. On the other hand, where work allows a participatory structure, the ongoing task of social construction becomes a major vehicle for the continuing development of the individual. Where people are able to participate in the continuing shaping of their organizations, they are able in the process to shape themselves.

From Liberation, *Vol. 19, No. 5, May 1975. The last section of this essay is taken from "Toward a Grounded Theory of Humanist Organization,"* Humanity and Society, *Vol. 4, No. 2, 1980.*

Part III

Bringing Democracy Into The Workplace

Chapter 7

Economic Democracy and the Future (1978)

The Theory of Self-Management

Self-Management falls within the tradition of direct democracy that has existed as a minor element within Western political theory and practice since the time of the Greeks. It has seen practical expression in a variety of places throughout history: the Canton of Appenzel in Switzerland has had a system of direct democracy for several centuries; the Diggers espoused it under their leader Winstanley in seventeenth-century England; some of the nineteenth-century Utopian experiments in England and America employed it; the Spanish anarchists practiced it in northern Spain before the Civil War; and lastly, the New Left and much of the civil rights movement practiced it in their organizing efforts in the sixties.

Arguments in favor of self-management fall into four categories: psychological, political, ethical, and prudential. The *psychological argument*, supported by contemporary humanistic and developmental psychology, stresses the importance of control over the immediate conditions of work and life as central in the development of competence and identity. The development of skills, manual or mental, allows for pride in accomplishment; they set a person off from others. Forms of competence that are recognized and valued give a secure sense of personal worth. Research has confirmed the Marxian notion of the centrality of "sensuous human activity" for human development by showing that psychosocial development is not merely a matter of inter-

personal relations but depends on the acquisition of skills and competence. Empirical studies of work indicate that the single most important
contributor to worker satisfaction is the ability to participate, while the
major factor in worker alienation is powerlessness. Self-actualization
goes beyond survival needs. In terms of work this actualization can only
take place in a non-coercive environment where people are free to
co-determine with their fellow workers the conditions and nature of their
work.

The *political argument* for self-management is rooted in an understanding of authoritarianism and of the psychopathology of power.
Elitists argue that government should be left to those few most fit to
govern. Yet the increased power of governments to determine questions
of life and death and their failure to meet human needs and to avoid
recurrent crises has rendered this theory suspect. In the private sector,
appeals to managerial expertise and capitalist ideology, e.g. survival of
the fittest, profit as primary, etc. are offered as the basis for elitist
management.

Direct democracy counters this elitism by arguing that one cannot
delegate to others the determination of what is in one's own vital
interests. It asks the ancient question, *quis custodet ipsos custodes*—who
will oversee the overseers? With increasing technological complexity,
the argument for elitism may have become stronger; but so has the
counter-argument, which points to the many ways technological and
managerial elitism victimize the average person.

The *ethical argument* for self-management is based on the doctrine of the primacy of the person—the dictum of philosopher Immanuel
Kant that human beings are never just means to an end, but are ends in
themselves. People exist for the sake of their own development, not as
raw material for someone else's. The necessary social expression of this
insight is organization that eschews all forms of domination or manipulation.

The psychological, political, and ethical arguments for self-management meet in the classical Greek concept that politics is the key to
the good life. For the Greeks, the essential elements in *Paedeia*, or
education, were ethics and politics. The German sociologist Jurgen
Habermas has noted that in classical Greek culture "politics was always
directed toward the formation and cultivation of character; it proceeded
pedagogically, not technically." Viewed in this fashion, self-manage-

ment is identical with direct democracy and has inherent value not simply as a means to human liberation, but also as the immediate expression of that liberation.

As for the *prudential argument*, consider first a dominant image of the future: that of increasing scarcity, which will place severe strains on the economic system. Those who predict this future argue that a corporate state will emerge, dominated by a system of planning and control instigated by and for the benefit of large corporations in conjunction with the state. What is likely to be lost in the process is the tradition of democratic government that has characterized the last few centuries in the West. A major thread in these arguments is that the present industrial system is based on the possibility of unlimited growth, and this continued growth makes the inequities and maldistribution of the system both within nations and between rich and poor nations endurable. But growth is reaching its limits, and as this happens the social pressures will build up, leading to explosions of discontent primarily aimed at the wealthy nations. Moreover, as industrial growth recedes, this discontent will be experienced within the wealthy nations as well.

Growing resource shortages combined with population pressures are likely to result in increasingly authoritarian political systems. Ecologists have seriously questioned whether the traditional *laissez-faire* mechanisms are capable of dealing with a world of limited resources. Given this increasingly likely image of the future, the alternatives are clear: either a world governed by some sort of amalgam of corporate-state control in which the citizen has little say or a world in which the present tendencies toward centralized control are countered by movements toward democratization and the restoration of popular control.

Moreover, other pragmatic—and more immediate—grounds favor the introduction of democracy at work. Workplace democracy has been shown to give workers a stake in expanding company productivity, to compensate them for accepting reduced wages, to promote feelings of ownership and pride in high quality workmanship, and to contribute to labor cost savings arising from the elimination of superfluous middle management or supervisory personnel. In addition, today's increasingly youthful workers—influenced by the protest culture of the 1960s and 1970s—require more than a decent paycheck; typically, they expect a greater measure of freedom and responsibility on the job. Democratic worksites can meet this sort of demand far better than those relying on old-fashioned, assembly line forms of organization.

Implicit in the self-management alternative is the principle of decentralism, which requires that all decisions about economic issues be carried out at the lowest level possible, leaving only coordinating functions to the highest level. The American corporate system is a particularly good place to develop a movement for decentralization. Having lost its monopolistic position in the world economy and faced with increasingly organized cartels controlling the vital resources that are in short supply, the American corporate system can no longer be the guarantor of the American Dream.

The degeneration and delegitimation which is manifesting itself at the base of the society does not take a glaring or startling form. Yet each year the statistics of social pathology grow, and with them, alienation and unrest. For those able to find work, the dichotomy expands between their expectations and the realities of increasingly depersonalized work in large organizations. But the system is unable to provide anything beyond subsistence-level living and unemployment or underemployment for an increasing number, somewhere over one quarter of the population (depending on where the poverty line is drawn). Here expectations enter in as well. If work cannot be intrinsically rewarding, at least it must be capable of delivering the standard consumer package that represents membership in the middle class—a late model car, appliances, big screen color TV, a house in the suburbs.

As the mythology of the Land of Opportunity fades in the face of urban crime and degeneration, meaningless work, cynicism about big business and big government, the remaining legitimacy of the corporate system is largely negative. It may be imperfect, even dehumanizing and unjust, but (supposedly) there is no system that can deliver the goods any better. This view is pragmatic; the system is justified because it works, even if not very well. Criticism becomes threatening, because there is no use knocking the only game in town. But herein lies the significance of a movement for the humanization of the workplace. The technological-industrial system determines the basic thrust and nature of the United States as an advanced post-industrial society. The workplace is the point where that technological-industrial system confronts human social organization; it is the logical place to begin a movement toward genuine, decentralized democracy.

A movement striving to bring to life viable and effective models of humanized work, capable of creating useful and consumer-oriented products while utilizing a high level of technology, would strike at the heart of the corporate system in a number of ways. It could appeal to the new consumer and ecological consciousness that is in part responsible for the low esteem in which the corporate system is held. It could appeal to the growing group of unemployed or those employed in positions below their skill and education level. And it could appeal to the large group of organized blue-collar workers whose disaffection at present takes the form of absenteeism, drugs, and sabotage. As André Gorz has said, workers are hardly likely to take to the streets for a fifty-cent-an-hour pay raise. But a movement creating not only jobs but also self-determination and freedom in work, committed to producing goods with integrity and usefulness, would not only appeal to basic material needs but would also provide a live basis from which a critique of both the dehumanization of work and the falseness of current consumer values could be made. In short, the actual creation of self-managed enterprises that furnish socially useful and ecologically sound products could be the first step in democratizing all of society's institutions.

On the Road to Self-Management and Democracy

To bring economic democracy to the United States it is necessary to demonstrate concretely that self-managed, democratic work organizations can function efficiently and at the same time be responsive both to workers' needs and those of the consumer. But establishing individual and isolated enterprises is not enough. Supporting institutions must be developed that can both assist the sound economic development of these enterprises and also link them together into a closely knit system capable of mutual support and cooperation. This may sound like a scheme to develop a self-managed conglomerate, but there is a critical difference: a conglomerate is linked through centralized control and through the funneling of all profits into the central holding company. A self-managed system, however, is linked by bonds of voluntary cooperation wherein control rests with the working members of each enterprise; there is only a voluntary contribution of profits to some central fund or bank in order to develop more enterprises.

A continuing educational effort, parallel to the economic effort, is also necessary. The present system of corporate managerialism is based on separation of intellectual skills from manual skills so that management monopolizes the former, and the production technology is deliberately specialized and limited to the most simple operations. In order to humanize work and allow workers to make use of their brains as well as their brawn, there must be a training program implemented in each self-managed plant that reintegrates management and work skills through rotation of supervisory and management functions, the democratic selection of managers from the workplace, and a continuing program of education in the elements of accounting, finance, law, marketing—in short, in management skills—for those interested. At present there is a clear division between those who engage in manual work, whether blue collar or white collar, and those earmarked for management. The latter are products of a specialized education, and typically come from a different class background. A democratic system of work organization must seek to counter this disparity in education by making management skills available to all.

Also needed are new sources of capital and forms of capital control. Pooled risk, mutual fund investment vehicles would eliminate the need for single large investors, and in the process do away with the demand for external control by investors. Such pooled investments can offer high fixed interest rates to reflect the risk or variable interest rates pegged to worker-productivity indicators. These investments would in fact be safer, on a number of counts, than those in conventional corporations, since the conditions under which a portion of the profits would be paid out could be clearly defined instead of being subject to the decisions of a self-perpetuating board of directors. Also, self-managed companies lack incentives, such as tax-loss benefits, to go bankrupt that conventional corporations have. Once control is vested in the working members themselves, there would be a maximum incentive to maintain jobs and preserve the company.

Mondragon, a Spanish network of producer cooperatives, has demonstrated for the past several decades of its existence that people can be motivated by broader goals than simply income. In Mondragon, the maximum wage differential was originally 1:3. Managers chose to stay with Mondragon despite the limitation on their income level because they formed part of a working community committed to values that extend well beyond profit-making. Moreover, jobs created in a self-managed system such as Mondragon are far more permanent than those in the corporate system; there have been virtually no layoffs in Mondragon since the system first began, and only two or three business failures. A cooperative credit union serves as the development bank for the entire system, providing both the technical expertise as well as the funding necessary to ensure that all the firms in the system (approximately ninety industrial firms, as well as a large number of agricultural, housing and consumer cooperatives) maintain their economic viability.

Economic Democracy and the Future

Economic democracy envisions a future deeply rooted in the history of the United States. The early system of representative democracy based on geographic divisions did not foresee the rise of large corporate systems operating on a national and multinational level, with the power to shape the physical and social landscape, to dispose of the country's national resources, and to dictate forms of transportation, products, services, and even culture. Such economic decisions affecting the lives of a large number of citizens are made today and will continue to be made. The question is whether these decisions will be made by a few, without public accountability and in the interests of a few, or whether a system can evolve that is capable of ensuring that these decisions are made democratically, in the interests of the majority.

This vision of the future questions the belief in progress through technology that characterizes both Western liberalism and much of Marxism. It seeks to humanize technology and make it serve human ends. It has therefore much in common with the "limits to growth" vision of a conserver or steady-state society. But it questions the ability of even a well-intentioned elite to plan the future, believing that the critical question is who plans for whom. It seeks to introduce popular and democratic control into the heart of the technological-industrial system where it affects people's lives most directly, namely in the workplace. Rather than seeking to legislate control from the outside, leaving the basic structure with its narrow orientation toward profits intact, it seeks to build in other kinds of goals, ones that will evolve integrally and organically out of the conditions of working life. The vision projected is decentralist, humanistic, and oriented toward community. Rather than creating ever-larger plants and increasing productivity, it sees work as central to human fulfillment and seeks to link work to other aspects of living, by having control over the workplace rest with those who also are the consumers and community members. Work itself is transformed. It becomes intrinsically meaningful, engaged in not for survival or to build up retirement income, but for its own sake. All citizens capable of working would have a right not to a guaranteed income, but to the possibility of worthwhile work in which they can develop their full humanity. In the political system, each person is equal, possessing one vote. Economic democracy would apply this same principle to the economic system, in this way combining technological and industrial development with the social values and vision embodied in the demo-cratic ideal.

From Clement Bezold (ed), Anticipatory Democracy, *1978.*

Chapter 8

The Challenge of Mondragon (1986)

In the Beginning...

The Basque region of Spain has, in recent years, seen the rise of a system of cooperatives that is unparalleled in its dynamism, growth, and economic impact on a region. The system, which spreads throughout the surrounding Basque region, is named after Mondragon, a town in the mountains of Guipuzkoa Province near Bilbao, the place where the first cooperatives started. Since its start over thirty years ago, it has gained an international reputation, with similar models now being developed in England, Wales, and the United States.

While its explicit connections to the anarchist tradition are unclear, the Mondragon system is an example of liberatory organization which, like its predecessors in the Spanish Civil War, has achieved success on a scale unequaled in any other part of the world.

The Mondragon network was founded by a Catholic priest, Don José Maria Arizmendi, a man who had narrowly missed being put to death by Franco as a result of his participation in the Spanish Civil War on the Republican side. With the help of collections from citizens of Mondragon, he founded an elementary technical school in 1943. The first graduates numbered among them five men who, in 1956, founded a small worker-owned and managed factory named ULGOR, numbering initially 24 members, and given to the manufacture of a copied kerosene stove.

This cooperative venture proved successful and developed into the "flagship enterprise" of the whole system which later was to come into being. At one point ULGOR numbered over 3,000 members, although this was later recognized as too large and was reduced. The structure of this enterprise served as the model for the latter enterprises forming the system. Following the Rochedale principles, it had one member-one vote; open membership; equity held by members and hence external capitalization by debt, not equity; and continuing education.

Additional Principles

However, it adapted and added to these principles in a fashion that made it differ significantly from industrial cooperatives developed hitherto. It is these additional principles which are responsible for its dynamism and success, in contradistinction to almost all industrial cooperatives which preceded it. The additions can be summarized as follows:

1. It developed a system of individual internal accounts into which 70 percent of the profits (a more accurate term is "surplus") of the cooperative were placed. Each member had such an internal account. Thirty percent were put into a collective account for operating capital and expansion, with a portion of that being earmarked for the community. The individual internal accounts noted receipt of the portion of the surplus earmarked for it, but this was then automatically loaned back to the cooperative, with interest paid. Upon leaving, members receive 75 percent of the accumulated funds credited to their internal account, while 25 percent is retained as the capitalization which made the job possible. This system essentially allows the cooperative to capitalize close to 100 percent of its yearly profit and gives it a capacity for internal capital accumulation unequaled by any capitalist enterprise. It also establishes an ongoing flow-through relation between the individual and collective portions of the surplus.

2. A membership fee was determined, now equivalent to about $3,000, which represents a substantial investment in the cooperative, and which could be deducted from initial earnings. This too is credited to the internal account. Both the membership fee and the share of the surplus represent methods of ensuring commitment through financial incentives. Unlike older cooperatives, which often determined the membership fee on the basis of dividing the net worth into the number of shares,

hence making the membership fee prohibitive, the fee is arbitrary and fixed at an affordable amount.

3. Unlike traditional cooperatives, members are considered to be worker-entrepreneurs, whose job is both to assure the efficiency of the enterprise but also to help develop new enterprises. They do this in their deliberative assemblies and also by depositing their surplus in the system's bank, described below, which is then able to use it to capitalize new enterprises. There is a strong commitment on the part of the membership to this expansive principle, and it is recognized that the economic security of each cooperative is dependent on their being part of a larger system, in ways that will become clear as we proceed.

4. A probationary period of one year was instituted, to ensure that new members were not only appropriately skilled, but possessed the necessary capacity for cooperative work. Whereas in a capitalist enterprise workers are considered "factors of production," in a cooperative they are members of an organization with both the rights and duties of membership, sharing also in the ownership of the organization. Thus while there is open membership, members must be able to participate not simply as hired hands but must be able to discharge their membership duties by sharing in the management of the enterprise. This requires a capacity for responsibility and group participation that in turn implies a certain level of maturity.

5. The "anticipo" or earnings that would in a conventional enterprise be considered as wages, was fixed at prevailing wage levels, minimizing conflict with other local enterprises. Also, the wage differential—the difference between the lowest and highest wage—is strictly limited to an agreed upon range. This ensures an egalitarianism between workers and the elected management (selected by the General Assembly of workers) that makes for high morale. Wage levels are determined by a formula which takes into account the difficulty of the job, personal performance, experience, and interpersonal skills. Relational skills have been given greater weight recently out of a recognition that in cooperative work they significantly affect group performance.

6. Above all, Mondragon represents a "systems approach" to cooperative development. In addition to the base-level industrial cooperatives there are a set of so-called second degree cooperatives which variously engage in research, financing, technical training and education, technical assistance, and social services. In addition there are

housing and consumer cooperatives which collectively are able to create a cooperative culture in which the basic activities of life take place. Members can operate within a context of interdependent and cooperating institutions which follow the same principles; this makes for enhanced efficiency.

A Credit Union Is Added

To continue the story, three years after ULGOR was founded, Don Arizmendi suggested the need for a financial institution to help fund and give technical assistance to other start-up cooperatives. As a result, the Caja Laboral Popular (CLP), a credit union and technical assistance agency was founded. The CLP contains an Empressarial Division, with a staff of over 100, which works intensively with groups desiring to start cooperatives or in rare cases to convert an existing enterprise. It does location studies, market analysis, product development, plans the buildings, and then works continuously for a number of years with the start-up group until it is clear that its proposal is thoroughly developed and financially and organizationally sound. In return, the CLP requires that the cooperative be part of the Mondragon system, via a "Contract of Association," which specifies the already proven organizational and financial structure and entails a continuing supervisory relation on the part of the CLP. The surplus of the industrial cooperatives is deposited in the CLP and reinvested in further cooperatives. This close and continuing relationship with the financial and technical expertise of the CLP is both unique and largely responsible for the virtually 100 percent success rate within the system.

The CLP is considered a second degree cooperative, and its board is made up of a mix of first level or industrial cooperative members and members from within the CLP itself. In addition to the CLP there are a number of other second degree cooperatives: a social service cooperative which assures 100 percent pension and disability benefits, a health care clinic, and a women's cooperative which allows for both flex-time and part-time work; women can move freely from this to the industrial cooperatives. Also there is a system of educational cooperatives, among them a technical college which includes a production cooperative where students both train and earn money as part-time workers. This, too, is operated as a second degree cooperative with a mixed board made up of permanent staff and students.

The Mondragon Network

Mondragon also features a large system of consumer cooperatives, housing cooperatives, and a number of agricultural cooperatives and building cooperatives. Today the total system's net worth is in the billions. Mondragon consists of 86 production cooperatives averaging several hundred members, 44 educational institutions, seven agricultural cooperatives, 15 building cooperatives, several service cooperatives, a network of consumer cooperatives with 75,000 members, and the bank. The Caja Laboral has more than 130 branches in the Basque region and has an office in Madrid as well as in Barcelona. This is significant, since it indicates a willingness to expand beyond the Basque region. The CLP's assets are over a billion dollars.

Mondragon produces everything from home appliances—it is the second largest refrigerator manufacturer in Spain—to machine tool factories and ferry boats, both of which it exports abroad. It represents over 1 percent of the total Spanish export product. With over 20,000 workers, it accounts for about 15 percent of all the jobs in Guipuzkoa Province and 5 percent in the Basque country. Although a major part of its products are in middle level technologies, it also produces high technology products. Its research institute, Ikerlan, regularly accesses U.S. data bases including that of M.I.T., and has developed its own industrial robots for external sale and for use in its own factories. This is typical of its approach to technology, which is to assimilate new technologies and make them its own. Mondragon has spent considerable time studying and implementing alternatives to the production line; its self-managed organizational system is now being complemented with the technology of group production.

The internal organization of a Mondragon cooperative features a General Assembly which ordinarily meets annually and selects management. In addition there is a Social Council which deals specifically with working members' concerns. There is also a Directive Council, made up of managers and members of the General Assembly, in which managers have a voice but no vote. This system of parallel organization ensures extensive representation of members' concerns and serves as a system of checks and balances. Mondragon enterprises are not large; a deliberate policy now limits them to around 400 members. ULGOR, the first co-op, grew too large and at one point in its early history had a strike, organized by dissidents. The General Assembly voted to throw the ringleaders out. But they learned their lesson. Size of its own accord can breed discontent.

To obtain the benefits of large scale, along with the benefits of small individual units, Mondragon has evolved a *system* of cooperative development. Here, a number of cooperatives constitute themselves as a sort of mini-conglomerate, coordinated by a management group elected from the member enterprises. These units are either vertically or horizontally integrated and can send members from one enterprise to the other as the requirements of the market and the production system change. They are able to use a common marketing apparatus and have the production capacity to retain a significant portion of a given market. This system was started initially by a set of enterprises in the same market banding together for inter-enterprise cooperation. Now Mondragon develops such systems from the outset.

Effectiveness of Mondragon

If one enters a Mondragon factory, one of the more obvious features is a European style coffee bar, occupied by members taking a break. It is emblematic of the work style, which is serious but relaxed. Mondragon productivity is very high—higher than in its capitalist counterparts. Efficiency, measured as the ratio of utilized resources—capital and labor—to output, is far higher than in comparable capitalist factories.

One of the most striking indications of the effectiveness of the Mondragon system is that the Empressarial Division of Mondragon has continued to develop an average of four cooperatives a year, each with about 400 members. Only two of these have ever failed. This amazing record can be compared with business start-ups in this country, over 90 percent of which fail within the first five years. I have seen a feasibility study for a new enterprise. It is an impressive book-length document, containing demographics, sociological analysis of the target population, market analysis, product information—just about everything relevant. When a new prospective cooperative comes to Mondragon seeking help, it is told to elect a leadership. This leadership studies at the

Empressarial Division for two years before they are allowed to start the cooperative; they thus learn every aspect of their business and of the operation of a cooperative.

Mondragon is not utopia. While it does not produce weapons, useless luxury goods, or things that pollute the environment, it does produce standard industrial products using a recognizable technology of production. It does not practice job rotation, and management is not directly elected from the floor—for good reason, since experiments elsewhere that have tried this have not worked. Members vary in the nature of their commitment. In fact there is something of a split in Mondragon between those who see Mondragon as a model for the world and those who prefer to keep a low profile and have no interest in proselytizing beyond their confines.

Mondragon has also been faulted for failing to produce mainly for local consumption. It is in the manufacturing, not community development business, and, while it creates jobs, its products are exported all over the world. It has exported machine tool factories to eastern European countries, to Portugal and to Algeria; a Mondragon furniture factory is now operating in New York State. Mondragon does not export its system with the factories however; they are simply products, bought and run by local owners. In general, it makes little attempt to convert the heathens; at present, it is swamped by visitors from all over the world, and it finds this hard enough to deal with without going out and actively spreading the word.

Mondragon has awakened worldwide interest. The Mitterand government in France has a special cabinet post for the development of cooperatives, the result of its contact with Mondragon. In Wales, the Welsh Trade Union Council is engaged in developing a system of cooperatives patterned after Mondragon. In England, the Job Ownership Movement along with numerous local governments, developed both small and large cooperatives on the Mondragon model. Progressives in the Catholic Church, seeing Mondragon as an alternative to both capitalism and communism, have helped establish industrial cooperatives in Milwaukee and in Detroit; and in Boston this writer worked with the local archdiocese to plan the development of a system of cooperatives based on the same model.

Why does Mondragon work so well? Part of the answer lies in the unique culture of the Basque region. Members of the staff of Mondragon with whom I have talked (those of Ikerlan, the research institute, and of ULARCO, the first of the mini-conglomerates) have doubts about whether the model can be exported, arguing that the cohesiveness and communitarian traditions of the Basque culture alone make it possible. But Anna Gutierrez Johnson, a Peruvian sociologist who has studied Mondragon extensively, believes that basically it is the *organizational pattern* that makes the whole system work, and that this is exportable. I share her opinion, but also believe that in the United States our culture of individualism and adversary worker-management relations is a major impediment. Workers have little ideological consciousness in this country; moreover, they have very largely bought into the capitalist system and often see work as a ticket into the middle class. But their lack of ideology is nonetheless a plus in one way, for *the secret of Mondragon is, above all, organizational, not ideological: it is "how-to" knowledge that makes it work.* Knowledge, for example, of how specific industry sectors work, of how to facilitate cooperation between the CLP and worker-entrepreneurs, of how to ensure that individual enterprises are integrated into the Mondragon community.

Mondragon has revolutionary implications, primarily because its structure of democratic governance, with worker ownership and control, challenges the capitalist system at its very heart. Where capitalism awards profit and control to capital and hires labor, Mondragon awards profit and control to labor. In the process, it has developed a worker-centered culture which, rather than infantilizing, empowers. Mondragon members are citizens of a worker commonwealth, with the full rights that such citizenship confers. This can be seen best in the steps that have been taken to make the formal system of participation into a working reality: different systems of leadership have evolved, and with them, a growing sense of teamwork. For example, a furniture factory now operates completely through work teams. Thus the formal system has led to the ongoing evolution of a democratic process which is the real indicator of its success in revolutionizing the relations of production.

Also, Mondragon has created a *total system* where one can learn, work, shop, and live within a cooperative environment. (On such total systems, see Antonio Gramsci.) In such an environment motivation is high because members share an overall cooperative culture which integrates material and moral incentives, and which extends into every aspect of life—work, community, education, consumption, and family.

A member of the Empressarial Division has underlined the uniqueness of Mondragon viewed as a total system, pointing out that this system goes far beyond what can be found in the Basque culture. The proof of this is to be found in the efforts needed to socialize new workers into the system; the simple fact of being Basque is hardly enough to guarantee effective participation.

Lessons of Mondragon

Perhaps one of the most brilliant achievements of the Mondragon organizational system is the way in which it has combined collective ownership with the incentives of individual ownership in a mixed system which recognizes both the individual and the collective side of human motivation. The system of individual accounts with automatic loan-back, along with the partitioning of the surplus into an individual component and a collective component, represents a method of giving the worker a sense of individual ownership along with a sense of collective participation in an organization which provides more than simply a meal ticket, even as it expects more than simply job performance.

A strong argument can be made for the importance of creating more networks like Mondragon—if one is to move toward social liberation. Its systems approach to job creation confronts the problems of economic organization and development head-on, managing at once to create freedom in work and enough jobs to have a powerful impact on a regional economy. Until it happened, it was easy to write off experiments in economic democracy as marginal and unrealistic utopian ventures, totally irrelevant to the task of affecting any sizeable portion of an existing economy. This can no longer be said, and hence both state socialist and capitalist arguments for the economic necessity of oppressive work are given the lie.

Moreover, Mondragon contains an important lesson. It demonstrates that to achieve freedom in work, a high level of organizational skill is needed, and that when such skills are present, the traditional opposition of democracy and efficiency vanish, and the two reinforce rather than oppose each other. Mondragon is important because it serves as a model of how this can be done. Here, ideological debate gives way to concrete know-how and another false dilemma bites the dust. Centralization in concert with modern technologies, entirely apart from the further coercions of capitalist ownership, contains pressures toward an oppressive machine form of organization. This is true both because of its large scale and its productivity requirements; these pressures are greatest in the case of mass production.

Taming this contemporary organizational beast thus represents a challenge which must be met if one is to create freedom in work. This type of organization, moreover, is central to advanced industrial societies. It would be nice, utopian fashion, to simply be able to leap over the problem and go back to small-scale craft production, thereby, admittedly, eliminating piles of semi-useless junk. But the first step in deciding what is to be produced or not produced is to regain control of the system. What should or should not be produced is after all not a given but a decision to be democratically arrived at. If the control is there, people may indeed decide in good time that mass production simply is not worth the effort—or they may not.

With control of the production process one can then at least begin the process of educating consumers to better products, or fewer products, or craft products, or whatever one happens to feel is an improvement over the present system. Moreover, one cannot change a whole culture in a day; if one wishes to wean people from an over-dependence on cars, for example, one way is to build better trains, which is at least a step beyond building more fuel-efficient cars. The fact that one cannot do everything should not be made into an argument for doing nothing.

I recall a debate a few years ago in the pages of *Social Anarchism* where Len Krimerman described his efforts to create a poultry processing cooperative. In the main his anarchist respondents were horrified: He had borrowed money from the government (the Small Business Administration)! Also, he had foremen and supervisors, rather than pure and total self-government! He trafficked with capitalist distributors! The whole thing was a desecration of anarchist principles, being centrally involved with capitalism, hierarchy, and the state. This is of course an old debate, but it is reminiscent of the Marxists' argument that, until the "objective conditions" for revolution exist, nothing can (and hence need) be done.

One can indeed preach purity, but talk is cheap, and moreover, people know that. The significance of Mondragon is two-fold. It represents a positive vision of freedom in work, a community that is democratically controlled by its members. The ideal of democracy, to which everyone gives lip service, is actually practiced here. But it also represents something that works, and that in turn constitutes a statement about human nature, establishing beyond controversy that people can manage complex social tasks via democratic organization. *If a picture is worth a thousand words, an effective working model is worth at least a thousand pictures.*

Probably the most frequent criticism of utopian thinking is that it flies in the face of human nature, which has powerful propensities for evil as well as good. This argument is not one that can be settled in the abstract. The value of Mondragon is that it speaks to the claim of the weakness and fallibility of human nature in specific and concrete ways. Whereas the Webbs and others have long argued against the viability of worker cooperatives on the basis that they tend to degenerate into capitalist enterprises, Mondragon has clearly shown that this is not true. Not only does Mondragon work, but it works a lot better than its capitalist counterparts, and it grows faster. By showing that one can combine democracy with efficiency, it gives the lie to a basic article of capitalist dogma about human nature: that people are naturally lazy and irresponsible and will work only when given the twin incentives of the carrot and the stick.

Another objection has been raised. Structure is brainlessly equated with hierarchy and bureaucracy, and hence the complex organizational structure of a system such as Mondragon is written off out of hand. But structurelessness breeds tyranny. Informal cliques develop and hidden leaders emerge who wield power behind the cloak of an espoused equality.

Mondragon is worth studying because it works, and the argument can be made that utopian theory must always confront the practical since the burden of proof is on the theorist. The problem with capitalism and, more generally, with coercive industrial systems of whatever persuasion, is not that they don't work; they do deliver the goods, but in the process grind up human beings. The only answer to this state of affairs is to prove that a better system also works; theory alone simply will not do. And, if we wish to claim that something better than Mondragon needs to be built, then it is incumbent on us to do it.

From Black Rose, *Winter 1986-7.*

Chapter 9

The Labor Movement and Worker-Management (1982)

The Role of Organized Labor Under Capitalism

In assessing the possibilities for worker-management in the United States, it is necessary to understand the role of organized labor within the capitalist system. (Worker management refers to democratic control by workers of their workplaces.) It is difficult to see how such democratic control could develop significantly without at least the acquiescence, if not the positive support, of organized labor. Organized labor today is very much a product of its historical origins; it is impossible to understand the constraints within which it operates without understanding something of its history. American labor has been shaped by its immigrant origins and by the possibilities of both industrial and geographic expansion. During its formative period, American society was never forced to face the effects of its own dedication to non-planning and pell-mell industrialization; there was always an open frontier to the west, with land to spare. Those who found the rapidly industrializing East too constricting for their ambitions could always journey westward.

Moreover, the ethnic variety of the immigrant groups was a factor which further impeded the development of worker solidarity and class consciousness and was indeed used to maintain the divisions within the working class. Organized labor, divided from the start, has never been able to do more than try to keep pace with the growth of capitalism in a society able to industrialize with few of the traditional restraints derived from older institutions. The technological and organizational transformations linked to capitalist development have created further divisions within labor. As blue-collar workers became organized into labor congresses demand has shifted to white-collar workers who were, until recently, unorganized. The increasing rationalization of work along the lines proposed by the corporate efficiency expert Frederick Taylor has created severe status differences between skilled and unskilled labor, blue collar and white collar, so that these groups have never developed overall solidarity. White-collar workers have resisted being organized into blue-collar unions. Added to this are the divisions resulting from racial as well as ethnic differences. As a result, the organized sector of American labor is significantly smaller than its European counterparts.

In the early part of this century, in contrast, American labor possessed a radicalism which has since disappeared, for reasons which will become evident. Unions sought to implement workers' control, setting up producers' cooperatives in the early 1900s and proposing a plan to take over failing railways through a national corporation which would be run by the workers, shortly after World War I. Since the 1930s, however, organized labor has formed an increasing part of the national consensus. In addition to the strength of the mythology of the Land of Opportunity (backed by continuing industrial growth and the access of the worker to middle-class status), two important causes can be listed for the siphoning off of labor militancy into economistic demands and the consequent integration of the labor movement into the corporate capitalist system.

The first cause historically, and the most important, was the successful channeling of labor militancy into acceptable and legally defined forms of conflict which agreed to the basic rules of the capitalist game. As Domhoff has shown, the legislation of the 1930s (including the Wagner Act, and laws creating the National Labor Relations Board and the Social Security System) was the product of initiatives taken by the liberal wing of the ruling class, often in the face of strong labor opposition. This legislation essentially involved a bargain accepted by Samuel Gompers, then the leader of the American Federation of Labor. The bargain amounted to an agreement that, in return for labor's right to organize and obtain government recognition, it would restrict its activity to economistic demands and foreswear overtly political activity and attempts to challenge the capitalist system.

The conventional historical approach has always been that the social legislation which benefited labor has been proof of pluralism in the United States, since it indicates a victory of the forces of labor over big business. This argument could be made because the conservative business groups represented best by the National Association of Manufacturers (NAM) did, in fact, oppose such legislation. But so did organized labor. It was the liberal wing of the ruling class which was farsighted enough to grasp the possibility that organized labor could be integrated into the capitalist system, and that, when it was, it could be a vehicle for the social control and discipline of the workers, while at the same time strengthening the ideology of pluralism.

Perhaps the best evidence of the passive or oppositional role of labor in social legislation affecting it is the Wagner Act. Often called "labor's bill of rights" because it guarantees the right of collective bargaining and sets up government mediating mechanisms, it was passed at a time when organized labor was at almost an all-time low. Union strength declined from 12 percent of the labor force in 1920 to 6 percent in 1933. While the Great Depression had weakened organized labor drastically, the Wagner Act was passed because labor militancy had risen, and there was fear that it would take radical political expression. The need was seen to strengthen organized labor, to assure that no organized radical movement would develop. With the help of the leadership of organized labor and the liberal wing of big business, the Wagner Act was finally passed, after a long fight with the conservative NAM wing of big business. This, too, has been mistaken for a conflict between labor and business; instead, it merely indicates the successful displacement of radical protest into reformist channels. Management's current half-hearted attempts to siphon off the discontent of the rank-and-file through job enrichment programs and other gimmicks is simply the latest in a long line of successful efforts to bypass organized labor. If the efforts are weak, it is because the leadership of organized labor has by now thoroughly made its peace with the system.

The Communist Scare

The second factor that served to guarantee a nonradical and economisticly oriented labor movement was the role of Communism in the movement. The depression of the thirties gave rise to the hope that the capitalist system was at last experiencing its predicted downfall, and Communism took hold within the labor movement. With the success of the New Deal and, above all, of World War II in bailing out the capitalist system, the Communists, by now entrenched in the labor leadership, maintained their belief in the eventual collapse of the system but simply postponed the date. Paralleling to a marked degree the behavior of the Communist Party-affiliated union, the *Confederation General du Travail* in the May Days of 1968 in France, they foreswore radical tactics and, instead, concentrated on building union strength within the context of the accepted ideology of collective bargaining. Moreover, they aligned themselves with the Democratic Party in the effort to become respectable, while continuing to work for positions of power within the unions. In light of the development of the Cold War and McCarthyism, and repressive legislation such as the Alien Registration Act of 1940 (commonly referred to as the Smith Act), the unions successfully purged themselves of most radical elements. As proof of their newly won status as junior members of the power elite, union leaders outdid big business in espousing Cold War ideology; the AFL-CIO cooperated actively with the Central Intelligence Agency in helping to assure that the Latin American labor movement would not become infected with leftwing ideologies.

What had happened was that the ruling groups within government and big business made it clear that the condition for continuing to enjoy the benefits of acceptance and protection through collective bargaining, and for continuing to be a junior partner of the power elite, was the renunciation of alien ideologies. Labor must accept the official definitions which equated freedom with the free enterprise system. It was all right to struggle for higher wages and for protective legislation—after all, business also seeks it own protective legislation and higher profits—so long as one accepted the basic rules of the free enterprise game. Ideological struggle was not permissible, even if the form it took was hardly revolutionary. This further clarification of what was required of organized labor to maintain its status as one of the organized groups within the ruling circles completed the assimilation and integration of labor into the American consensus. By the time it happened, the leadership of organized labor had already enjoyed status as members of government commissions, and in many cases, were friends with members of the ruling class. Big labor had the experience of working closely with big business and had found it was possible to establish a *modus vivendi*.

The result of this continuous and forced process of integration of organized labor into the role of junior member within the capitalist system has been to fatally narrow its scope, and in the process, render it vulnerable to the demands of its own rank-and-file. It could not question the authority of management to control the workplace or to determine the goals of production and profit levels. Hence, management was able to pass on wage raises to the consumer, often with a handsome increment of profit thrown in. For every dollar of wage increase the United Auto Workers wrung out of General Motors, GM was able to raise the price by three-and-a-half dollars. The result has been that the leadership of organized labor has been unable to meet the growing demands of the rank-and-file for improved conditions of work. And, with respect to the great majority of those outside the ranks of organized labor, it has become more and more an exclusionary interest group, dividing the interests of those within from those outside its doors. The spate of wildcat strikes, work stoppages, and so on, and, more recently, the organization of black and women's caucuses are proof of the decreasing capacity of the leaders of organized labor to maintain their control of the rank-and-file while continuing to follow the demands imposed on them as "responsible" members within the American consensus.

If a movement for self-determination and freedom in work arises, it will have to arise outside the institutions of organized labor. For, behind the rigidity and autocracy of the AFL-CIO leadership, there are the power-political facts of life which that leadership understands far better than do the young dissidents within the rank-and-file. The history of American labor is a living illustration of the power of the capitalist system to both accommodate and integrate dissent into its own social and political definitions of reality.

Organized Labor and the Present Situation

At a time when hundreds of thousands of workers are losing their jobs, organized labor now finds itself largely unable to safeguard those jobs and unable to make its demands keep pace with the rising cost of living for those who remain at work. The capacity of the unions to raise wages has been significantly reduced. The growth of conglomerates and multinationals has caused many jobs to move overseas or into areas of unorganized labor in this country, largely the South. As suggested, unions are powerless to affect this trend.

The loss of jobs to other areas provides an opportunity for the development of worker management which may just possibly affect the attitude of unions towards it. An example is the textile workers' unions in the Northeast. For several decades, textile mills have been moving south to areas of lower labor cost. The garment industry, in particular, has also suffered from foreign cheap imports, and the result has been the devastation of towns like Fall River, Massachusetts, which have become poverty areas.

This brings up the distinction between *worker management* and *worker control*. Proposals for worker control have been developed by writers such as G.D.H. Cole, Anton Pannekoek, and Antonio Gramsci in the last century and in the early part of this one. More recently André Gorz has urged workers to develop a strategy of encroaching control. However, none of these writers saw labor unions as the originators of such a movement, feeling that, even in the case of the European labor movement, the unions were too hierarchical and bureaucratic to react in any way but negatively to the idea of worker control. *Worker control* in this context has been understood to mean direct efforts by workers to organize councils and assemblies in existing capitalist workplaces in order to carry on struggles for control over the conditions of work. Such struggles have taken place in several European countries, notably in the north of Italy, but have never reached the point where the actual control and ownership of an enterprise fell into the hands of the workers, although the possibility existed briefly at the Fiat automobile plant in Turin, and workers did succeed in operating the LIP watch factory for a period in France.

Worker management, although it is a broad term covering all aspects of the operation of an enterprise controlled and owned by workers, has come to refer, in practice, to those enterprises, notably in Yugoslavia, but existing also in Great Britain, Spain, and elsewhere in Europe, which are totally controlled by workers. In almost all cases, these enterprises have developed either as the result of government policy, as in the case of Yugoslavia, or from a start-up or changeover to a system of worker management where outside ownership either did not exist or voluntarily gave over control to the workers. The existing examples of worker-managed enterprises have not arisen out of workers' struggles for control, but rather as a result of conscious decisions on the part of either governments, entrepreneurs, or founders to develop such enterprises. This suggests the truth of the organizational axiom, expressed by Kenneth Boulding amongst others, that it is a lot easier to start a new organization from scratch than it is to try to radically alter the structure of an existing organization.

But let us return to the present and to the potential role of organized labor under a system of worker management. Unions are now structured to represent workers' interests, or some of them, within the capitalist system. The organization of unions along trade lines (and, in Europe, along party and religious lines), the exclusive focus on economistic issues, and the acceptance of managerial definitions of the scope and nature of the job and the reward scale are contrary to the demands for worker management. Unions could serve in several important roles under a system of worker-management, but, to do so, they would have to be organized so as to represent a single enterprise as a whole; and, while some of their present functions would become irrelevant, other functions would have to be extended and still other new functions developed. With the prospect of continued stagflation and continued unemployment, there are incentives for unions to encourage job creation and counteract plant shutdowns by at least accepting the idea of worker-management, even if they do not take an active role in bringing it about. But, for this to happen, it is necessary for the advocates of worker management to answer the question posed by one high UAW official, who accepted the idea that worker management could save jobs but wanted to know the role his union could play.

The Role of Unions Under Worker Management

It is possible to envisage the role of unions vis-a-vis a movement for worker-management in terms of a number of stages. Only the initial stages are based on experience at this point, but, in view of the history of organized labor in this country, the experience so far seems to lead to cautious optimism. Because the core of union demands at the local level centers around wages, many unions have insisted that, whether the enterprise became worker-managed or not, the existing wage levels must be kept. This creates a number of problems for a worker-managed enterprise. In the first place, who is the wage contract to be made with? Secondly, the requirement that the existing wage contract be maintained means that the enterprise loses the opportunity to lower the income level in the event that business is bad and the earnings are insufficient to pay income to the workers at the contract level. The workers may well wish to continue without resorting to the conventional solution of layoffs. For, in a worker-managed enterprise, the concept of wages no longer applies; as owners, the workers earn income and should be free to set the level for themselves, either lower or higher than their previous wage levels.

If the basis of the union contract is eliminated as the very first step in the transition to worker-management, however, it is unlikely that the union will continue to support the project. At the same time, it is a general practice of worker-managed enterprises to choose to lower overall income in the case of a business downturn rather than to lay off working members (who, after all, have a share in the business).

A solution here would allow the union to maintain the centrality of the wage contract, while at the same time allowing the workers to reduce income in the event that earnings dip. A wage contract is made out and a wage level is set, according to the union's wishes. It is a contract between the union representatives and the board of the enterprise, elected by the workers. The enterprise is so structured that individual worker accounts are set up, representing earnings at decided-upon income levels to reflect differences in skill level, seniority, work time, and so on. (The decision on income differentials is a separate problem which also must be worked out.)

The organization's surplus earnings may be defined as everything beyond what is needed to meet the decided-upon income level, operating expenses, and a portion set aside for reinvestment and growth. Individual workers receive into their accounts on the organization's books a portion of that surplus—a dividend on their work, so to speak. In the event earnings are insufficient to pay the worker's income at the agreed-upon wage level, the difference between what is actually paid out and what is agreed upon simply becomes a debt to the accounts, to be paid later, when earnings warrant it. Since there is some flexibility in determining costs to the enterprise, and it is the workers who determine these costs, they may decide to reinvest their earnings in advertising, market expansion, operating equipment, or other items, while debiting their accounts in the event that it is impossible to both make these investments and pay themselves income at the contracted wage level.

The incentive for a union to go along with such a scheme is that the union can maintain dues-paying members. In several cases, workers have been reluctant to consider continued union membership for that very reason, feeling that the union did little enough for them before and would do less in the event that they became worker-managed. However, it is possible to negotiate with a union an arrangement that part of the dues goes into a fund to assist workers in other enterprises to buy out their company in the event that it is to be shut down.

Also of potential relevance to worker buyouts and worker-management are union pension funds. These funds are an enormous source of potential capital to be used to buy out enterprises. But, in most cases, these funds are under the control of trustees made up of management and banking figures, with, at best, a minority of union representation. Unless unions were willing to make efforts to gain control over their pension funds, it is impossible to conceive of those funds as a source of capital. However, worker-managed enterprises could set up pension funds under their own control, and these could finance the growth of worker-management. Unions have at various times set up credit unions, health clinics, and consumer unions. Self-managed enterprises could encourage unions to perform these services which are both in the union tradition and close to the tradition of worker cooperatives.

Unions might well accept the validity of worker-management, if faced with the existence of a number of such enterprises created from plant shutdowns. In that case they could, perhaps, be induced to leave the matter of wages to the internal decision of members of the enterprise and concentrate instead on such matters as industry-wide standards and take on the role of arbiter in disputes between a worker or groups of workers and the management of the enterprise, representing the workers as a whole. This would correspond to their traditional function of being responsible for grievance procedures and would prevent the danger of the tyranny of the majority over individual members. Moving beyond this, they could take up the idea of developing a workers' bill of rights covering hiring and firing procedures and workers' rights on the job.

Before the American labor movement became successfully integrated into the capitalist system, unions at various times sponsored worker-management in the form of cooperatives which either failed or, more often, were crushed by industry groups such as the NAM. It seems unlikely that the labor movement of today will show much interest in repeating such experiments. But, if others help develop worker cooperatives, it is in the unions' self-interest to admit them to the organized labor movement. If these cooperatives were capable of growing with anything like the dynamism shown by the Mondragon system of cooperatives in northern Spain, the union movement would then be forced to take serious notice of worker-management, and this might possibly help introduce something of the older union spirit by demonstrating that there existed an alternative to being a junior partner in the capitalist system. However, this is speculation. Union leaders recognize that, as things stand, they are powerless in the face of loss of jobs. At least some of them are willing to help, albeit cautiously, when workers seek to maintain their jobs under conditions of worker-management.

On the national level, organized labor could serve as an important lobbying force to introduce legislation favoring worker-management as a solution to unemployment. The new national cooperative bank explicitly includes worker cooperatives in its purview. Legislation is being planned to allow federal funds equivalent to a small percentage of unemployment insurance to be used for investment in worker-owned enterprises as an answer to plant shutdowns. So far, unions have not been involved in any of these efforts. But the health of organized labor has depended on an expanding economy and the possibility of real wage gains for its members. Now, with stagflation a continuing feature of the economic landscape, any program which gives promise of successfully creating jobs or of preventing the flight of jobs abroad and to non-union areas must, of necessity, be attractive to organized labor. Perhaps, though the task is certainly difficult, worker-management can fulfill that promise.

From Frank Lindenfeld and Joyce Rothschild-Whitt (eds), Workplace Democracy and Social Change, *1982.*

Chapter 10

Political Education
for Worker-Management
(1980)

What Political Education Involves

Political education for workers can be distinguished from the education needed to effectively operate a worker-managed firm, although in a broader sense the latter also is of course political. However, we shall focus here on the education that extends *beyond* the self-managed firm and that can serve to bind workers together into a movement for worker self-determination. In general, worker-management projects in the United States have concentrated on the skills and knowledge necessary for workers to operate their own firms. But given the changing global situation, it would seem important now to go beyond this and to develop a program for political education that operates in tandem with the program for internal education in worker-management. Such a program must take into account the particular history of labor in the United States. The lack of anything beyond a capitalist ideology in the labor movement and a corresponding bread and butter approach to collective bargaining, contrasts with the European labor movement where ideology plays a role, although often subordinated to short term goals. European labor has been able to rely on the existence of fairly strong social democratic parties and in some cases—such as Sweden— this support now encourages worker-management.

What this suggests is that a movement to politically educate workers in this country must develop its own institutions to substitute for a lack of broad-gauge union and political support. The level of worker consciousness in Spain before and during the period of the Spanish Civil War can serve as a model of what can be achieved. Workers in Spain had experienced over fifty years of political education, largely by travelling anarchist organizers; this helped enable them to develop a system of self-managed factories, communes, and farms where prices were determined by political rather than market considerations, and close cooperation between different towns and regions was the norm.

This commitment to a political perspective on worker-management and worker control is important in ensuring participation within the firm as well. As a 1981 study by Espinosa and Zimbalist confirms, the most important variable affecting participation among Chilean workers during the Allende regime was the political ideology of the workers. The ideology went clearly beyond material self-interest.

In Mondragon, the system of worker cooperatives in northern Spain, similar attitudes are expressed. The workers are collectively committed to expanding their system so as to create more jobs. This operates through the institutions of the system, where a portion of the surplus is retained for expansion and further job creation. While the Chilean workers who were most successful in implementing worker-management shared a socialist ideology in which worker-management and workplace democratization played an important role, the Mondragon workers see themselves as helping to create jobs for their fellow Basques; their organization is more nationalist than socialist and is based on strong cultural and community ties.

Because of the lack of a socialist tradition in the United States, it would seem that the most direct way to develop a program of political education should resemble Mondragon more than the more ideological approach of the Chilean workers under the presidency of Salvador Allende. The focus would be on the necessity to expand and develop more jobs under worker-management, with the ultimate goal being the creation of a strong worker-managed sector in the United States. The arguments for doing this are defensive as well as offensive: Small and isolated worker-managed firms existing within a capitalist environment are subject to both political and economic pressures, which they would have difficulty withstanding alone. Maximal security would exist when a system of self-managed firms emerges, with relatively self-contained financing, education, research and development, and technical assistance facilities, and when the size and number of firms is such as to create a significant impact on local and regional areas. There would still remain an external dependence on markets and to a lesser degree on suppliers; but just as Mondragon is now concentrating increasingly on international markets, a large system of industrial cooperatives could likewise seek sales both internationally and in those areas where support for cooperatives existed.

Cooperative Consciousness: The Goal of Political Education

Thus, the primary focus of political education would be on the task of developing a set of institutions capable of partially insulating worker-managed firms from the dangers inherent in an alien and potentially hostile environment. Put positively, such a system would create the possibility of strong mutual reinforcement mechanisms, especially if the result were what could be termed an *institutional ecosystem*—a system of cooperatives which embraced the major aspects of daily life. Thus Mondragon has created food cooperatives, agricultural cooperatives, housing cooperatives, health care cooperatives, cooperative disability and pension programs, and so on. At this point, a form of consciousness has been created, and it is this consciousness which most directly creates commitment to the cooperative idea and to democratic governance as a set of cultural values and as a way of life.

The purpose of political education, as perceived here, is to create a sense of solidarity and of commitment to the idea of economic democracy. This is seen as an overarching set of values which extend beyond the immediate and personal benefits of humanized work, greater job and financial security, and a generally improved quality of life. These values constitute a form of consciousness because they suggest a vision which comprehends a set of personal values and personal behavior, as well as a set of institutions which help generate and reinforce these values. Consciousness thus represents a linkage between personal experience and institutional systems. The political dimension of this consciousness is expressed by the commitment to both defend the values involved and to propagate them out of a belief that they represent a better way of life for others. Such a consciousness would create a sense of solidarity and mission, far more than any classroom exercises or texts, and would constitute the most reliable defence against the incursions of capitalist cultural values with their tunnel vision, narrow focus on profitability alone, manipulativeness, and competitive individualism.

But how to develop this form of consciousness? And how to do so, concretely, beginning from the relatively undeveloped form of the movement for self-management and economic democracy in this country?

Institutional Dimensions of Political Education

The stages of development of political consciousness through the creation of critical supporting institutions are sketched below. The outline is necessarily tentative; as conditions change, changes in the strategy may be needed. There are five progressive stages:

1. The development of a *communication linkage system* via conferences, networking, newsletters, periodic seminars, speakers, visits between cooperatives, and so on.

2. The development of *economic linkages* via vertical and horizontal forms of integration, joint enterprises, spin offs, turnkey projects, and so forth.

3. The development of a set of *supporting institutions* such as research and development units, common accounting units, credit unions, small business investment companies devoted to cooperatives, investment funds, schools, and technical assistance organizations.

4. The development of *common membership organizations*, regional associations of self-managed enterprises with lobbying and political functions, or some combination of the two.

5. The development of *more inclusive systems* or *communities of self-management* in which the major institutions of work, education, services, consumption, housing, planning and governance are all self-managed as well as highly linked and interdependent.

Although these categories are roughly sequential, it is likely that events will dictate what opportunities can be seized, and when particular institutions can be developed. The development of a *communication linkage system* is perhaps the first affirmation that the effort to develop self-managed firms constitutes a movement with a shared common cause. Linkages would probably be most appropriate on the regional or city level and might quickly result in local federations, much as consumer cooperatives in different regions have formed federations. It has been the experience of representatives of worker cooperatives attending regional conferences featuring cooperatives of all varieties that the concerns and orientations of representatives from housing cooperatives, consumer and energy cooperatives, and worker cooperatives differentiated them as much as they united them. A strategic issue for worker cooperatives would therefore be whether it would be better to develop their own linkage system ultimately resulting in a federation or whether to throw their lot in with existing federations or united federations in the making.

Part of the function of such a system would be a program of continuing education for member cooperatives, featuring the discussion of common problems, information sharing, skills workshops, and so on. Another function would be to explore possibilities for economic linkages. An overall purpose would be to develop an awareness that the cooperatives are not alone and are working in a common cause. The overcoming of a sense of isolation within an alien environment, the sense of a larger movement of which the members are a part, the institutionalizing of contacts via newsletters and other forms of continuing communication would all be possible results of the development of this primary linkage system.

The development of *economic linkages* is already taking place in the area of consumer cooperatives. Wholesale cooperatives are selling to consumer cooperatives, while other consumer cooperatives are dealing directly with systems of farm suppliers, although the latter are not cooperatives. It is likely that for a considerable time to come such linkages, although economic in nature, will be partial and have no significant economic impact on the cooperatives involved; there are not enough cooperative publishers around to fully occupy a cooperative printer, and the same is true in other fields. However, the contacts with like-minded organizations are valuable in themselves, and foster a sense of solidarity among those involved. The creation of research and development cooperatives devoted to creating spin-offs would be a method for creating closer linkages among member cooperatives, as would a franchising cooperative which specialized in creating cooperative franchises where the advantages of technical assistance, quality control, product identification, pooled advertising, financing, and a tested market would be available.

The development of *supporting institutions* is also taking place. On the regional level there are technical assistance groups, community loan funds, and credit unions devoted to financing worker cooperatives. At some point soon it would be helpful to have a research and development group capable of developing new products for cooperative production. Several higher education campuses—including Cornell University, Boston College, Hampshire College, Kent State, and Utah State University—have programs devoted mainly or exclusively to education for worker-management. Technical assistance organizations like the Industrial Cooperative Association offer workshops on employee ownership and worker-management throughout the country. However, there is a need also for ongoing educational facilities that could offer theory courses, skill development, and hands-on types of training to practitioners and other interested persons. Such a facility would be best linked to operating worker cooperatives so that students could gain experience in actual working conditions.

Membership organizations would most logically be regional in scope, evolving where worker cooperatives were most numerous. One immediate service that they could provide would be to set up region-wide health care and health insurance systems, and pension funds. They could also facilitate the setting up of day care centers, the encouragement of flex-time and part-time work, and set standards for maternity leave, leave of absence, and similar matters.

As an industry or trade association, the federation could represent the interests of the cooperatives taken as collectivities, promoting the sale of their products, the development of new cooperatives, linking in with regional banks and financial institutions, and providing publicity and promotion for the regional worker cooperative movement. It could seek favorable legislation at the state level, especially the development of a body of law specifically tailored to worker cooperatives. It could develop regional macroeconomic analysis and forecasts to assist cooperatives in their own economic planning. In short, it could perform the functions of a regional lobbying group. National lobbying would be undertaken presumably by a third level federation of federations.

A strong argument can be made for the development of *community systems of cooperatives,* since they would provide greater evidence of the meaning of cooperatives considered as a way of life and as a form of cultural and social hegemony. The removal of cognitive dissonance between work life and community life should facilitate activities in both spheres, and the development of a system of institutions possessed of similar structure and values should provide significant reinforcement for the individual units making up the system. Such systems would most likely develop where a number of industrial cooperatives existed together in a relatively small community. If their collective impact on the culture and the economy of the community were great, they could then most easily proceed to set up other forms of cooperatives, thus involving members of the community beyond those working directly in the cooperative sector.

My focus here has been on the institutional and social structural aspects of political education for economic democracy. Thus I have not dealt with dialogic methods of *conscientization* (see here the many works of Paulo Freire) which need also to be developed, and which would in part serve as the content for the conferences, seminars, and other educational approaches proposed above. However, another and more substantial reason for not suggesting what a dialogic program for political education might look like is that there is strong and justified opposition to teaching workers about what values or political attitudes they should adhere to. Instead, the proposed approach is to develop organizational structures calculated to assure that internal democracy is maximally facilitated. The values that emerge from this are the product of free choices on the part of working members, and the belief is that if these choices are made within a context of free and humanized work, they will express values which are themselves humane.

From Changing Work, *No. 7, Winter 1988. This essay is a revised version of a working paper delivered at the Sixth Annual Self-Management Conference, Howard University, Nov. 20-23, 1980.*

Chapter 11

Putting the Reins on Technology (1982)

Combatting the Culture of Industrialism

It is important to understand any disease before proposing a cure. If the only problem confronting activists today was social inequality resulting from abstract historical forces or from the single-minded quest for profits, then counterposing to this a struggle for an egalitarian worker's state might have some meaning. But if the deeper problem is learning how to combat the thrust toward ever-greater technological power and organizational giantism, then only participatory, decentralist solutions—embodying a humanized technology subject to broader social purposes—will do. Much of socialism has swallowed the reigning mythology of industrialism and technology. But anarchism has inherent reasons for allying itself instead with the new ecological consciousness. These reasons derive from an understanding of how the popular consciousness has been formed by the technological fix and of how extensive investment in technology leads to social domination as well.

The culture of industrialism has inevitably made work into a machine-like activity, subordinating the majority *as workers* to the technological dreams of grandeur of those who possess the means and knowledge to master the machines. But *as consumers*, this majority shares in the dream by possession of the products that result from technological mastery; oppression in the workplace is countered by participation in the technological marketplace. Thus although a majority of the workforce is now involved in service and maintenance functions—in government, education, social services, and the like—the dream is still there: The power and the glory belong to the instrumentalities of production since it is here that the magnification of human powers is experienced most directly. Note that this is also experienced by those who operate the state apparatus—and through identification by their underlings—through the extensive involvement of the state in weapons systems possessed of a power and destructive potential that are unique. The nuclear weapons, the jets, the missiles, the radar and communications, the tanks and battleships—all form part of a vast technological apparatus dedicated to destruction. This apparatus derives its rationale from the existence of similar systems of warfare technology possessed by other states.

Nowhere is the addictive character of technology seen more clearly than in the setting up of systems of mutual destruction, to the detriment of living standards, security, and peaceful forms of human progress. The urge to power thus finds its most apt expression in the warfare state, which links state domination with the technology of warfare; Randolph Bourne's observation, "War is the health of the state," takes on a magnified meaning here. This meaning is clarified by the understanding of how technology contributes to the natural tendencies of the state toward self-aggrandizement at the expense of its people and at the same time makes these tendencies infinitely more lethal. The private corporation and the warfare state are the twin loci of the contemporary disease; the two are closely intertwined—on the material level by the urge to profits and on the cultural level by a shared investment in power through technology.

Worker Co-ops and Social Values

Some self-management advocates argue that it is important not to involve the worker cooperative movement in attempts to instill social values. Worker cooperatives should be free to produce whatever they want—particularly given their general marginality and the difficulty they experience in obtaining financing, skilled workers and management, and adequate markets. For those who have experienced the difficulty of developing successful examples of self-management, this argument has some clear force. On the other hand, those in the ecology movement or those who espouse an appropriate technology which is neither capital nor energy intensive frequently have a pronounced interest in creating more democratic forms of production. My own view is that the proponents of worker-management should recognize that the product does matter, and that worker-managers who cater to the prevailing technological fix only narrow the scope of their potential influence.

In the last ten years or so a powerful critique of the present thrust of technology has developed which is too important to be ignored. It steps outside of the prevailing assumptions regarding technology and critiques both its methods and its goals. An essay written in 1909 by C.R. Ashbee previsioned a number of central themes. Writing of Indian village communities, he questioned whether technological progress has improved the quality of life. The essay anticipated the contemporary critique of technology by investigating whether machines have not created social costs greater than their benefits. This issue was echoed in the writings of Ivan Illich, who pointed out that labor-saving devices usually do not save labor. When production and maintenance time is factored into the overall life of a car, the average speed is reduced to around five miles an hour. Likewise, labor saving appliances, when the wage labor costs to consumers are figured in, end up substituting the labor required to earn them for whatever labor time is saved.

Technology and the Workplace

This analysis is powerful, because it suggests the irrationality inherent in the present commitment to technology. We sacrifice freedom in work in order to be able to purchase appliances, vehicles—the accoutrements of technology—which supposedly add to our sense of power. But the Faustian bargain is that we sacrifice the power to determine how or when we work and for what purpose. We can thus see how intimately related are the critique of technology and the critique of the workplace, if we subject both to rational evaluation.

Technology and workplace democratization are closely related on several levels. As Harry Braverman has shown, technology has never been neutral when it comes to the workplace. The development of the technology of production owes far more to considerations of *efficiency of control* than it does to any abstract desire for efficiency as such. Work has become highly rationalized; mental work has been split off from manual work; jobs have become mechanized. All of this subjects workers to lower wage scales and makes them more replaceable through de-skilling, hence increasing managerial power over the workforce.

The development of technology has been fueled by the urge to dominate nature. The vision of vast extensions of human power and human perception has allied the quest for scientific knowledge with the quest for domination. And the result of this is a social order in which the control of technology and its magnification of human power has led naturally to the control of other human beings.

On the positive side, this means that freedom in work requires an appropriate technology, based on a human scale, where neither the technology nor the organization of work make workers into machine-tenders. Any efforts to create freedom in work must bring the present runaway technology under control. Moreover, the lack of concern for human beings as workers is of a piece with the manipulation of human beings as consumers: passive workers, following orders, and passive consumers, advertised into buying. Just as there should be worker control, so there should be consumer control, so that products last, are reasonably priced, and meet needs as defined by consumers, not by the producers. Technology in general, not simply its application in the workplace, needs to come under democratic control.

We live in a society which is fragmented and devoid of the stability, rootedness in place, localism and cultural institutions which together can provide emotional security. In this fragmenting society, people addictively turn to massive industrial technology to compensate for their lack of power and emotional security. It is hence not enough to combat this technology without also seeking to change the social and political landscape by returning power to the local level and in the process building community. *The answer to our runaway technology is social reconstruction.*

Social Reconstruction

The primary focus for a social critique should thus be the extent to which the contemporary investment in technology has deformed both work and community life together. If this is true, there can be no real freedom in work without a freeing of the imagination from the dominance of and preoccupation with technological forms of power and mastery. Democratizing automobile assembly lines is not enough; the real question is whether cars themselves are necessary or should be replaced, and whether there are not priorities that are so much more pressing that cars—and jets and space shots and much else—should simply be abandoned in favor of projects that contribute more directly to human growth and human wisdom. Thus the *aims* of technology, and not simply the organizational methods which it uses, must be put into question. Its deformation of the social landscape, as well as its pillaging of the natural landscape must be challenged.

Again, if the simple motivational model obtained and technology served the profit of the masters only, then the workplace could easily be seen as the primary field of struggle. But humans are the willing consumers—and slaves—of the technological imperative. While the constraints of human nature, entropy, and organizational size are always with us, these constraints differ from that imposed by technology in that technology alone not only resists efforts to organize in a liberatory fashion but pulls in its own, and contrary, direction. The lure of the Megamachine, its power and its glory, captivates both by its logic and its magic. Its logic is that technology must be free to go where it will, and social forms must accommodate it. Its magic is linked with nationalism—another magic—and with corporate greed. But while greed is decried, and the current lethal form of nationalism is suspect, there is little general questioning of the general goals of technological advance. The ecology movement is a partial exception—partial in that it questions the impact of technology on the natural environment without fully enough exploring its impact on the social environment.

The challenge is to accord technology a place within a larger vision which consciously controls subordinate elements in the interests of human growth. But to accomplish this, a level of consciousness and planning is necessary which at present does not exist. The primary expression of such a consciousness should be in the organizing of communities and workplaces which are deliberately structured so as to be participatory, coherent, ecologically sound, and continuously responsive to the needs of the inhabitants. The result would be a different social reality, a culture which would act back on its members so as to encourage different behavior patterns and different norms.

As an ideology of reconstruction, anarchism must move beyond its current involvement with largely cultural and educational alternatives and develop a capacity to deal with the larger functions of formal organizations, including mainly those functions which address technological power. Thus it should concern itself with democratic work organization, especially in those new areas of communication and information technology which are most likely to become the carriers of the dominant technological thrust. Above all, it should be concerned to develop liberatory organizations in product and service areas which are close to the heart of the present technological thrust, demonstrating through this, how it is possible to create both liberatory organizations and a liberatory technology.

From Changing Work, *No. 7, Winter 1988. Adapted from a paper given at the Anarchos Institute Conference, "Intellectuals and the State," Montreal, June 5 and 6, 1982.*

Chapter 12

Building Support Systems for Worker Cooperatives (1982)

Theory Sets the Stage

At various times in my life, I have worked in teaching, publishing, community organizing, business, research, and as an administrator-or-ganizer in the peace movement. I have never worked in any area, however, where the need to embody theoretical understandings in organizational practice was so pronounced as in the national Federation for Economic Democracy (FEDO) and the regionally-based Industrial Cooperative Association (ICA), two organizations set up to provide technical assistance to workers wishing to develop self-managed businesses.

Those of us involved in these support organizations learned about self-management, in part, by trying to help workers develop it and by attempting to apply it within our own organizations. Most of us came from professional, and particularly academic, backgrounds. As professionals, we had been for the most part trained to work alone, not in close conjunction with others or in teams. We all espoused the ideal of economic democracy and were eager to implement it, but often our personal styles became a major impediment. We learned that if we were to work effectively with others, we ourselves had to become an effective working group. Out of this came our collective recognition of the intimate link between theory and practice.

For example, prior to developing FEDO in 1975, I came to know Jaroslav Vanek, one of the major theorists of worker-management in this country. He had ideas about why traditional producer cooperatives had failed and proposed some solutions. He believed that to implement worker-management within the essentially alien environment of the corporate capitalist system, it was necessary to have a "shelter organization" capable of giving educational, financial and technical support to worker-managed companies. This supporting organization could provide capital on a loan basis without the strings that equity investment entailed. It could help develop a network of worker-managed companies to offer reinforcement and mutual support for each other. It could provide continuing assistance and advice. I began to see in Vanek's ideas how some of the traditional problems which had plagued cooperatives—their isolation and their need to be self-financing, with consequent distortions in their system of control—could be avoided. Theory in this case was to precede and guide practice.

Building Shelter Organizations: Phase One

In addition, by this time I had become convinced that it would be possible to engage seriously in the effort to build worker self-management. Because the major thrust of the American system is to create increases in productivity and profits through technological advance, I believed that the industrial system was the place to start, even though its work force was shrinking in relation to the service and public sectors. The contradiction between the monotonous and highly repressive conditions of factory or office work and the official mythology of democratic governance make the production system the weak link in terms of legitimation. As Braverman and Gorz have pointed out, contemporary efforts to legitimate the system are couched in terms of the need for managerial expertise, but an accumulating body of evidence shows that efficiency of control, rather than of production, is the real goal and that such control can actually reduce production efficiency. Much of managerial overhead is often superfluous.

Self-management represents a new form of legitimation more in consonance with the strivings for participation and equality which characterized the sixties. On the one hand, people remain hopeless in the face of the vastness and the power of the corporate system. On the other, the friction costs, and inefficiencies of the system are increasingly apparent. This creates the opportunity for alternatives so long as they can prove their viability in terms of capacity to meet productive demands and utilize the existing technology.

A further desirable characteristic of such self-managed alternatives is that they be on a scale capable of challenging mainstream organizations. Also, although the nature and uses of existing technology are being questioned, the idea of a high technology is broadly accepted; organizational alternatives must demonstrate their ability to employ a complex production system and a high technology. Such alternatives must be humanized and democratic in structure but not utopian in the sense of demanding heroic measures of their members, such as rejection of private property, total equalization of income or a zero-profit orientation. Although these latter features characterize some of the work collectives of the counterculture, they would not appeal to the majority of workers. The latter, however, might welcome the opportunity to own their own jobs and could come to recognize the benefits and security that derive from a democratic form of governance.

Traditionally, efforts to create social change are aimed at organizing the poor or other dissident groups, or at organizing for protest. Our efforts were different. The small group who got together in Ithaca to form FEDO wanted to develop successful operating examples of economic democracy. Because of time considerations and because of our lack of experience in enterprise development, we decided to concentrate on plant shutdowns —situations where a viable business had existed but had been closed down for reasons extrinsic to its basic potential. Such shutdowns occur irregularly and are dispersed. We therefore needed an organization which was itself dispersed, with chapters located preferably in industrial areas. The plan was to develop an organization with chapters that would eventually cover major centers along the East Coast and with a governing board made up of delegates from each chapter as well as from public figures committed to worker-management.

The first step was to develop an initial board of Ithaca-based members. However, because of a failure to clarify organizational goals, several of the initial members saw the organization as Ithaca-based and as oriented toward assisting small, zero-profit cooperatives of the sort that had begun to develop locally. Later, as more chapters developed and sent delegates to the board, the thrust toward the development of larger enterprises won out, but the opposition between many of the original Ithaca members and the new majority continued and remained a source of friction. The Ithaca members, for instance, were suspicious of foundation fundraising. They advocated an organizational approach based on voluntarism and unpaid staff, a concept which fitted in with the idea of developing small cooperatives but contradicted the goal of developing a professional staff capable of putting together larger projects. As the Executive Director, I was the fundraiser. I was also a major proponent of working outside of Ithaca to develop larger enterprises. As a partisan in these issues it is difficult to claim objectivity. Both approaches were viable, but they had different goals.

Plant shutdowns require immediate initiatives if they are to be salvaged before the work force goes elsewhere and the sales deteriorate. Due to the need to make rapid decisions, a Steering Committee was set up in Washington to evaluate and approve projects and to decide whether to commit staff resources. The Ithaca members, however, wished to retain control over these decisions; they insisted on maintaining monthly board meetings and required that all board members be polled before a project was officially begun. As more chapters were formed, those chapters developed their own agendas and made their own demands on central staff resources. Conflicts thus developed over who should enjoy the scarce resources of staff time and the allocation of any extra funds after staff and overhead expenses were paid. These conflicts were not resolved at the board level, and as other conflicts accumulated, they eventually overwhelmed the organization. Thus we found ourselves in the paradoxical situation of working in an organization dedicated to implementing self-management which seemed, in the end, unable to manage itself.

Phase Two: Bringing Technical Support Back Home

The Steering Committee decided it would be better to disband the central office and allow those staff members who so desired to continue working with specific chapters. It was largely a commitment to long-term work that impelled many of us to continue despite the demise of the national organization. Aside from the centripetal force within FEDO which made the idea of a federation with a central staff unworkable, there were cogent, objective reasons for decentralizing. The experience of working with a number of projects made it clear that extensive staff time was needed for each project. Local technical assistance was the only answer because it was impossible to expect staff who lived elsewhere to spend weeks and even months away from home. I joined forces with what had formerly been the Boston FEDO chapter to form ICA. I had worked closely with its members and identified with their approach of developing sufficient expertise to work effectively on projects of a significant size.

ICA began with a cohesive board composed mainly of members who had worked together on other projects. Remembering the problems of our parent organization, we added to the board slowly, bringing in potential new members on a probationary basis. As a result, a cohesiveness was maintained which facilitated making difficult organizational decisions regarding allocation of staff and resources. At that time ICA saw itself as a regional organization which mainly restricted the scope of its activities to within driving distance of Boston.

In doing this, we were following the organizational principles which we had learned were necessary for worker cooperatives as well. Unlike consumer cooperatives which maintain the principle of open membership, we had learned that worker cooperatives involve a far closer and more intensive form of association. Working members must fit in, and while membership is in principle open to all, those who apply must prove their capacity to work effectively with their cohorts, and also to take their share of responsibility for participating in the control of the organization. The kinds of decisions our board had to make were by no means *pro forma*; they involved financial and organizational viability, potential for creating or saving jobs, and operational choices about whether to develop and support funding proposals that often were in the hundreds of thousands, and occasionally in the millions, of dollars. We needed people with judgment and business experience who had a strong commitment to what we were doing. We also needed people with whom we felt personally comfortable. Our work was pragmatic as well as based on theory. We needed to be flexible, to be able to learn from our mistakes—which we certainly made—and to learn from each other. Ideologues could easily have destroyed the effectiveness of our board as a working group. Fortunately, we attracted only a few of these, and when we did, they found their views were not shared and they left.

At ICA our problems were mainly external to the organization. We were freed from the internal conflicts that had characterized FEDO. This meant we had to develop a coherent approach to implementing worker-management which involved not simply working with projects, but also creating a climate within city and state government, within relevant federal agencies, within local unions and within foundations that would be favorable to our work. A person whose background included extensive experience in both organizing and professional fundraising indicated interest in joining the staff. We engaged him, and, as he successfully raised funds, we were able to hire additional staff—a business analyst, a co-coordinator responsible for education and administration, an economist who had gained business and organizing experience with FEDO and an administrator who also had business experience.

Our basic strategy was unchanged from FEDO days. We worked primarily with plants shut down because of mismanagement and in one case bankruptcy, although we also helped a couple of small new cooperatives start from scratch. Our major concern was to develop an effective track record which could assure us further funding. We realized that we were involved in a long-term project and that it might be a decade or more before our work bore real fruit. To supplement foundation funding, we developed a system of charging the cooperatives with which we worked, the payment determined by profitability of the enterprise and capacity to pay.

The Dangers of Growth

As ICA grew it became more professionalized. From a voluntary organization with no staff and a working board, it became an organization with a growing staff and less board involvement in project work. Board meetings became information sessions where the staff described their activities and occasionally asked for help or counsel. Board meetings were changed from biweekly to monthly, then from monthly to quarterly. We were undergoing a process of informal differentiation which could lead, as Holleb and Abrams have shown, from what they call consensual anarchy to bureaucracy. Organizations, as they develop, encounter certain critical choice-points. If they simply allow the forces of growth and differentiation to have full play, they can easily end up with bureaucracy and top-down control. Countering these forces requires maintaining democratic control by the members as a whole over both increasing differentiation and the newly developed administrative apparatus.

We faced this issue, but only after we had moved toward a situation where the board had become an appendage of the staff with little more than *pro forma* exercise of power. Dissatisfied with the extent to which we had become similar in structure to conventional voluntary organizations, we set up two committees which split the decision-making functions of the organization. The Outreach Committee took care of external relations, publicity, attracting new board members, and had a personnel committee to evaluate new staff applications. The Projects Committee was responsible for all project evaluations and decisions. A final issue was to decide who set the agenda for the board meetings; this too was resolved as a committee function. Board members were expected to serve on one or the other of the committees and, in addition, to make some contribution to the organization such as working with staff on projects. Although there was still a division between the extent and nature of staff and board members' involvement, the growing split was contained and rendered manageable. Board members were once again involved in the ongoing work of the organization, while staff members sat on the board.

The dangers encountered by ICA, as a result of growth and differentiation, were not the conventional dangers of organizational growth wherein a group of managers become differentiated from the larger group of workers. In this case it was the staff who had become the managers while the board became an inactive appendage. However, this form of regression is characteristic of voluntary organizations which seek to maintain democratic participation. As Holleb and Abrams point out, the lack of a defined organizational structure along with external pressures are factors tending to precipitate regression. At ICA, the original structure was informal, pragmatic and without differentiation between staff and board since initially there was no paid staff and later only one such person. As the staff grew in size it assumed control, partly as a result of the passivity of the non-staff board members (including myself) and partly because it was easier to make decisions among those who worked together on a day-to-day basis than to make the greater effort of involving the other board members. However, this tendency was reversed and board members became once more involved in the full decision-making process.

Counter-Institution Building as a Profession

Only recently have I given any thought to the skills, training and attitude requirements of work in such organizations as ICA. In part I have been motivated to do so by the recognition of a need for many more people with similar skills. And in part my interest began when I realized that a watershed had been reached. By 1980, ICA had become, in a critical sense, professionally competent. After about three years of working, we finally came to identify the skills needed to achieve successful implementation of worker-management and began to develop some successful worker-managed companies. Just as important, we developed a successful organization which passed through a stage of organizational development and crisis.

Most of ICA's work is done in teams of two or more and involves continuing assessments of many aspects of a constantly changing situation. We have learned the wisdom of having several points of view and the value of having input from members with specific training in business, development, and organization. Although it seems to conflict with democratic ideals, we learned that in the initial stages of enterprise development it is important to have a central figure with the necessary skills and leadership ability who is capable of getting a new project off the ground.

Related to organizing skills are organizational development and process skills, although some organizers are notably lacking in these areas. The ability to teach these skills to the members of worker-managed companies is also needed. An organizer must not only organize but must teach others how to organize, how to run meetings, and how to achieve consensus.

The role of management in worker-managed systems is a difficult issue. Much more is demanded of managers in a self-managed enterprise than in a conventional one. On the one hand, their authority is limited by the fact that final authority rests with the members as a whole. On the other hand, they must implement policy decisions in the most effective way, but do so in a consultative fashion which takes account of their own subordinate position. Managers must thus be process-oriented as well as business and goal-oriented. They must be sensitive to the feelings and needs of other members but also responsive to the performance demands placed on the organization by external constraints.

By 1981 we had a complete team to call on—with specialists in business, organizing, cooperative structure, and education. Thus we were no longer quite the generalists we were in the beginning. But evaluations of performance and of next steps were almost always group evaluations, many of them involving either a committee of the board or the board as a whole. In this we functioned much like the cooperatives we worked to develop. We were all involved collectively in policy decisions. To make them, we sought a synoptic view of our projects comparable to that taken by the board of directors and top staff of a conventional corporation. Much of the challenge and excitement of our work derived from this. We were very much aware that we were a frontier organization doing pioneer work.

Moreover, we were fortunate in attracting members who, whatever their backgrounds, had the capacity to work well with bankers, workers, and government officials. This required a pragmatic orientation as well as practical skills. Our organization did not attract many ideologues, who preferred to watch skeptically from the sidelines. To activists, however, it offered a whole new arena for action, and a number of original board members had all but moved out of academia to work continuously on developing self-management. Part of the attraction lay in the promise of creating long lasting institutions rather than temporary ones. A number found, as I did, that the challenge of developing new skills and the opportunity to make a difference in people's lives by creating jobs with greater dignity and freedom, was worth considering as a career.

From Clinical Sociology Review, *Vol. 1, 1982.*

Part IV

Steps Toward
A Libertarian Community Life

Chapter 13

The Decentralist Implications of Nuclear Free Zones (1986)

An Unorthodox Perspective

The development of campaigns for nuclear free zones suggests a strategy which can educate and radicalize local communities. Indeed, by extending the logic of the nuclear free zone idea, we can begin to flesh out a libertarian municipalist perspective which can help move our communities several steps toward autonomy from both the central government and the existing corporate system. The examples offered here are intended to be suggestive, however, rather than definitive. Without actual experimentation and organizing it will not be possible to determine just what approaches will prove attractive in any given community. Nor do I believe it is possible to predict how far beyond standard liberal views of government and the state people concerned about peace and justice issues are prepared to go.

The nuclear issue is not only an over-arching one. It is also one which has the potential for most clearly revealing the *nature of governments as power-oriented special interest groups* whose real policies and actions are not only obfuscated but also concealed from its citizens. These policies moreover constitute a costly and planet-threatening power game played by power-oriented individuals seeking to further their own positions of political domination at the expense of the rest of humanity. The problem is that to accept unauthorized versions of political reality requires a 180 degree attitude shift from the orthodox definitions.

Cold War Double-Speak

The anarchist perspective has an unparalleled relevance today because prevailing nuclear policies can be considered as an ultimate stage in the divergence between the interests of governments and their peoples. Moreover, although the extent of this divergence is generally concealed, the implications when revealed serve to raise fundamental questions regarding the advisability of entrusting governments with questions of life and death. Assumptions regarding the democratic character of governments are faced with the fact that with the adoption of nuclear weapons a single person or at most a very few can decide the fate not only of Western civilization but of all life on earth. There is thus a pressing impetus to re-think the role, scale, and structure of national governments so as to decentralize and limit their powers and to create more direct and accountable forms of democratic governance.

Governments, especially those of the U.S. and NATO powers, have carefully masked their real policies and often their actions from their peoples. The United States has been without doubt the chief instigator of nuclear threats. As Daniel Ellsberg pointed out in 1981, ever since the United States attempted to press tactical nuclear weapons on the French for use at Dienbienphu in 1954, to avert their being driven out of Indochina, and even before this under the Truman regime, the United States has persistently resorted to the threatened use of nuclear weapons to achieve geopolitical objectives and maintain U.S. hegemony.

What becomes evident if one examines the history of the Cold War is that the U.S., with the connivance of England and other NATO allies, has practiced a continuing deception on the peoples of the world. Its resort to nuclear threats has for the most part been cloaked in secrecy; its commitment to a first strike policy has never been publicly stated. There is therefore a paramount need to educate peoples—especially the citizens of the U.S. and its close allies, including Canada—regarding the continuing commitment to first strike policies and nuclear threats, in particular those mandating nuclear retaliation against non-nuclear Soviet initiatives.

I believe that the most useful approach to the understanding of national governments in the West is to see them as special interest groups, consisting of interlinked political, corporate, and military inter-ests, all of which officially equate their activities with the national interest. The legitimacy of governments derives from the fact that they fulfill certain public administrative and welfare functions (many pre-empted from the local level because economic centralization and private control of resources has rendered communities incapable themselves of providing necessary life support and other social services). This pseudo-legitimation allows national governments to engage in costly and complex power games, which enhance the power of its representatives as well as the profits and power of those interest groups with which governments in capitalist countries are intimately linked.

Liberal ideology assumes that the contemporary growth of governments which results in the welfare—more accurately, welfare-warfare—state is a basically rational development. Hence to change these assumptions involves a considerable effort at demystification and re-education. While an important part of this re-education must treat directly with the issues of Cold War policy, another part must relate these issues to the domestic institutionalization of militarism via the military-industrial complex. This can be done in local communities by working for the adoption of a community-wide anti-nuclear stand which will thus inevitably confront those manifestations of the military-industrial complex which exist locally. Such confrontations can reveal the motives and attitudes of warfare industries more directly than any perusal of texts.

A further step is to examine ways that the corporate system pre-empts resources from local communities, creating net dollar outflows (such a study was done by Lee Webb in Vermont), which in turn requires a centralized national government for bail-out operations. This kind of study should lead to an understanding of how the centralization of economic power leads to a centralization of political power so that taken together they result in a colonialized society made up of communities that are dependent economically on corporations with distant headquarters and dependent politically on decisions made in Washington, Bonn, or Paris. Both the private and the public sector can then be understood as representing a set of intimately linked special interest groups, allied in their exploitation of the hinterland.

Nuclear Free Zones

The nuclear free zone (NFZ) movement, a late starter in the United States, has achieved considerable momentum in Europe and the Pacific

Basin. Wales also has declared itself a nuclear free zone, as have New Zealand and 20 other countries; 200 towns in Great Britain have declared themselves nuclear free. There is strong pressure for the declaration of a Nordic nuclear free zone involving Finland, Sweden, Norway and Denmark. Among others, Germany, Japan, Italy, Belgium, Canada, the Netherlands, and Ireland each have over 100 towns which have declared themselves nuclear free. In the United States, about 175 locations with close to 17 million people have declared themselves nuclear free; many more have active NFZ campaigns. In Cambridge, Massachusetts, a center for defense research, a referendum to declare the city a nuclear free zone lost narrowly with a 42 percent vote in favor.

The idea of what a nuclear free zone involves varies somewhat, but in general, nuclear free zones are local areas that have declared a prohibition on local research, production, transportation, and deployment of nuclear weapons. A nuclear free zone renounces the right to be defended by the use or threat of nuclear weapons, and requests to be taken off the target list of all other governments employing nuclear weapons. The obvious virtue of such a move is that it forces everyone within the political area in question to consider the nuclear issue as having local relevance—something which must be confronted *as a community* in the same way people deal with other local ordinances, school bills, municipal bonds and the like. Another virtue is that by declaring itself a nuclear free zone, a town takes an official stand which flies directly in the face of official federal policy; it is a declaration of local independence, of opting out.

The idea of a nuclear free zone goes considerably beyond the nuclear freeze. It does not make reciprocity or verifiability a precondition for halting the nuclear arms race; also, it addresses itself to those who see a connection between nuclear arms and nuclear energy. Finally, it represents a local initiative that does not depend on the federal government for action. Thus it is a step toward local empowerment and away from the large category of social actions which are aimed at reform or change in policies at the federal level, including redistributive programs which would increase food stamps or welfare payments and reduce military expenditures. The reformist approach certainly represents an improvement of conditions, but structurally it changes nothing. Steps that increase local autonomy change the power relations between the center and its colonies and thus have a structural as well as a material content; they can thus contribute to sustained empowerment.

Further Initiatives

The nuclear free zone movement has a thrust which is clearly congruent with anarchist ideas. But it is worth exploring other ways in which the notion can be extended in the direction of a full scale critique of the over-extension of the state and its suppression of local autonomy. There are a number of paths which can be taken, many of them complementary. They represent an extension of the idea that local communities can opt out in those cases where they are made into dependent colonial zones by the centralized power of the state and the corporate system. The same motives which go into the declaration of a nuclear free zone would dictate that in other areas where the state and the corporate system's services are dysfunctional and involve excessive costs, they too should be dispensed with.

It is quite possible, at least in Europe, that eventually whole regions and then countries may declare themselves nuclear free zones. If other equally reasonable steps toward the limitation and decentralizing of state and corporate power could be successful, the ultimate result could indeed be revolutionary. What follows is a grab-bag of initiatives, intended to follow or build upon the declaration of a nuclear free zone.

Initiatives directed against state dependency

1. Begin a research project to better understand the overall input-output structure of all federal taxes, individual and corporate, and all federal benefits. Such studies have already been done for several communities, e.g. that of Lee Webb mentioned above. This could serve as a basis for community-based protest against federal appropriation and use of funds. The possibility of litigation against the federal government could be explored; for instance, a nuclear free zone could argue that it was being forced to support weapons production to which it was officially and legally opposed. Out of this might come further actions suggested below.

2. The issue of taxes going for nuclear weapons could be approached in other ways: A community could seek to supplement its income by calling on citizens to pay a peace tax to go for local amenities.

As a further step it could organize so as to persuade its members not to pay a portion of federal income taxes. If the balance withheld were then used by the community, this would give the action a social legitimation in the eyes of the community. Tax resistance at present is mostly an individual matter. This is far less effective than a community-wide commitment, agreed to by public referendum in the same fashion as a nuclear free zone. Those who voted against it might be excused from participating. It could be implemented only when a certain number of citizens supported it. Such tax resistance, with community legitimation and large numbers, would be extremely difficult to prosecute; prosecution would take on the character of a prosecution of the community as a whole by the central government.

3. As a further strategy for preventing the federal government from taking legal action against individuals, the local government could pass an ordinance requiring individuals to hand over all taxes to the municipal government. The federal government would then have to take the municipal government to court to collect its taxes. It would undoubtedly win, but at the least, the idea would focus national attention on the action and the ideas behind it. Or it could force the federal government to attach its tax revenues, thereby highlighting the difference between revenues going for local services and the same revenues going into armaments.

4. On a more modest level, a community could declare itself a "free town" somewhat along the lines of Reagan's "enterprise zones." The free towns would promote the growth of socially responsible industries, which provided needed social products and services at reasonable cost, and were democratically managed. A portion of corporate taxes on such industries of choice would be forgiven in return for a contract wherein the corporation contracted not to leave the area, and perhaps also to support certain social services. The corporations could then defend their failure to pay federal taxes by claiming that they had signed a binding contract with the municipality for those same taxes.

Initiatives against external corporate dependency

1. A community that had enacted nuclear free zone legislation could engage in a conversion study with the objective of assisting a proscribed war industry to convert to peace-oriented production. It

could then give the industry various forms of assistance including tax breaks, low interest loans, and so on.

2. A study comparable to the tax and revenue study suggested above can be done on the local private sector to determine the net status of outflows and inflows. This need not cover every single business. The important areas to examine are energy expenses, the food distribution system including grocery and fast food chains, branches of large corporations headquarters elsewhere, and absentee landlords. Although this study may not cast light directly on the military-industrial system, it can reveal the outlines of the colonialization of local economies. In this way, the study should throw light on how economic dependency leads to political dependency, and hence taken together, to the warfare state.

3. Some communities are already requiring a contractual *quid pro quo* from industries attracted as a result of tax breaks, industrial parks and the like. Local ordinances could be passed requiring all industries to sign a contract which would require prior notice of shutdown, a commitment never to leave, and beyond that possibly the placing of local public members on the board, supporting worker participation, and sustaining certain forms of local community assistance.

4. A program of import substitution and local growing could be introduced with funding made available for the starting of such businesses. A study of import-export patterns could be made so as to minimize redundancies in transportation, and create substitutions first for those businesses which operated with a net export of money flows from the community. Import substitution would be especially aimed at companies involved in nuclear protection. For example, it has been thought to be cost effective to produce light bulbs locally; this could accord with the boycott of General Electric products in the U.S., G.E. being a major nuclear weapons manufacturer.

5. For any of these steps toward community autonomy a considerable amount of organizing would be necessary, resulting in some form of citizens' committees, advisory boards, and broad representation and inputs from citizens' groups. Initial mobilization around the nuclear free zone idea could then lead to ongoing study groups to research how the community could move to reclaim autonomy in other ways.

Conscientization

An extensive program of *conscientization* (Paulo Freire's term seems most appropriate here) would be necessary to bring a community to a point where it was willing to begin to declare its autonomy in different ways from the central system. As suggested, the nuclear issue would seem the best place to begin. The impetus to work for autonomy in other ways would come from the delegitimation process occurring as a result of the public's greater understanding of the central government's power orientation (both domestically and globally) and the resulting contradiction between the government's and the citizens' interests.

Beginning with the nuclear free zone idea, and extending the principle of local control to other areas, local communities might begin to move in the direction of greater independence from central state authority. (This might be a natural issue for local Green parties.) The extent to which this will happen will be dependent on local circumstances and local leadership; it will be facilitated by a process of intensive community organizing and *conscientization.*

This previously unpublished essay was written in 1986.

Chapter 14

Militarism and Local Tax Reform (1985)

Federal Taxes Breed War-making

Historically, taxes and military activities are closely related; in the 17th century, for example, over 60 percent of all the taxes in Western Europe went to finance religious wars. In the United States, federal income taxes were first initiated at the time of World War I. Since war-making constitutes probably the largest item in the state's budget, we cannot avoid asking whether its power to tax the citizenry has been abused and ought to be withdrawn or at least curtailed.

This line of questioning is particularly relevant at a time when the state's monopoly on the means of violence includes nuclear weapons, and with it the power to destroy both civilization and life on earth. Also, the development of government in this country is generally recognized to entail both the growth of the administrative and bureaucratic apparatus at the expense of more democratically oriented legislative functions, and the subordination of all branches of the government to powerful vested interests, such as the military-industrial establishment, and other corporate giants. As a 1976 poll commissioned by the People's Bicentennial Commission showed, a majority of citizens perceive their government to be responsive mainly to Big Business interests.

It is, in other words, the compulsory tax system by which the worst features of centralized government are fed. Through this system, it can bypass the democratic process to support unpopular wars and subsidize powerful special interests. Through this system, it is able to grow without limit or control. And through this system, it endangers not only the lives of its citizens but all of life on this planet. Conventional tax reform efforts are unlikely to alter this system. Their aims are too narrow, and they usually accept the war-making activities of the federal government. However, there is another approach which might work.

Why Not Localize Taxation?

If these problems do derive from the central government's power to tax, then the solution certainly is to weaken that power, if not eliminate it. If taxes were both collected and distributed by local jurisdictions, they could be brought under the governance of direct democracy: town meetings, local referenda, votes on the specifics of local collection methods and expenditures.

What would such a decentralized system look like, and how could it be achieved politically? Essentially, it would be a system in which local jurisdictions would collect for local needs. They would have full freedom to collect corporate and income taxes, sales taxes, property taxes, or whatever other form of tax they could devise. One core element would be the right of local jurisdictions to use the full spectrum of tax collection mechanisms, rather than being limited to the property tax and the sales tax. The other element would be the right to have first, not last, claim on taxes—all taxes.

Basic Elements of Decentralized Tax Reform

The basic elements of decentralizing taxation are thus: first, tax collection would be the prerogative of local jurisdictions alone. Second, some method would then be worked out to fund higher level jurisdictions on a basis that was both equitable and retained the local jurisdiction's right to decide on both the kind of taxes and the amount to be collected. Third, claims would be established by a process which involved periodic consultation with the jurisdictions from which the taxes derived. (For example, minimums would be established for basic services, and communities unable to meet these minimums out of their own revenues would have a legal claim on revenues at the next higher level.) Fourth, these claims would be treated not as permanent, but rather as temporary, claims for both social services and development toward self-sufficiency.

Some Possible Strategies

The strategy of working toward such a decentralized tax system would involve first developing a broad-based coalition that would span the political spectrum. The argument, "no taxation without representation," would have some weight; although taxes are decided by elected representatives, the government budgetary process is out of control, and the only way to return it to control is to return the tax function to the local level. Conservatives might balk at the establishment of floors on social services, but actually this is far cheaper than the present system of largely uncontrolled spending in all sectors—social services as well as national defense.

A strategy of achieving incremental gains toward local control of taxes would have to be developed. One danger would be that states rather than local jurisdictions might seize the initiative here. To counter this, a national organization with a clear platform of tax reform requiring genuine local control would be needed. It might start by attacking the fiscal irresponsibility and bureaucracy of the federal government—something difficult to deny or defend—and arguing for a return of the taxing power to local jurisdictions.

What would happen then is anybody's guess. If the movement were strong enough, politicians would undoubtedly jump on the bandwagon and a political party possibly might result. (Tax reform would be a good issue for the emerging Greens.) At the very least, such a program of tax reform would allow for the articulation and dissemination of a critique of the government as a special interest group unrepresentative of the people at large. Such a critique echoes, and gives expression to, a broad-based sentiment already in existence.

Who Would Benefit from Tax Decentralization?

Since taxes provide the basis for the government's war-making capacity, the anti-war movement should be an ally in the demand for local control of taxes. In no area is the government's power to define the terms of acceptable debate, as well as the government's character as a special interest group, more evident. Local control of taxes would inevitably democratize the foreign policy debate, placing the guns-or-butter issue in a context which would reveal it as a conflict between a nationally-based special interest group and the needs of localities and their citizens.

There are many additional interests which would stand to benefit by the decentralization of taxation. Small businesses would benefit since they would be much more likely to receive local than national support, being important to the community's economic well-being. Labor would benefit from greater control over plant closings and over other negative corporate decisions. Communities as a whole would clearly benefit; they could begin to truly flourish, to fully meet their citizens' needs, instead of remaining welfare recipients dependent on a warfare state and powerful corporations. We would all gain by the restoration of democracy to the local level—a vital range of decisions would be made by municipal neighbors at town meetings. The slogan, "Get Big Brother Off Our Backs"—now a hollow sham—might become a unifying cry of liberation.

From Changing Work, *No. 7, Winter 1988. This paper was originally written in 1983 and revised further in 1985.*

Chapter 15

Growing a Local Economy
(1984)

Preparing for an Economic Crisis

At present there is a general sense of an economy which is out of control. Polls indicate a widespread distrust of both Big Government and Big Business, and in New England, especially, the tradition of local democracy and local autonomy still persists. If economic conditions worsen, as economists from a number of positions predict, then we are likely to find an openness to alternatives which have not been thought of since the depression of the 1930s. The argument made here is that, first, it is important to plan for a possible economic crisis, since it is not only practical, but also can serve as a method of mobilizing a community in creative ways. Second, such planning allows for a broad systems approach, capable of transcending the shallow assumptions which constrain most urban and community planning.

Orthodox economic analysis assumes that a local economy has only a very limited set of responses in the face of deteriorating macro-economic conditions; as the private sector deteriorates, so will the public sector. It is also assumed that both the nature and the degree of dependency on the external macro-economy is unchanging. This paper will start off from a very different perspective. It will consider the totality of resources available within the community and then consider what changes could be made so as to enhance the use of these resources and hence improve the quality of life within the community.

The approach suggested here works best in small to medium-sized communities of perhaps 20,000 to 100,000. But some of the solutions it points to have historically been used in cities as well as in smaller communities. Two assumptions govern it. First, the present concentration of economic and political power is excessive and has destructive consequences; local communities are largely devoid of significant economic or political control over their own functioning. Second, countering this trend toward concentration of power can create not only empowerment but efficiency; decentralization, in many cases, reduces costs.

Using Energy Credits to Build a Local Currency

Historically, at times of severe inflation or capital shortages, communities have been forced to rely on their own resources. During the Great Depression, many cities printed their own currency; this works to the extent that a community is able to maintain a viable internal economy which provides the necessities of life, independent of transactions with the outside. In post World War II Japan, there were essentially two currencies: the official yen currency and a secondary currency of promissory notes. Unlike ordinary credit, which is non-transferable, promissory notes could be signed over to another creditor and this process would continue for the life of the note, which was usually of several months duration. These notes, circulating with the endorsement of each subsequent user, represented a short-term secondary currency, based on the promise to pay in the primary currency. Thus they added to the money supply at a time of capital shortage.

Given a shortage of needed capital (assuming a high level of government borrowing, such shortage seems likely to continue for some time), it is worthwhile to inquire how a community uses alternate forms of financing to avoid the national and international situation. A couple of examples may clarify both the possibilities and the problems to be overcome. A community might decide, in one case, *to construct a local hydroelectric utility* which could significantly lower local energy rates if not hooked into the national grid. The community could finance the project by first establishing a limited partnership able to make use of energy tax credits, depreciation, and possibly research and development costs; this would be an effective tax shelter pass-through for investors, thereby reducing the need for high investment return. Second-stage financing would be via the issuance of energy credits, in kilowatt-hour denominations, bought with investment dollars. These energy credits would be redeemable in electricity at the then-current rate, thus representing a hedge against inflation.

To the extent that there were sufficient energy credits within a community to allow for significant internal transactions to take place with their use, these energy credits would then constitute an internal commodity-based currency. On the hypothetical assumption that, in any given year, there would be no more than one-fifth redemptions, five times the total energy output of the hydro facility could be put into circulation as energy currency, thus extending the usage of the currency from simply paying for electrical energy used, to paying for a number of other goods and services.

A community would need—to give a second example—*a program of local economic development* to support its locally initiated currency. There might be rewards for dealing locally, as in the mutual benefits exchanged in barter systems. In addition, local businesses could be subsidized and external transactions taxed. Beyond these measures, the community would need an *import substitution and local job creation program* that could utilize the sort of tax breaks that are now used to entice outside industry to settle. One bold example of a way this could be done in the energy field would be to begin to develop a *system of solar ponds* (following a Department of Energy study using the town of Northampton, Massachusetts as a model). Such a system could, when completed, provide for virtually all of a town's heating needs, since solar ponds provide an optimal method for "banking" solar energy and making it available through the cold months when it is most needed.

A staged program of import substitution addressed to energy needs—the major import of any community—could start with electricity, as suggested, then move to heat use, and finally to transportation. The latter is probably the most difficult area for local substitution, requiring local production of ethanol or methanol, electric buses or streetcars, and gas savings via group taxis and dial-a-buses. Financing could include municipal bonds, private investment with tax write-offs and deductions, and some arrangement with the state that could capitalize the savings in welfare and unemployment benefits resulting from local job creation.

Going Beyond Energy

Dependency and self-sufficiency can be viewed in terms of the four categories which together take up the major portion of an individual or family budget: energy, housing, food, and medical care. In the case of public spending, human services and public maintenance must be added.

We have seen that energy costs can be lowered by local substitutions. There are substitutions as well for major reliance on the private automobile and gasoline. The same holds for land and housing, including finance costs. As for medical care, local health maintenance organizations can significantly lower costs by eliminating redundancy, using para-professionals, and substituting fees-for-service for salaries. For many communities, local food production is now, at a time of high transportation costs, an increasingly attractive option; it is happening already. It can be both rationalized and hastened by the development of a local warehousing and distribution system. With such a system in place, planning and incentives would help to create agricultural diversification, and local storage facilities would serve to lengthen the availability of local produce throughout the season.

Admittedly, local food self-sufficiency could at best be only partial, given the penchant for year-round fruits and vegetables. However, food costs could be lowered greatly. At present, communities with an agricultural base are at the mercy of distribution systems located in urban centers. These force food which is locally produced and locally consumed to travel first to an urban market and then back again, in the process suffering both the transportation costs and the high volatility characteristic of such markets. Also, supermarkets often price local products at the import price in order to maintain price consistency throughout the year. Finally, various methods of intensive cultivation, e.g., permaculture, could be employed to both diversify and increase yields.

Mobilizing the Community Around a Resource Plan

How might a city or county organize a comprehensive program to utilize its own local resources? To return to Japan: It is probable that the small business sector in Japan resorted to an extensive promissory note system after World War II because of the destruction of the economy and the extensive capital shortage. But the fact that these notes were made transferable was the product of a high degree of cultural cohesiveness and trust. These conditions could be most easily replicated on a local level, given either successful mobilization efforts within a cohesive community or hardship conditions brought about by an external economic collapse.

Mobilizing a community around the goal of becoming more reliant on local resources could itself be an effective method for achieving the necessary cohesiveness. This could be done by first obtaining support from local voluntary organizations, banks, and other leading business institutions, as well as the county and municipal government, for a *planning conference* on the subject. Out of this would come a series of task forces focusing on energy substitution and conservation, transportation, housing, job creation, human services, food and agriculture, and medical care. The task forces would be made up of a mix of specialists in the area, possessed of the requisite knowledge and vision, along with representatives of interested local organizations. Planning groups approximating this model were put together by the Montreal Citizens' Party, which produced position papers embodying significant alternatives in a number of areas; they then got several members elected to the city council. A similar system of task forces has been put together in Brattleboro, Vermont. Any plan resulting from such an effort would have to involve staged development, while taking into account the particular character of local needs and local resources. It would call for development in the overall degree of self-sufficiency in critical areas, enhanced capacity for self-financing, and the establishment of new public-private institutions aimed at solving major community problems. These might include a local development corporation, a community-owned utility, a community investment fund, and a large-scale bartering network involving both individuals and local businesses. These programs would be modest at first, but as they took hold they would stimulate bolder programs in the specific areas marked for development. Tax incentives could be used to stimulate energy conservation through industrial cogeneration, retrofitting, and solarization, to abet the work of the new institutions suggested above.

Further steps might include dial-a-buses or public taxis along the lines of Latin American "colectivos," a local Health Maintenance Organization (HMO) or community clinics with sufficient consumer input to rationalize and control medical costs, a retrofitting and firewood cooperative, and a garbage and waste recycling cooperative that could profit from resale and reprocessing of materials collected. The projects should be chosen for their capacity for community involvement and should be structured so as to encourage it; hence the importance of the HMO, the local development corporation, the public service cooperatives, the bartering system, all of which are institutions which enable—indeed, presuppose—extensive community membership and involvement.

Without going further into the details of a local development and financing plan, it should be evident that it can develop incrementally, in ways that do not seem "far out" or fly in the face of established custom, yet also lay the groundwork for full-scale alternatives which would then be perceived as logical extensions of the existing programs. A poll conducted in Great Barrington, a western Massachusetts town of several thousand, indicated a positive response to a list of suggestions for local economic development. These included cooperatively owned businesses, a community-owned credit union, cottage industries, as well as the development of a public transportation system, greater energy efficiency, waste recycling, community gardens, canning and food preserving centers, community wind farms, and so on. There was almost no opposition among the local organizations and businesses polled, only skepticism as to whether such programs could be initiated.

In creating a local development plan, the resource optimization approach leads to the idea of community mobilization, and this in turn contains presuppositions. At one extreme would be a pure conflict model which will not allow community mobilization, since such mobilization requires alliances between citizen groups, mainstream voluntary organizations, businesses, and the local government. At the other extreme would be a consensual view of community structure and community relations which also is not implied. The assumption is rather that there exists a fairly widespread and shared recognition of the failure of centralized institutions to respond to local needs and interests. The basic dependency of local areas runs counter to strong and continuing instincts of localism and self-reliance within the American tradition. These instincts can be appealed to so that the localist thrust results in new institutional, social and technological arrangements, the net effect of which is progressive. This does not deny the existence of conflicting and vested interests. But the effort to optimize the use of local resources is a goal which, if the Great Barrington poll is any indication, would be broadly supported. Opposition would exist, but could not easily coalesce around any broadly acceptable ideological position.

An Embryonic Example in Massachusetts

Thus, in Great Barrington, on the heels of the survey mentioned above, a local investment fund has been created which illustrates the possibility of alliances between local progressive groups and local opinion leaders. The local bank has agreed to house the fund, which has loan criteria that include democratic management, labor intensity, local consumer benefit, ecological soundness, and local development value. Called *Self Help for a Regional Economy* or *SHARE*, it provides local loans and investments collateralized against SHARE depositors. The SHARE strategy, in three separate ways, provides a model of how alliances can be made with mainstream institutions oriented to progressive goals. First, in the SHARE system, loans are approved first by the SHARE loan committee in terms of social criteria and then by the loan committee using financial criteria. A system of associations already exists in the fields of wind generation and agriculture. New associations are being formed along these same lines. These associations propose projects to SHARE and subsequently give technical assistance to ensure their sound development. Thus development is not placed solely in the hands of existing institutions, complete with their external dependencies. Rather, a joint system of control is created which draws on the facilities and legitimization of the bank, so as to give the program credibility and to demonstrate, to the bank, the viability of social investments. Second, the program provides broad citizen input into the loan process, via the SHARE membership and the linked associations, and a system for joint control via the SHARE loan committee. Third, it is focused squarely on local benefits and local economic development, an objective capable of uniting mainstream and progressive groups in a number of areas. An alternative approach would be to have a consortium of banks develop a low interest loan program for local economic development. But this approach would lack the essential ingredients of citizen involvement and local citizen control; financial considerations would most likely predominate over social criteria, rather than operating conjointly.

A *Window of Opportunity*

The approach outlined here departs from mainstream economic articles of faith: e.g., that taxes must be increased to maintain community services and that only remote corporations and public agencies can bail out local economies. Communities that finance themselves generate lower costs, through import substitutions and the avoidance of artificially high interest rates, for necessities like energy and food; they do not need to raise taxes to provide needed services. Hence, a program to develop local self-sufficiency can appeal to the current widespread dissatisfaction—expressed in tax revolts on various levels and frustration with local funding of excessive systems of "military defense" with continued use of taxation in a shrinking economy. A window of opportunity, in short, may be open to alternative approaches which transfer control of investment and development to democratic and face-to-face groups. Such approaches go beyond dividing a static pie more equitably; they reveal how to make more—and better—pies or stocks of resources.

In addition, relying on local resources leads naturally to non-market—and community mobilizing—vehicles such as barter, community development corporations, community investment funds, and cooperatives. These all combine economic with social functions, much as SHARE relies on both social and conventional criteria to disperse loans. Moreover, in the process of building from within, we can eliminate the need and the high cost of paying tribute to a large central (and largely unaccountable) government and industrial system.

The reasons for "community resource mobilization" are many and diverse. What remains is to follow SHARE (and others, including ARABLE in Eugene, Oregon) in bringing our economies back home.

From Changing Work, *No. 7, Winter 1988. This essay was originally written in 1984.*

Part V

Commentaries

$$\overline{\textit{Chapter 16}}$$

A Paradox of Size

Jane Mansbridge

The era of the 1960s and 1970s produced a generation of social thinkers and activists animated by the human goals of Marxism and the organizational goals of anarchism. These practical "organizational anarchists" were concerned with building functioning organizations. They saw human liberation as requiring human solidarity, and worked to create actual institutions that fostered such solidarity. They were not "philosophical anarchists," concerned primarily with theory; nor did they focus primarily on libertarian freedom from others' control.

It was this group of thinkers and activists who struggled both in practice and in theory with the problems that increasing size poses for maintaining fulfilling human relations. George Benello was central to this generation.[1] His activist concern for making organizations work combined with a vision of human possibility gave him an eye for the telling detail (the coffee bar at Mondragon), energy in pursuing actual experiments (FEDO and ICA), and realism in drawing lessons from their successes and failures.

Although the great wave of widespread experimenting with collective organizations in the United States has now momentarily passed, a legacy of many alternatively organized collectives and worker-owned enterprises remains, along with a new infusion of humanist ideas into the American tradition of decentralization and a legacy of theorizing about problems like the problem of size.

In this essay, I will single out learning and power among the means to the humanist goals I share with George Benello, then pose the democratic paradox that the learning that is best for the individual and the power that is most effective at the level of greatest scale seem to require two different and separate kinds of organization. I will also develop an understanding of power that contrasts with that expressed by Benello.

Shared Human Goals

As George Benello once put it, "We live in a society today in which both the scale and the structure of human organization represent forces powerfully opposed to the possibility of human growth and freedom." That scale and structure undermine the human need for *relationships* based on wholeness, openness, self-disclosure, honesty, and an ethic of mutual aid. Large-scale and bureaucratic structures also undermine the human need for *work* based on a sense of personal efficacy and intrinsic motivation. "Solidarity and meaningful activity" are the two central human goals that Benello identified as unchanging human needs.

The kind of solidarity that George Benello considered a basic human need works best, as he pointed out, on a scale that makes it possible to know other people in depth. His is not the solidarity of the nationalistic *levee en masse* or the allegiance of thousands of followers to a leader larger than life. It is the solidarity of "people working in face-to-face relations with their fellows in order to bring the uniqueness of their own perspective to the business of solving common problems and achieving common goals." Large scale makes these face-to-face relations impossible.

The kind of meaningful activity that Benello considered basic involves both mastery and engagement, dealing with "the obstinacy of matter"[2] and finding self-actualization in interaction with others. This meaningful activity, this work, should lead to self-awareness and self-understanding. It thus requires that the individual be able to participate significantly in those areas of work or public life that affect his or her own existence. The kind of work that involves only following orders—a kind of work promoted by large-scale and bureaucratic structures—cannot produce this result. To help all members of the community to develop, work must be organized to draw on each individual's problem-solving capacities and productive collaboration with others.

The Organizational Means

Because he correctly saw many Marxist analyses of social change as "statist and grandiose," Benello focused on the ways that the organization of work and political life on a small scale could improve the lives of those who worked, lived, and did politics together. He focused less on how the small-scaled organizations that produced the best human relations could bring about social and political change on a large scale.

To address changes on the scale of the modern nation state, Benello employed two principles, decentralization and federation. The decentralist principle, with which I (and even many capitalist management theorists) would agree completely is: "Decentralize all functions to the lowest possible level."[3] The problem here comes in the tradeoffs that arise within the concept of "possible." Different members of a group are likely to disagree on what is the "lowest possible" level, that is, when the costs of decentralization in restricting the reach of decisions exceed too greatly the many benefits of decentralization. If building a highway, for example, is not to depend on the cooperation and willingness to pay of each component, localities must be empowered to deliberate and make decisions for the whole. To be effective, some decisions need only apply to a locality, but others—many ecological and commercial decisions, for example—need a larger "reach." They need to apply to more people. Decentralization has costs when it undermines policies or blocks decisions that should apply across local boundaries. Reach is particularly critical if decisions involve power, rather than pure consensus.

Centralization itself, of course, has great costs, primarily in the human terms that George Benello described so well, but also in many other areas like efficiency (dampening the process of experimentation) and peace. Both in nations and in simpler societies, the larger the society, the more likely it is to go to war.[4]

The federative principle in its anarchist form postulates that large scale decisions require a decision structure based on a pyramid of face-to-face groups "which communicate both vertically and horizontally through a system of delegates whose power is limited by the groups they represent."[5] In practice, in a polity the size of the United States, such a system would require a minimum of three levels. Imagine that the bottom unit, a small neighborhood, included 500 adult citizens, the very largest group one can conceive operating on a face-to-face basis (even this would need to be broken down into groups of no more than 20 for each member to know the others well). The second level up, an assembly of no more than 500, could thus accommodate the views, through delegation, of 250,000 adult citizens.[6] The next unit up, again limited to 500 as the outermost limit of face-to-face interaction, could accommodate the views of 125,000,000 adult citizens, a little under that of the United States today. In such a system sovereign authority would always lie with the lowest possible level. The primary source of authority would be the individual citizen, and the secondary source the neighborhood. All other sources of authority would derive from these two.

A pyramidal system like this could be limited to only three layers, at the cost of having huge assemblies (state legislatures usually number about 200; the Senate of the United States has 100) and of omitting regional government, which might be important in ecological and other issues. Yet even with only three layers, a pyramidal system would place greater distance between the individual citizen and the council that deals with the largest scale than do present systems of representative government. In the early days of the American republic, conservatives devised systems of "indirect election" that bear some resemblance to the pyramidal council system precisely in order to distance the representatives from the people. With no direct election, the layers of selection that intervene between the bottom and the top create considerable psychological and actual distance between citizen and national representative. In theory, this distance could be eliminated by insisting that all delegates be strictly mandated, that is, that they take no action on which they have not been given exact instructions from the council or people that elected them. Whenever an unanticipated issue arose, each delegate would have to return to her council for instructions, and the members of that council would return to their local citizens, gathered in assembly, for instructions.

In my experience the strict mandate system is unworkable. In 1973, I observed decisions in a workplace of forty-one members, divided into subgroups of two to twelve each, in which decisions that applied to all were made by all, through discussion and consensus in both an assembly of the whole held whenever anyone requested it and in a council of nine representatives from the subgroups.[7] The nine (rotating) council representatives were strictly mandated, and had in addition strong personal commitments to not making any decision without consulting the other members of their groups. Yet with the best will in the world, and with ample opportunity for consulting the others in their groups (with whom they worked daily), the council members could not avoid making some decisions, even important ones, with inadequate consultation. Sometimes the representatives were unaware of the implications of a decision, as when they approved a suggestion to join in a city-wide "March Against Drugs" without realizing, as some subgroup members could have told them, that the march had political implications they might want to avoid. At other times, the representatives did not hear, and therefore could not report, the views of members of their own group who had missed a group meeting. But even when every subgroup member had attended every meeting and the representatives had heard all views, those representatives found it impossible adequately to convey in the council the arguments on both sides and the shades of meaning that different subgroup members had expressed.[8]

The process by which this council made decisions without full consultation was incremental and subtle; it involved little or no conscious intent to amass power.[9] In a large-scale pyramidal system, ensuring that the delegates only made decisions that arose directly from consultation with individual citizens would be impossible, even if there were never any need to make an immediate, pressing decision. Any practicable system would have to allow some discretion to its representatives, and would thus have to rely, for accountability, on the standard representative forms of accountability, namely retrospective voting, supplemented by the unwieldy and therefore rarely used mechanism of recall.[10] A system that promised thorough consultation would soon create cynicism about its workings. Rotation in the councils would diminish expertise in the job, although it might alleviate cynicism by showing everyone through practice that some modification in the ideal was required no matter how good anyone's will.

I have concluded that on some issues—issues of large-scale ecology, like acid rain, or large-scale economic issues, like redistribution to geographically disadvantaged areas—people need ways of making binding collective decisions at the scale of the modern nation-state or beyond. As all of us begin to understand the many kinds of effects each of our actions can have upon our neighbors, including the neighbors who live thousands of miles away, we need social forms that let us take collective control of the negative "externalities" of individual and local collective action. In some way, people from the different regions affected must meet to find ways to keep the actions of some from hurting others. Those ways might include enhancing mutual empathy, promoting relevant moral principles, distributing social praise and blame, and instituting material rewards and disincentives to promote desired behavior.[11] Geographical separation should not prevent people who affect one another negatively, and thus have a common problem, from meeting to try to work out solutions to that problem. Some such problems will require representatives from the scattered parts of a whole continent to meet. Other problems will require representatives from more than one continent. If such meetings limited themselves to purely consensual outcomes, they would deprive the collectives they represent of the valuable human tool of agreed-upon mutual coercion.

When collective decisions are necessary on the scale of the modern nation-state and beyond, I would argue for some kind of directly elected representative system. Perhaps such bodies could meet infrequently, or limit themselves to one problem, as in the recent conferences on the law of the sea. Undoubtedly they should be supplemented by devices like the neighborhood town meetings and two-stage multi-option referenda that Benjamin Barber proposes,[12] or by "policy juries"—groups of citizens selected by lot and paid to confer for a period from a week to three years on specific policy questions and either decide themselves on these issues or advise the elected representatives.[13]

We should, I believe, reduce the role of large-scale government to those questions that demand a large-scale analysis. We should also institute participatory innovations that would reinvigorate democratic life, promote deliberation on large-scale issues, and give citizens a greater impact on collective decisions than they do in the United States at present. Yet even this reduction and these innovations would not eliminate the probability that any group that met to consider large-scale action would, by acting in the name of some of the citizens (probably the more powerful citizens), oppress other citizens. To protect against such oppression, and to make people aware of the issues in large-scale decisions, it would therefore still be necessary for sub-interests in the population to organize collectively in order to try to influence decisions on the larger scale.

The small-scale, face-to-face organizations that Benello correctly argued foster solidarity and many kinds of meaningful activity among their members, can generate two kinds of influence on the larger scale: the gradual change of deeply held attitudes throughout a population and the day-to-day resistance of oppressed groups to their oppressors. Such groups are less appropriate for ongoing large-scale decision-making. I will argue that the very characteristics that make small groups so effective at developing solidarity and meaningful activity among their members, creating sweeping changes in consciousness, and resisting daily oppression also make them less effective at making or influencing specific decisions on a large scale.

The Problem of Power

George Benello's essays and my own thinking diverge at one critical point. Benello wanted to avoid completely a politics based on power, that is, on making others act against their own interests.[14] Indeed, he frequently recommended "the dissolution of the political into the social," meaning by the political the realm of power. I believe, however, that collective decisions on the large scale require either majority rule or, less damagingly, proportional outcomes, if they are not to give disproportionate weight to the status quo. Decisions by consensus give too great a weight to the status quo. The alternative to the status quo is some coercion. When a large-scale collective adopts either majority rule or a system of proportional outcomes,[15] it adopts, in effect, a system that decides issues through the application of coercion. The adversary theory of democracy legitimates such a system through the equal weight given each citizen in the decision.[16]

Anarchist theory does not, by and large, countenance the coercion of one group of citizens by another, with the exception of informal social coercion in small communities.[17] I will argue here, however, first for mutually agreed on formal coercion and second for coercion through majority rule or some form of consociationalism.

First, I contend that in order to produce universally desired collective action a collective may legitimately use not only social censure (and approval) on the small scale but also, on either the small or large scale, mutually agreed upon disincentives (coercion).[18] Such disincentives make collectively undesirable actions also individually undesirable after the disincentive is added to the calculus of individual costs and benefits.[19] Moreover, formal disincentives (coercion) for collectively harmful behavior can protect the great majority who may want to act cooperatively for principled and empathetic reasons from being "suckered" by the few who lack either principles or empathy.

Just as I would argue for decentralizing on all issues to the lowest possible level, I would also urge keeping all coercion, even mutually agreed upon coercion, to a minimum. What that lowest possible level is on different policy issues is best discussed in a specific context, like, say, acid rain. Here I argue only that some collectively agreed on coercion is a useful tool in managing the collective action problem.

I will now go further, however, and argue for coercion on some issues through either majority rule or proportional power-sharing ("consociationalism"). Anarchist theorists, like many more mainstream democratic theorists, espouse a deliberative theory of democracy, in which citizens come together to discuss and resolve matters of the common good.[20] I too see much greater scope for a politics of the common good than present American politics or political science credits. Moreover, in a more human, egalitarian, worker-owned, highly decentralized system many present-day conflicts would not arise. Yet I believe that any polity, of no matter what size, will always generate some issues on which members of the polity have irreconcilable conflicts of interest, and on which it is not in even the deepest, most human interest of those members to submerge those conflicts in the attempt to create a common good.

In some issues in interpersonal relations both parties may be better off when each openly espouses his or her self-interest and the pair reaches a settlement under procedurally fair rules. So too a political system that either makes self-interest morally unacceptable or provides no means for settling disputes other than unanimous agreement or mandating the status quo leaves the collective in a position of discouraging self-awareness or promoting political injustice.

I would argue, in short, that even in the best society any decision-making body would find itself in the position of having either to endorse the status quo or make some decisions for some group of its members against the interests of the others. *Not* making a decision—continuing an open debate, for example—*is* making a decision to leave the status quo (which may be oppressive, or just inefficient) unchanged. While it is critically important to restore deliberation on the common good to its central role in democratic theory and practice, it is also critical to devise legitimate ways of exercising power in moments of conflicting interest. Adversary theory, with its mandate of equal weight for each citizen in the determination of social coercion, takes a step in that direction.

If my argument is correct, any collective that does not want simply to endorse the status quo will have to exercise power on some issues—issues of fundamentally conflicting interest—some of the time. Collective bodies that make decisions for entities as large as half the North American subcontinent may have to do so frequently. If this is so, citizens will have to organize themselves to exercise power both to provide a balance against the power of others and to influence policy.

The Paradox

Alexis de Tocqueville was the first observer of the American scene to document the great importance of small groups in American life. In these groups, de Tocqueville noticed, citizens both learn skills and change their desires. "[T]hey converse, they listen to one another, and they are mutually stimulated to all sorts of undertakings."[21] "Feelings and opinions are recruited," he argued, "the heart is enlarged, and the human mind is developed only by the reciprocal influence of men upon one another."[22]

For de Tocqueville, local government was the principal bulwark against the potential despotism (his word) of a national-scale government. Only local governments, and, we might add, democratic workplaces and voluntary associations, could become countervailing centers of power against the far-reaching power of national government.

At the time that de Tocqueville wrote, the United States was a relatively decentralized system, based on strong local government. But that system soon became more centralized, under the impact of corporate capitalism and the Civil War, dramatically reducing the ability of local political institutions and voluntary associations to serve as countervailing centers of power against the central state. The New Deal and the postwar welfare state further reduced the power of local governments. Local power diminished even more in the 1960s, with a growing popular commitment to universal egalitarianism on the national and state levels—expressed, for example, in concern for equal funding in school districts from unequally wealthy areas in the nation or equal representation in state legislatures. Since de Tocqueville's time, the growth of towns and cities, city incorporation movements, and school consolidation have also expanded the size of local units, thus reducing citizen opportunities for participation in political life. Radical decentralization can reverse this process, but in practice it is unlikely that the full effect of nineteenth and twentieth century centralization will ever be reversed. In this case, even a three-tier system, if any decision rule but unanimity were allowed, would still have to rely on organization in collectives and workplaces as much as on local government to resist the power of majorities at the national level. The collectives we create should thus both expand our capacities for solidarity and meaningful activity and also serve as nationally influential centers of countervailing power.

The collectives that do best in helping us expand our capacities, however, do not always do best in exerting power at the national level. Small groups like those that Benello advocated, and the highly decentralized, polycephalous structures that characterize social movements are the most likely to stimulate the expansion of individual capacities for solidarity and meaningful activity. Each subgroup in such a structure can be small enough to give every member the experience of responsibility. Each member can find out at first hand how his or her interests interact with those of the others in the group and the outside world. Each can come to know the others with the kind of wholeness that derives only from experience with many different aspects of their lives. Such decentralized structures are also highly innovative and adaptive. In moments of massive political repression they may be best adapted to resist coercive governmental power.

Such groups are also the best structures for promoting deep attitudinal and behavior change.[23] Women who have participated in a consciousness-raising group can confirm this account. By and large, face-to-face relations have been responsible for the slow but pervasive change the women's movement has wrought in gender mores in the United States.

Yet in periods of normal governmental functioning, small face-to-face groups are *not* the most effective counterweights to large-scale collective power. Small groups are hard to organize into federations. The small groups on which social movements are based are often relatively short-lived. Nor are they organized to bind their members in a way that allows the organization to deliver reliably on political promises after negotiations. In a polity in which political power often functions through groups organizing to promote their interests, highly decentralized structures often cannot sustain themselves long enough or act in a disciplined enough manner to counter with their power opposing interest groups acting through the large-scale governing bodies.

On the other hand, groups organized to defend their members' interests effectively on the larger scale—say, on the national level—are likely themselves to be nationally centralized, and to rely extensively on nationally-based legal, political, media, and business experts. Associations organized in this way can promote the interests of a group of citizens at the national level. They do not, however, provide much experience in participation, and hence in democratic learning, for the average member.

Solutions to the Dilemma

A common solution to this dilemma utilizes a division of labor. It accepts the seeming fact that it is difficult, if not impossible, for the same voluntary association both to provide wide opportunities for participation, responsibility, and solidarity for its members and to organize itself to exercise power effectively on a national scale. Perhaps, however, the same association need not do both these jobs. Citizens could belong to many different types of associations, some of which would provide experience in participation and some of which would represent their members' national interests effectively.

Today, in the United States—a much more centralized system than the ideal—this division of labor reflects the bifurcated pattern of participation of those citizens who are politically active. Many Americans who do not belong to any explicitly political groups either on the local or national level get involved in "communal activities"[24]— their church, garden clubs, the YMCA, and so forth—which provide experience in solidarity and meaningful activity. With the spread of workplace democracy each workplace could also become, as Benello predicted and hoped, a place where each individual in interaction with others could develop his or her best capacities. With a revivified participatory democracy, neighborhoods and workplaces could promote opportunities for deliberation and decision on both national and local issues. In addition to the face-to-face environments that provided solidarity and meaningful activity, citizens could also belong to national producers' collectives or contribute to organizations trying to influence national opinion. In this relationship they would be relatively passive members of highly organized, relatively centralized interest groups. Each kind of association would do a different job, but the whole would add up to an effective combination of self-development and countervailing power.

This solution to the dilemma, however, runs into trouble when the system must integrate information from small-scale and large-scale sources. A central function of participation, both in explicitly political associations and in non-political ones, ought to be to help the participants come to understand their interests, broadly speaking, more clearly.[25] Ideally, participation ought in some cases to help impart "public spirit"[26] and interest "the greatest number of persons in the common weal."[27] But participation ought also to alert the participants to moments in which their interests conflict with others', as when trying to produce change reveals a power structure otherwise obscured. Deliberation must often be combined with action for the process to reveal rather than obfuscate.

A system that divides the job of exercising effective political power on the large scale from the job of self-development through participation does not perform very well the function of helping participants come to understand their own interests. On the local face-to-face level participants may be "drawn from the circle of their own [narrow] interests" and be made constantly to "feel their mutual dependence."[28] But the process will not necessarily generate the information the participants require to understand all their interests. Even when the concerns of the small decentralized group are explicitly political, as they are in a social movement, the members of the small group may not be able to get the information they have generated to the national level, or themselves gain access to information generated at the center. The division of labor between the small decentralized group whose members create solidarity and engage in meaningful activity and the large centralized core which exerts national power makes less likely the confrontation of ideas and action on which learning about one's interests depends.

These conclusions derive from my study of the struggle to ratify the Equal Rights Amendment in the United States from 1972 to 1982. There I concluded that legal experts at the center of the national movement had, without any conscious desire to curtail debate, prevented crucial ideas from getting to the activists at the state level.[29] Access to those ideas would, I believe, have changed dramatically the local activists' discussions, which were constantly informed by lessons drawn from their own actions. Discourse was curtailed through a process of "decision by accretion," with no malice or manipulation intended.

The same bifurcation of individual learning and the exercise of power vis-a-vis the central state occurs again in today's anti-nuclear movement. Centralized groups like SANE have relatively easy access to large donors and can exert significant power at the national level. Yet they have a fairly passive mass membership. Decentralized groups, like the Nuclear Freeze Campaign before their merger with SANE, provide almost unlimited opportunities for taking responsibility at the local level, but have trouble organizing to exert power at the national level. Many activists can tell this story of bifurcation from their personal experience with existing political groups.

If a thin and curtailed dialogue results from a division of labor between organizations that promote citizen solidarity at the local level and those that exercise countervailing power at the national level, the remaining solution is to experiment with organizational forms, trying to discover some system that can both create solidarity and meaningful activity at the bottom and consolidate power at the center. In today's United States, Common Cause has experimented with these forms; so have the Democratic Socialists of America. Common Cause has succeeded in wielding effective political power but not in the promoting extensive participation or a discourse informed by local-level individual action. DSA has succeeded in promoting participant discourse but not in wielding effective political power. Cities and towns that are large enough directly to affect national decisions are themselves too large, without massive internal decentralization, to provide the individual development through face-to-face relations that a humane vision of political life demands.

The best solution to this dilemma is to reduce as much as possible the number of issues collectively decided on a large scale. Beyond this, it might also be possible to devolve responsibilities onto such intermediary organizations as Mondragon, the Basque cooperative network, the newly formed Federation for Industrial Retention and Renewal, which includes some 25 labor and community coalitions, and the various Progressive Alliances now sprouting up in many states within the United States.[30] But to avoid the problems of self-selection, citizens affected by the decisions who are not members of these occupationally selected or self-selected organizations must have institutional means to work with these associations in agreeing on a final decision.

The goal of combining the solidarity and meaningful activity possible in face-to-face groups and the power necessary to protect against oppression or influence collective decisions on the large scale has not yet been proved impossible. This essay suggests, however, that the task is difficult and may involve major institutional incompatibilities. The institutions of liberal "adversary" democracy may particularly hinder the development of groups that must engage in a dialogic process to discover and create their collective interest.[31]

At least in present day America, and perhaps even in any polity we could imagine, we are left with a paradox. In practice, the institutions that help us find a solidarity based on the encounter with another's whole self and not on the sharing of a principle alone are different from the institutions that organize influence in collectives that must address problems that cover wide geographical areas. The organizations that can do one of these jobs cannot easily do the other. The workplaces and small collectives that permit intensive participation cannot easily deploy power on the large scale, while those that can deploy such power cannot provide the opportunity for much effective participation. We may have to settle for a division of labor in which citizens participate in both kinds of associations for different ends. The result is to separate participation from power and to undermine that critical part of public discourse which should be informed by citizens exercising power on matters that by acting in the real world they have come intimately to understand.

Endnotes

1. My thinking has been greatly influenced by George Benello and people like him. While George and I disagreed on many things, particularly the issue of power, the conversations we had together were always productive. I regret again as I write this, as I have so often since his abrupt death in 1987, that I can no longer discuss these issues with him. His death was a great loss to activism and social thought in the United States.

2. Benello, "Towards a Grounded Theory of Humanist Organization," *Humanity and Society,* Vol. 4, No. 2, 1980. Benello would probably have agreed, however, with more recent ecological and feminist critiques of the mastery model. See e.g., Isaac D. Balbus, *Marxism and Domination,* (Princeton: Princeton University Press, 1982).

3. Robert Dahl, a mainstream pluralist political scientist, enunciated the point in two principles: "1. If a matter is best dealt with by a democratic association, seek always to have that matter dealt with by the smallest association that can deal with it satisfactorily. 2. In considering whether a larger association would be more satisfactory, do not fail to consider its extra costs, including a possible increase in the sense of individual powerlessness." Robert A. Dahl, *After the Revolution? Authority in a Good Society,* (New Haven: Yale University Press. 1970), 102. Dahl, with Edward R. Tufte, in *Size and Democracy,* (Palo Alto: Stanford University Press, 1973), poses the general paradox I investigate here as a tension between "citizen effectiveness" and "system capacity."

4. For the dehumanization of large scale organization, see Kirkpatrick Sale, *Human Scale,* (New York: Coward, McCann and Geoghegan, 1980). For the relation between size and war among nations, see Bruce M. Russett and R. Joseph Monsen, "Bureaucracy and Polyarchy as Predictors of Performance: A Cross-National Examination," *Comparative Political Studies,* 8 (1975), 5-31, especially 14, 23, and 25. In simpler societies, Melvin and Carol Ember, using the Yale Human Relations Area Files, have found a significant relation between size of community and likelihood of war (work in progress, reported by C. Ember, October 1990).

5. See also C.B. Macpherson, *The Life and Times of Liberal Democracy,* (Oxford: Oxford University Press, 1977), Model 4A ("Participatory Democracy"). On pages 108-9, he argues that "the simplest model that could properly be called a participatory democracy would be a pyramidal system with direct democracy at the base and delegate democracy at every level above that. Thus one would start with direct democracy at the neighborhood or factory level—actual face-to-face discussion and decision by consensus or majority, and elections of delegates who would make up a council at the next more inclusive level, say a city borough or ward or a township. The delegates would have to be sufficiently instructed by and accountable to those who elected them to make decisions at the council level reasonably democratic. So it would go on up to the top level, which would be a national council for matters of national concern, and local and regional councils for matters of less than national concern."

6. This number is a group equivalent to just over half the size of our smaller states—Wyoming, Arkansas, and Vermont—or about the size of New Haven, Connecticut or Newark, New Jersey, or a ninth the size of Chicago, or a twentieth the size of New York City.

7. See the study of "Helpline" in my *Beyond Adversary Democracy,* (Chicago: University of Chicago Press, 1983).

8. *Ibid.,* 213.

9. I later came to call such decisions "decisions by accretion" in my *Why We Lost the ERA,* (Chicago: University of Chicago Press, 1986).

10. On the reasons for the infrequent use of recall, see Thomas E. Cronin, *Direct Democracy: The Politics of Initiative, Referendum, and Recall,* (Cambridge: Harvard University Press, 1989).

11. For a discussion of non-material means for enhancing a concern for the common good, see my essay, "On the relation between altruism and self interest," in my *Beyond Self-Interest,* (Chicago: University of Chicago Press, 1990).

12. For institutional innovations, from joint citizen work to teledemocracy, that would go far to bringing democracy back to the people, see Benjamin R. Barber, *Strong Democracy: Participatory Politics for a New Age,* (Berkeley: University of California Press, 1984), chap. 10.

13. For experiments with policy juries, see the publications of the Jefferson Center for New Democratic Processes, 530 Plymouth Building, 12 South 6th Street, Minneapolis, Minn. 55402. For a proposed randomly selected advisory assembly at the national level in the U.S., see Robert A. Dahl, "On Removing Certain Impediments to Democracy in the United States," *Political Science Quarterly,* 92 (1977), 1-20. For decentralizing government to functional councils, selected by lot from those who nominate themselves for the office, which decide for the whole by negotiating among themselves, see John Burnheim, *Is Democracy Possible? The Alternative to Electoral Politics,* (Berkeley: University of California Press, 1985).

14. For power as action against another's interests, see Steven Lukes, *Power: A Radical View,* (London: Macmillan, 1974), 32.

15. See my *Beyond Adversary Democracy,* 265-268, for a discussion of "consociationalism" as a legitimate democratic process and proportional outcomes as legitimate when a lack of cross-cutting cleavages in a polity make it unlikely that an individual who loses on one issue will win on another. When cleavages in a polity do not crosscut in a way that lets everyone be in a majority on at least some issues of importance to them, majority rule will be unacceptable, even if every individual exercises equal individual power in the decision. In a country where the southerners speak French, have an economy based on agriculture, and are Catholic, while the northerners speak German, have an economy based on industry, and are Protestant, whichever group is in a minority on one important issue is likely to be in a minority on all important issues, and will, in consequence, be outvoted every time. Countries like these (e.g. Belgium and Austria) have instituted "consociationalist" systems of power sharing that in theory guarantee outcomes in proportion to numbers. If thirty percent of the citizenry are Protestant, they will get thirty percent of the budget, the ministries, the state television time, the schools, and so forth. Even proportionate outcomes, however, do not guarantee equal satisfaction.

16. In no real polity, of course, does each citizen have exactly equal weight in decisions. In large-scale nation states, whether capitalist or socialist, some individuals have incalculably more weight than others. In adversary theory, decisions are more legitimate the more the process approximates in fact the ideal of equal weight.

17. In *Anarchism: A Theoretical Analysis,* (Cambridge: Cambridge University Press, 1980), Alan Ritter points out that many anarchists approve of the coercion inherent in informal social censure. Indeed, Godwin, Bakunin, Proudhon and Kropotkin relied heavily on such censure in the anarchist communities they prescribed.

18. On the argument for unanimous direct democracy, see Robert P. Wolff, *In Defense of Anarchism,* (New York: Harper and Row, 1970). For arguments against, see Ritter, 62-63.

19. See "On the relation between altruism and self-interest" in *Beyond Self-Interest.*

20. Non-anarchist theorists as diverse as John Rawls, *A Theory of Justice,* (Cambridge: Harvard University Press, 1971); Michael Walzer, *Spheres of Justice,* (New York: Basic Books, 1974); and Benjamin Barber, *Strong Democracy* adopt a deliberative understanding of democracy, based on the potential for discovering or creating common interests, and not an adversary understanding based on the coercion inherent in majority rule.

21. Alexis de Tocqueville, *Democracy in America,* Francis Bowen trans. (New York: Knopf/Vintage, 1960), Vol. 2, 127.

22. *Ibid.,* 117.

23. See Kurt Lewin, "Group Decision and Social Change," in Theodore M. Newcomb and Eugene L. Hartley (eds.), *Readings in Social Psychology,* (New York: Henry Holt, 1947).

24. Sidney Verba and Norman H. Nie, *Political Participation in America,* (New York: Harper and Row, 1961).

25. See my *Beyond Adversary Democracy,* 244-246. In one's "interests" I include other-regarding interests and interests in a principle. One may think of interests defined this way as "enlightened preferences."

26. de Tocqueville, Vol. 1, 69.

27. *Ibid.,* Vol. 1, 70.

28. *Ibid.,* Vol. 2, 109, 110.

29. See my *Why We Lost the ERA,* chapter 10. Specifically, the feminist constitutional lawyers who advised the local activists did not tell those activists that the Supreme Court might well use the war powers clauses in the Constitution to interpret the ERA as not applying with full force to the military. If the activists had known about the probable effect of the war powers clauses, they might have decided not to argue to the legislators and the public that the ERA would send women draftees into combat on the same basis as men.

30. Accounts of all of these can be found in Len Krimerman and Frank Lindenfeld (eds.), *When Workers Decide,* (Philadelphia: New Society Publishers, 1991). See also Jeremy Brecher and Tim Costello, *Building Bridges,* (New York: Monthly Review Press, 1990).

31. See Claus Offe and Helmut Wiesenthal, "Two Logics of Collective Action: Theoretical Notes on Social Class and Organizational Form," in Maurice Zeitlin (ed.), *Political Power and Social Theory*, (Greenwich: JAI Press, 1980), Vol. 1, 67-115.

Chapter 17

Women: The Neglected Majority

Walda Katz-Fishman

George Benello presents a theory and praxis for social transformation. He draws on a body of theory that is humanist—from both the Marxist and anarchist traditions—and on a growing body of experience in workplace democracy and community transformation in the United States, Spain, and elsewhere. His observation of the dehumanization, oppression, and exploitation of workers and communities under advanced capitalism is undisputed. These ravages on the human condition are intensifying.

The contradiction between wealth and poverty, between opulence for the few and oppression for the many is a stark reality in the United States today—the richest country in the world. More than 32 million people live at or below the poverty level, including 20 percent of all children and roughly half of children of color. Several million people are homeless while many millions more are on the verge of eviction. Thirty-seven million have no health coverage. More than 20 million are hungry or malnourished. Unemployment, which surpassed seven million workers by the end of 1990, is unacceptably high. Real wages are falling as the rich get richer and the poor get poorer. (These figures are "official" government estimates. Actual numbers are higher. For example, the total number of jobless, including discouraged workers no longer looking for jobs and those no longer in the labor force, is close to double the number counted as officially unemployed. Those who are forced to work part-time, but would prefer to work full-time, are also excluded.) If you are a woman, especially if you are a single head-of-household, and particularly if you are a woman of color, your chances of being in these desperate conditions is several times as high as a white man. Of course, only workers—no capitalists—have any of these survival problems.

Benello's program for social transformation calls for workplace and local community initiatives. Women, however, are largely invisible in his analysis and in the program for change. History and experience in the progressive movements of the 1960s and 1970s suggest that the oppression of women will not "automatically" be addressed and resolved. We must be clear about what that oppression is for women, especially women of color. We must specify what measures are necessary in the process of social transformation to eliminate that oppression. Thus, to Benello's general analysis we must add the particulars of the oppression and exploitation of women. To his program for change we must add the steps necessary for the participation and, indeed, leadership of women who are the most exploited and oppressed—the poorest of working class women, including women of color.

The number of women in the American paid labor force, including those with infants and young children, has been soaring. Most women, however, are concentrated in sex-segregated jobs (e.g., "pink collar" jobs—clerical, nursing, teaching, poultry processing, producing textiles and garments, etc.). They earn between half and two-thirds of what white men earn. Many work part-time because full-time work is not available. They have few, if any, benefits. They are subjected to sexual harassment on the job. Day care for their children often consumes most of their earnings. When they go home, they are expected to perform all or most of the "unpaid" work of nurturing and housekeeping.

Half of all women are still outside the paid labor force (as are more and more men)! This is often not by choice. But when child care costs are more than earnings, it does not pay to work in the paid labor force. Women on welfare and their children are stigmatized. The ruling class and its spokespersons assert that they are lazy, ignorant, cheats ripping off the taxpayers, and certainly not capable of their own liberation.

In their personal relationships, including marriage, and in other social relations women are subjected to male domination. They are the object of violence—rape, incest and other forms of abuse. Women are even denied the right to control their bodies with regard to health and reproduction. Male supremacy and male domination are deeply embedded in the social institutions and culture and are reinforced continuously by the mass media and educational institutions.

Poor women and women of color most often live in communities segregated along economic and/or racial lines. The men in their communities are also victimized by the capitalist system. Working class men, and especially men of color, are increasingly unemployed and underemployed. Thus, the rise in female-headed families and in abuse against women is rooted in the fundamental economic relations of capitalism. Along with the men in their communities, women are blocked by the realities of corporate capitalism from access to decent housing, to quality education and health care, and to environments free of toxins. This is especially the case for women (mostly of European descent) of Appalachia, the women of the Black Belt South, the women of the Indian reservations, the women of rural America, and of the inner cities.

These realities of women's exploitation and oppression cannot be eliminated simply by workplace democracy. Many women do not work in the paid labor force, and much of the special oppression of women is not located, at least exclusively, at the workplace. Women's exploitation and oppression also cannot be eliminated simply by local or community initiatives since the communities in which the most oppressed women live are themselves—including the men of these communities—disadvantaged by their history of exploitation and forms of racial and national oppression.

I share with Benello a vision of a socialist society that is egalitarian and democratic, that is based on participation and decision making at the workplace and in the local community. But, given the location of so much of women's oppression at other than the work site, and the location of the most oppressed women in communities that have been especially exploited and oppressed by capitalism and imperialism, I differ with Benello in the specific steps needed to arrive at our common vision.

Benello's embrace of anarchism makes him highly suspicious of centralized planning and the use of workers' power organized as state power in the transition from capitalism to an egalitarian and democratic classless society. He believes they are antithetical to grassroots participation and local decision making. I would argue, to the contrary, that local and workplace initiatives and centralized planning backed up by workers' state power are interconnected and interdependent. Neither aspect of the total process, taken alone, can accomplish the transition of society from a dehumanizing, oppressive capitalist form of organization to an egalitarian, participatory and democratic socialist form.

This requires a planned economy, not just at the workplace and locally, but nationally and even internationally (given the international division of labor and the flight of capital to the cheapest labor sources). It requires explicit policies to eliminate the specific oppression and exploitation of women—at work, in the family, in personal relationships and in social relationships in the larger society and culture. Policies and mechanisms for enforcement are necessary to rectify the historic discrimination economically, socially and politically suffered by the communities in which the poorest women and women of color live. These remedies, which call for the dismantling of capitalist oppression and exploitation, necessitate more than workplace and local community planning. Rather, they require national planning and policies supported by the authority of a workers' state to guide the process of creating the egalitarian and non-discriminatory society that both Benello and I envision.

Among women in struggle there is a growing internationalism expressed in the assertion that "sisterhood is global." The lot of women in the United States of whatever race, nationality, and color cannot be improved at the expense of the further impoverishment and degradation of working class women of color world over. Thus, it is increasingly necessary to consider planning and policies that are international in scope to eliminate the realities of imperialist domination for women (as well as men) of the Third World.

One final point of difference with Benello deals with the question of advances in technology and their meaning for the human condition. Benello finds high technology to be, in the main, dehumanizing, alienating, and destructive of the environment. In contrast, I view advances in the technology of production as the very foundation of human history and social transformation. Stone implements were replaced by iron tools, the hand production of the feudal era was displaced by machine production and the factories of capitalism. Washing machines, dishwashers and vacuum cleaners have replaced hand washing and hand cleaning. Sewing machines have replaced hand sewing. The printing press, typewriters and copy machines have replaced the scribe and handwritten documents. Tractors and combines have replaced planting and harvesting by hand. Cars, trucks and metroliners have replaced the horse and buggy. Few would suggest that we should go back in history to the pre-machine era.

The 1990s mark a very advanced stage of technological innovation. Today's revolution in the technology of production is based on the microcomputer chip and rapid advances in automation and robotronics. We are presented thus with a qualitatively new situation. In the past period of mechanical production and industrialization, technology essentially enhanced the productive quality of human labor power. Automation no longer *enhances* human labor power, but rather *permanently displaces* human labor power from the productive process altogether. Thus, human labor is a superfluous commodity within capitalist production. Automation means more goods and services with much less human labor. This reduces the cost of production for the capitalists. At the same time, however, the displacement of workers from production means that less money is in the hands of the worker-consumer and her or his family.

Increasingly, the result of this technological revolution will be that workers are unable to purchase the necessities of life and the capitalists are unable to sell all the commodities their newly automated farms and factories are putting out. Commodities cannot be circulated and markets are actually contracting nationally and internationally. This superfluity of human labor in production is thus causing the break-up of the wages system and the market as the mechanism for the distribution and circulation of the necessities of life. For all workers, but especially women workers and those of color, the effect is a heightened struggle for survival. Their historic inequality and oppression are intensified as they strive to get a "decent" job (or any job at all) and maintain a meaningful family life.

The advances in technology make capitalism and the market obsolete as the mechanism for *distribution*. These same advances in technology make possible the *production* of an abundance of the things necessary for life—food, housing, clothing, medicine, books, computers, cars, etc. Humanity is thus poised for a revolutionary transformation of society. Much as machine production undermined the social organization of feudal society, automated production undermines the social organization of capitalist society.

Throughout the history of capitalist society women and other oppressed groups have struggled for their equality. These have usually been reform movements within the context of the existing class relations—the demand for more jobs, for better jobs, for affirmative action, for pay equity, for the "Equal Rights Amendment," for the right to control their health and reproduction, for a healthy environment, and for peace. Today, however, the social struggle of women and others who are oppressed is taking place within the larger struggle for the economic transformation and reconstruction of society. Capitalism in the United States (and elsewhere)—organized around machine production, the drive for maximum profits, and the market system—can no longer sustain a liveable quality of human existence for a majority of the people. The survival of humanity—of women and their children, of the men in their lives—requires the reorganization of society. Its form must be a socialist participatory and democratic system based on the distribution of the necessities of life to satisfy human needs.

Corporate capitalism organizes social relations in the workplace and the local community. It also defines national markets and international aspects of capital investment, production and commerce. The oppression of women is at the workplace, in the home and family, in social relations that are society-wide and even global. The elimination of women's oppression will require a process that addresses all of these dimensions. The socialist transformation and reconstruction of society must thus address conditions in the workplace, conditions in the home and in the family, conditions in the local community, as well as conditions embedded in the economic, political, and social institutions nationally and globally.

To do this we will need planning at all levels—the workplace, the community, nationally, and internationally. Policies must be articulated and backed up by the power of the workers' state to mandate in law and in actual practice equality for women and an end to their oppression in every aspect of their daily lives.

Benello notes the importance of grassroots education and participation in the process of social and economic transformation. Democracy and input into decision making and planning by those most affected are essential. We should, he says, be creative, innovative, and be guided to get us through what must be a difficult process with many obstacles, pitfalls, and detours.

Clearly, women, especially those who are most oppressed today, must be in positions in their local communities and nationally to develop the policies to guide society in its social reconstruction. What Benello argues for at the workplace and in the community—grassroots partici- pation and participatory democracy, responsiveness to the needs of those most directly affected, creativity, etc.—must be present in the development of a national plan for socialist transformation.

Today there is emerging a social struggle for survival led by those on the cutting edge. More women than men are being organized into the trade union movement. These are most often women working in the worst conditions—clerical workers, nursing home workers, poultry pro- cessing workers, garment workers, etc. Women on welfare, tired of being abused by the system, are fighting back through their own orga- nizations, e.g., the National Welfare Rights Union, the "Up and Out of Poverty Now" campaign that began in Massachusetts and is now na- tional. The homeless, tired of being controlled by shelter providers, organized themselves as the National Homeless Union, which has a woman president. Those fighting against hunger are organized in the National Anti-Hunger Coalition, in which women are in the leadership. The traditional women's movement (organizations such as the National Organization for Women) is being challenged by the emergence of this new leadership from within the ranks of those women most victimized by corporate capitalism.

These women who are most oppressed are organizing locally and nationally to make the changes in society—at the local and national levels— necessary to end their oppression. They are challenging the capitalist state and its unjust laws. They are demanding the distribution of the necessaries of life—food, housing, clothing, health care and education—based on human need. They are demanding child care and an end to their abuse. They are the grassroots in the process of socialist transformation. Their participation and their leadership in confronting the injustice and inhumanity of capitalism and its state and in creating a just and humane society is, in fact, an expression of George Benello's vision.

Chapter 18

Empowering
Communities of Color

An interview with Chuck Turner

Len Krimerman: Chuck, for close to a decade you worked with George and the Industrial Cooperative Association developing worker-owned enterprises and providing hands-on education to employees in the process of becoming owners. Do you now see this lengthy experience with worker-ownership and workplace democracy as significant and useful for people of color? Is it relevant, for example, to your present work with the Center for Community Action?

Chuck Turner: Workplace democracy and democratic ownership of one's work raise critical, but largely neglected, issues for low income communities and in particular for communities of color. One illustration of this is the meeting which just broke up downstairs here at the Center. This was one in a series of workshops with community organizers from various Boston neighborhoods who work in either the public or non-profit sectors. Many of them speak of feeling alienated from Boards and Directors who make basic decisions but do little or no work, who lack respect for them as workers with distinctive skills and responsibilities, and who go beyond establishing policy and try to determine day-to-day workplans. These organizers, for example, are often called upon to do office work, instead of the face-to-face organizing they were hired for. In short, they are disempowered by their work situations. And given this daily diminishment of their humanity, how can they be expected to encourage an attitude of empowerment in the communities where they work?

LK: Sounds familiar.

CT: Yes, in a way it's not surprising: just another dismal confirmation of the influence exerted on all sections of worklife by the prevailing forms of power and organization. Still, it reveals that the ideas behind worker democracy have very clear implications for workers in the public sector and in non-profit organizations. Those ideas speak to extremely important, but as yet largely unrecognized, needs of these workers, many or even most of whom are people of color.

LK: How do you see this changing? What can be done to give those needs greater legitimacy and recognition?

CT: We are working on this here at the Center—in ways which I've come to see draw heavily on my previous experience with democratic workplaces in the industrial sector. For example, we offer a kind of advanced course for these same organizers, one which applies the democratic ownership model in an educational setting. The educator's role shifts to being a facilitator or consultant. We stipulate that our students, the organizers, tell us how they want to utilize our time and our resources. We don't determine what issues or skill development areas are important; they do. In this way, they not only become familiar with each other's perspectives and find common threads and problems, but they get important experience establishing agendas and priorities.

LK: Besides this extension of workplace democracy to help empower public and human service workers, how else do you see this concept as crucial, and as connected to community empowerment?

CT: If we're thinking of black and other communities of color, there are several important connections. In the first place, consider today's minority youth. People in their teens or twenties today were born into an era of rising consciousness, an era that saw the dawning of new democratic rights and responsibilities. Our young had to be affected by these vibrations all around them. One key by-product is that they are no longer willing to accept abusive or demeaning relationships, to submit docilely to corporate hierarchies, be they in the industrial, insurance, fast food, or public sectors. Conformity is not on their agenda. Nonetheless, these young people, like any other, need workplaces, and they are needed in the workforce.

LK: Why is that? Couldn't our economy run as well without their participation?

CT: Not any longer. The white population has been getting steadily older and smaller, while the workforce has become increasingly female, young, and of color. And it is primarily this population, these new workers, who need a different kind of workplace—one that meets their enhanced aspirations and their intuitive sense of their role and rights in a democracy.

One model with increasing potential and relevance is the "labor cooperative." Instead of being hired employees, ordered about by supervisors and assistant managers, workers would collectively own enterprises that contracted with private or public organizations to provide anything from secretarial and janitorial to carpentry and catering services. They would then receive not only salaries, but a fair share of year-end profits. In short, instead of what's now offered—a kind of dehumanized wage slavery—new and enhanced work relationships would be created for people who today are systematically devalued.

LK: *Isn't there a danger here, though, of developing very transitory, dead-end enterprises? How would these labor cooperatives differ from the overflow of temporary positions which have recently surfaced?*

CT: There are lots of differences. For one thing, while labor cooperatives might provide some of the same services now offered by temporaries, these co-ops would of course be self-managing. Workers would have the opportunity to decide together what work to take on (and how much), how best to get it accomplished, what hours to work, etc.—everything they are now kept from deciding. Secondly, an education and training component would be included, so that human development as well as business success remained a key priority. This would be good for profits as well, for it would make these labor co-ops far more flexible—adaptable to different markets as well as to changing workforce aspirations—than "temporary" firms. Finally, as a labor cooperative becomes more profitable, each member's share of surplus revenues also increases. This practical incentive for worker involvement is totally absent from typical temporary employment. No matter how hard or smart they work, temporaries usually do not share in the success or growth of their company.

LK: *So you see the labor cooperative as providing a distinctive kind of work situation tailored to the needs and self-image of the "new workforce"—young, female, and persons of color?*

CT: Yes, mainstream corporations and public agencies cannot keep pace with the changing and rising aspirations of these workers. In particular, they cannot address the issue of how to restructure work so that it is a humanizing or empowering experience for all workers in all sections of the economy. But in addition I see a more long-range role for labor cooperatives.

LK: What is that?

CT: Once these labor cooperatives, which basically supply services to industry and government, start to thrive and not merely survive, they will begin accumulating capital. Furthermore, in a decade or two, they will have among them not only the capital resources, but the human skills and business experience to challenge traditional corporations, even in manufacturing or industrial areas. We may then begin to see an economic withering away of capitalism in its traditional form, at least in certain sectors.

LK: That's certainly an attractive picture, but isn't it overly rosy?

CT: I don't think so. Remember that we are talking here not about isolated worker co-ops scattered in disconnected regions of the country or among many separate industries, but those created primarily by people of color in their own communities. This gives them two important advantages: they will tend to think locally, i.e., to produce for local community needs; but at the same time, these cooperatives will see themselves as participants and partners in important global and national changes. Let me spell out both of these points in some detail.

Production for local needs (as George repeatedly insisted) makes both ecological and economic sense. Transportation costs are frequently a misuse of resources, and they often contribute to lowered product quality, e.g., in the food industry. Beyond this, by producing for local needs, a cooperative workforce can provide itself with a steady and uniquely valuable flow of feedback from its *customers.* This sort of producer-consumer communications can only improve worker motivation and product quality.

In regard to the wider or global context, here the demographics will be crucial. Even in the industrial sector, and throughout the labor movement, workers of color are becoming a more and more significant influence. A growing number of them have their primary loyalties to the countries and continents of their origin—to South America, the Caribbean, and Asia—and they will look there for ideas on worklife as well as for economic partners. In addition, models such as the Mondragon association of cooperatives will continue to gain influence, for these enable planned growth while facilitating cooperation between housing, service, agricultural and industrial enterprises.

LK: In other words, labor cooperatives are just one expression of some very far-reaching and widely diffused changes in our economy.

CT: Yes. The system initiated by Franklin Roosevelt to patch up the damage left by the Great Depression—the ruling troika of government, corporate, and union elite—is about to explode. It may take two years, or six, or ten, but it is bound to self-destruct. For decades, it's been running on subsidies, creating phony throwaway products, financing itself though junk bonds or federal deficits: pumping air, rather than new blood, into its veins. The ruling troika never did much for people of color; we were excluded from any benefits it dispersed. So as the system totters, and union leaders (as well as rank-and-filers) of color begin to dominate, there will be little loyalty around to keep it shored up. New models will be sought, new questions will become central. The main debate will not be over wages and benefits alone, but over how (and by whom) work is to be controlled, and over how to link it to both local community needs and those of global liberation.

LK: These are very fundamental changes. Where do you see them beginning to emerge in the next few years?

CT: One key area would be the current crisis in our youth community. Community-based labor cooperatives, with their empowering potential, might be able to help turn around the drug and gang phenomena, e.g., by building viable bridges between school and worklife. They could help harness a lot of this youth energy by directing it away from short term highs towards longer term goals, such as gaining social, economic, and political power.

In my neighborhood, for example, a community-based security company has provided shelter and jobs for youth who had been involved in muggings. The young people are also getting their equivalency diplomas at a local community college. There are group meetings every afternoon from four to six p.m. which bring together about 20-25 youth to think through their past and plan their future. It's not an easy process, but it illustrates how negative group energy can begin to be positively focused.

Beyond this, the wider community is beginning to edge towards a major recession. Massachusetts, with its nearly one billion dollar deficit and increasing private sector layoffs is moving in this direction, despite all the claims to the contrary. "Official" unemployment has risen to around 10 percent. Public sector and low income workers (and hence people of color disproportionately) are faced with increasing cutbacks and layoffs. This sort of crisis period could well become an opportunity for the incubation of new ideas to rebuild our sagging and unraveling economy—ideas like that of the labor cooperative, community-based production, and regionalization. But we will need to be ready with the crucial elements: working models, training programs, technical assistance, to name just a few.

LK: How, though, do you see all of this reaching people—those recently laid off public sector employees, for example—during this coming time of turmoil? How can we start developing a wider constituency for democratic control of work?

CT: It won't be easy. But there are two promising approaches, ones that have not yet been very fully recognized or utilized by the worker ownership movement in this country. The first of these is the development of a *land movement,* a movement that would secure homes, protect farmers and their croplands, and enable city dwellers and neighborhoods to acquire land to help meet their basic housing and food needs.

LK: Sounds like what some of us in the worker ownership movement, including George, have called "local self-reliance."

CT: Yes. However, the worker ownership and indeed the labor movement generally have largely ignored their relationship to *land.* But without a secure home in a secure community, how can people sustain a long term interest in work, however much improved or democratically reorganized? Land is a crucial element in all wealth, and, if we view it solely as a source of profit for private developers or real estate corporations, we risk reviving a cycle similar to that which led to the Depression of 1930s: farmers and others lose their lands, workers' jobs and savings dry up, the ranks of the homeless and the foodless swell. To forestall this sort of cycle, and to make room and provide stability for new forms of worklife—labor cooperatives and similar innovations—*we need strong rural (and urban) land development policies.* These policies would ensure access to land for neighborhood or cooperative groups as well as for small farmers; the land thus acquired could be used for both homes and subsistence and could in addition support numerous types of labor intensive enterprises.

These might include, for example, remanufacturing—taking old equipment and renewing it. Or, given our food crisis, the area of hydroponics needs to be carefully examined. In addition, crafts production should not be overlooked: wood and metal products, glass blowing, sweaters woven from the wool of New England sheep. Let us use our imaginations to construct an economy of the future that can be housed in buildings, and on land, owned by the community.

LK: *What's the second potential path for building a wider constituency for democracy at work?*

CT: This involves what I've called "education for ownership." Up to now, surprisingly, very little of this sort of education has been introduced within worker-owned companies in the U.S.. Weirton Steel in West Virginia is perhaps a good model, since it uses worker education to enlist the consciousness of worker-owners in re-designing their own shopfloor procedures. Not only does the Weirton workforce have access to crucial company information, but they are given—through labor-management teams—the opportunity to use that information to improve both the way they work day in and day out and the larger workplace as well.

As I see it, what's essential in "education for ownership" is that responsibility is decentralized: planning, work schedules, resource acquisition and allocation, feedback from the firm's clients and customers, are all distributed throughout the entire enterprise. What this full-scale decentralization achieves is an increase in worker motivation. In fact, different sorts of motivation—beyond wages and benefits—come to life. Workers feel empowered, their creativity and intelligence are tapped, and they become more productive, more professional, more concerned with the quality of their own work and that of the company's products. It turns out, as Hackman and Oldham among others have claimed, that if you treat someone as if they have a brain, they will then learn to use their capacities, but, if you continually tell them what you want them to do, they'll shut down and won't do anything until they're told to do it.

In short, if we want to reach (and hold onto) more and more workers and communities, we will need more than new notions of ownership. In addition, we will have to find ways of *making work empowering, of shifting key responsibilities, awakening creative powers.*

This in turn will require a re-educational process, one which puts the learner (and future owner of work) in the driver's seat and provides opportunities for the exercise of initiative and judgment. One illustration of this education for ownership model, which I've already mentioned, is our advanced workshops with community organizers in which they tell us—the students tell the teachers—what they want to learn and how they want to utilize our time and skills. In addition, labor cooperatives can provide a setting for this re-education process. And a further example would involve blending the cooperative ethic and practice with the Junior Achievement model of youth learning business at an early age. [This blend has actually been achieved by the Rural Entrepenurial Action Learning (REAL) programs in three southern states. For more information, see Chapter 5 of Len Krimerman's and Frank Lindenfeld's *When Workers Decide,* 1991.]

Chapter 19

Beyond Sustainability
What Green Activists Can and Can't Learn
From C. George Benello

Steve Chase

Historically, radical social movements have advocated programs to remake society in an effort to improve the quality of our common social life. It is primarily out of this tradition that the late C. George Benello wrote the essays in this collection during the 1960s, '70s, and '80s. Interestingly, during these same years, a new concern began to emerge and take center stage for many activists. For these people, the primary goal became to remake society so that its members could simply survive. In the 1990s, it is naive to dismiss this survivalist emphasis as foolish or paranoid. The Wasteland Culture so insightfully critiqued by Benello has indeed become lethal. Ours is a "people-killing culture."

While many human beings in history have struggled for their lives against racist genocide and imperialist wars of aggression, the post-Hiroshima peace movement was the first social movement to raise the apocalyptic question of global species survival. Its focus was thus, above all, on nuclear disarmament. The environmental movement which emerged in the 1970s raised the question of human species survival even more widely and argued for some sort of industrial disarmament which would protect the capacity of our planet's overstressed eco-system to sustain human life. From the 1970s to the present, books such as the Club of Rome's *Limits to Growth,* Anne and Paul Erlich's *Population Explosion,* and the Worldwatch Institute's annual *State of the World* report have become influential best-sellers.

Not surprisingly, sustainability has become the key watchword for many in today's Green movements. As the German Green Party Manifesto argues, "We must stop the violation of nature in order to survive in it."[1] The British Green Party is even more explicit. Its program argues that "The overriding, unifying principle [of Green politics] is that all *human* activities must be indefinitely sustainable."[2] Given our current society's unrelenting commitment to industrial expansion, polluting technologies, and exhausting nonrenewable resources (a commitment shared by most Marxists, social democrats, progressives, and liberals), it appears that only minority radical political parties and social movements such as the Greens are offering a program that can ensure long-term survival. Given the reality of the ongoing global ecological crisis, what could be more radical?

Sustainability and Green Politics

This new survivalism is an ambiguous basis for a new politics, however. By itself, it is inherently reformist (at best) and does not fully address the need to, in Benello's words, enhance the "compatibility of social settings with the broader natural environment" or "their capacity to contribute to human growth and freedom." While environmental sustainability is an absolutely essential component of any political perspective with a claim to sanity, it is hardly a sufficient foundation for a radical Green politics. Several possible social and economic systems can ultimately be made sustainable. Not all of these possible alternative futures are equally desirable. Some are not desirable at all.

French political philosopher André Gorz may well be right that the environmental limits to growth theory "already has enough converts in the ruling elite to ensure its eventual acceptance by the major institutions of modern capitalism."[3] He thus sees the possibility that when "capitalism begins to work its way out of the ecological impasse, it will assimilate ecological necessities as technical constraints and adapt the conditions of exploitation to them."[4] Gorz even goes so far as to sketch out the very likely prospect of an "eco-fascist" future, where our species' survival is ensured by technocratic environmental engineering and human social life becomes even more stratified, oppressive, and authoritarian.

Is this what Green politics will ultimately come to stand for? Perhaps. Margaret Thatcher began calling herself a "Green" in the late

1980s. George Bush described himself as "Greenish" during his first campaign for U.S. President. Certainly, ruling elites, including powerful international groups such as the World Bank, are increasingly trying to co-opt the sustainability rhetoric of the Green movement. Even more troubling is the fact that such elites are finding junior partners from within the Green movement itself. The reformist *realo* wing of the German Green Party, for example, and its kindred tendencies in the U.S. Green movement such as the Green Party Organizing Committee, have increasingly talked of working within the system, "Greening" capitalism, and gutting Green programs of all radical demands besides those that relate to sustainability. As English Green writer Andrew Dobson notes, this reformist "light Green" faction is coming to increasingly dominate the Green movement, muting the radical thrust of what he calls the "dark Green" faction which originally animated and organized the international Green movement.[5]

Green politics once meant much more and, to many people, it still does. From the very beginning of the movement, radical Greens have attempted, admittedly tentatively and often intuitively, to integrate the ecological ethic of naturalists such as Henry David Thoreau, Aldo Leopold, and Rachel Carson with the political wisdom of the left libertarian, democratic tradition of utopian socialists and anarchists such as William Morris, Peter Kropotkin, and Emma Goldman. While all radical Greens are passionately committed to the goal of environmental sustainability, their programs also include far more ambitious social and ecological quality-of-life proposals. For a radical Green movement to survive and thrive, this tendency will need to further clarify and elaborate a fundamental alternative to Greenish reformism and the limited politics of sustainability.

Benello's work makes a valuable contribution to this effort by insightfully integrating the radical decentralist social tradition with environmental sustainability concerns. Indeed, Benello's own political career spanned from his active work with the anti-nuclear movement and the New Left in the 1960s through his work with local Green groups in Massachusetts before his death in the 1980s. I believe that consideration of his work now could help today's Green activists move beyond a vision of mere sustainability to a more developed and radical vision of sustainability, participatory democracy, decentralization, social responsibility, liberatory technology, and worker-community control of the economy. Benello's political perspective is thus an important bridge between the new survivalism and the historic humanistic left commitment to radically improving the quality of social life.

Understanding the Social Ecology of Alienation

Perhaps Benello's most fundamental contribution to Green politics is his insight that our modern, and now nearly global, Wasteland Culture degrades our natural and social landscapes in very similar ways. Just as modern industrial societies destroy the health of complex, stable, and symbiotic eco-communities through habitat take-over and the wholesale destruction of species diversity, they also destroy or domesticate the interconnected web of independent, face-to-face, grassroots social organizations that have historically made social life fulfilling and democratic. According to Benello, our society has devolved into a simplified, unhealthy, and unstable human community characterized by powerless and atomized individuals on the one hand and a few powerful, elite-dominated institutions, such as nation-states and multi-national corporations, on the other.

Gone, or significantly tamed, are the primary institutions that could stand between individuals and the dominant institutions of state and corporation. Indeed, according to Benello, top-down, corporate bureaucracies have become "the model for the other major organizational forms through out the society: the universities, churches, professional associations, and unions." Rarely is there any significant "continuity of rank and file participation" in these institutions. Over many generations, the independence and vitality of extended families, small businesses, family farms, cultural and nationality groups, neighborhoods, villages, towns, cities, provinces and regions, smaller governmental bodies, voluntary organizations, and grassroots political parties have been eroded—sometimes by the conscious design of ruling elites, sometimes as the unintended consequences of other social forces.

Benello's recognition of the social costs of this loss set him apart from conventional leftists who see industrialism, massive urbanization, and the rise of the bureaucratic welfare state as historically flawed but basically benign and rational trends in human history. In stark contrast, Benello argued that the destruction and domestication of grassroots organizations inherently involved in these social processes ultimately destroys a community's integrity. One of the key consequences he saw of this "progressive" loss of social richness and connectedness is the historic rise of a culture of alienation, a culture marked in our time by uninhibited selfishness, soul-numbing consumption, passive mass culture spectacles, widespread alcoholism and drug addiction, commodified sex, suicide, self-destructive rebelliousness, harmful crime, and urban violence.

Benello was able to see this destruction of community and organizational diversity as a problem because he looked at society through the lens of social ecology rather than through the lens of the atomistic philosophy of individualism that has long dominated liberal and progressive ideology. Individual things in such an atomized, individualistic worldview are seen as fundamentally separate from each other and infinitely more important than the relationships in which they are embedded. As political scientist Benjamin Barber points out, "the liberal portrait of human nature" projects "the human essence as radically individual and solitary, as hedonistic and prudential, and as social only to the extent required by the quest for preservation and liberty in an adversary world of scarcity."[6] In this view, social bonds and community life are seen as a necessary evil submitted to in order to enhance individual security and survival.

Ecologists see individuality very differently. While not denying the value of individuals, they argue, in the words of eco-philosopher J. Baird Callicott, "that a thing's essence is exhaustively determined by its relationships, that it cannot be conceived apart from its relationships with other things."[7] In the case of human beings, even a person's genetic make up is vitally influenced by the social and natural relations of his or her ancestors. To ecologists, community—whether natural or social—is an essential factor in any organism's individuation.

This ecological view of individuality and community made sense to Benello. As an avowed social ecologist, he saw relationships, groups, and communities as fundamental to his analysis. In his view, human association, relationships, and community life are not just the result of a social contract for individual protection. Indeed, he found community life to be a vital component in human growth and development. These social relations make us, in large measure, who we are at our at our best (and, of course, at our worst). As human ecologist Paul Shepard points out, the evolutionary development of human intelligence and consciousness required the intense interaction of homo sapiens with a complex, species-rich, natural environment.[8] Certainly, early homo sapiens also developed their remarkable human capacities through the intense social interaction of their small face to face communities.

It hardly seems far fetched then to argue, as Benello does, that "the basic unit of society is the group, not the individual." Nor does it seem far fetched to claim, as Benello does, that individual human beings develop and mature best when they can directly participate in face-to-face democratic groups which "carry out the basic purposes of society, involving work, education, culture, and community." Such groups are essential sites of human freedom, conviviality, and psychological maturity. In Benello's view, such groups are vital organizational "species" in any healthy social ecology. Their destruction by the Wasteland Culture is the social equivalent of the Wasteland Culture's harmful simplification and destruction of the natural world.

The Strategic Problem of Social "Defoliation"

This analysis of social alienation is at the heart of many of Benello's essays. Yet, Benello did not limit himself to a cultural critique of alienation. He also repeatedly pointed out how people's social alienation from the decision-making processes of the dominant political and economic institutions in society leads almost inevitably to further domination, exploitation, and the general misdirection of social evolution by the well-organized political, economic, and military elites who control the expanding centralized organizations. Indeed, he believed that the loss of grassroots organizational diversity within society eroded peoples' collective capacity to protect their natural and social communities from domination and exploitation.

To understand this process, we need to clearly understand the nature of social institutions like the nation-state and corporations. While social institutions are often seen as solid, all powerful, and permanent, they actually are very similar to biological organisms in that they require a constant flow of external energy to maintain their form and structure. In the case of institutions such as the state and corporations, the human "energy flow" on which they depend is the social power made available through the willing or unwilling cooperation, submission, and obedience of citizens, consumers, and workers.

This line of analysis leads, of course, to the fundamental insight of nonviolent action theory which is that people can control and even disintegrate ruling institutions, whenever these institutions are unresponsive to popular needs and desires, through broad-based, coordinated, and strategic withdrawals of popular cooperation. The strategic problem in nonviolent action theory is, as political scientist Gene Sharp readily admits, that "the sources of a ruler's power are normally only threatened significantly when assistance, cooperation, and obedience are withheld by large numbers of subjects at the same time, that is, by social groups and institutions."[9] Thus, in the absence of a significant number of independent social groups and grassroots institutions which control resources, train people for self-reliant collective action, and provide mutual aid in times of repression, any effort to actualize this latent power potential of people is almost always doomed to failure.

Unconnected, isolated individuals who are almost completely dependent on centralized institutions pose little or no threat to entrenched power. They are simply too unorganized. However, when independent grassroots groups do exist, or are successfully created in the course of a social struggle, democratic social movements have been able to win significant reforms, block military invasions, change government policies and leadership, take over key economic enterprises, paralyze empires, and dissolve dictatorships—often through nonviolent means alone. As Gene Sharp points out, "If power is highly decentralized among strong and vital independent institutions, that condition will be of great assistance in emergencies in which struggle is required to control a ruler. It will greatly strengthen the capacity of the subjects and their institutions to withdraw the sources of the ruler's power in order to impose such controls."[10]

The strategic lesson here is that if a radically transformational movement like the Greens is going to be successful, it needs to directly focus on the "defoliated" institutional condition at the grassroots of our society and help organize or renew human-scale, participatory organizations and institutions at the grassroots level. This is Benello's fundamental strategic argument. As he said over and over again, "To counter the power of the present elites, on the one hand, and the alienation of the citizen and worker on the other, a combination of organization and insurgency must create new centers of power..." While he recognized the value of professional lobbying, national elections, and other formal constitutional procedures in his strategy, Benello placed his primary emphasis on transforming the existing power structure by increasing the existence, independence, and internal democracy of grassroots organizations at the base. Without such an organized effort, he felt it would be impossible to restore an underlying social ecology conducive to a successful popular struggle for peace, democracy, and ecological sanity.

The Effectiveness of a Revolutionary Decentralist Approach

This is clearly an unconventional political perspective. As Benello notes, "all liberal thought, and unfortunately a lot of socialist and progressive thought, turns to the state to cure us of our ills." The liberals lobby elites, legally protest government and corporate policies, and vote for the lesser of two evils presented by the establishment parties. Most progressives and socialists seek to realign the Democratic Party, or build a national third party, in order to go on to win state power through national elections. A few others argue that a disciplined Marxist-Leninist vanguard should seize state power through armed struggle and rule in the name of the people.

According to Benello, such statist-oriented activists are victims of the realpolitik delusion "which views politics as the art of the possible" and then goes on "to define the possible in terms of the existent." They are unable to see beyond what is and thus only seek ways to work within today's current institutional boundaries. These reformers and revolutionaries are painfully aware of the fact that the state is powerful and the grassroots weak. Yet, given their untested assumption about the impossibility of strengthening the grassroots, they seek, above all else, to persuade existing political elites of the correctness of their programs or, in the case of most progressives and socialists, to replace the ruling elites within the state by hook or by crook. This is the only way statist-oriented activists believe they can have effective influence and be powerful in the real world, whether they like it or not.

Greens, unfortunately, are not immune to this conventional political "wisdom." This statist approach is particularly compelling to those Greens who are committed to the very urgent and limited politics of the new survivalism. They argue that, in the face of nuclear terror and the ecological crisis, we need to be "realistic" and avoid "utopian" decentralist programs like Benello's. The once promising West German Green party is already showing significant signs of being seduced by the tantalizing fantasy of getting into power and has dramatically reduced its grassroots work. The many U.S. Greens who think that the only effective way forward is to build a national electoral third party show similar symptoms even though their chances of national electoral success are even dimmer than their German counterparts.

In order to counter these tendencies, Benello repeatedly tried to explain how "the development of a movement dedicated to the building of self-administering, free institutions...is both the most absent and most needed ingredient in a movement for social change." He argued that if we are serious about making a "change in the organizational structure" of society we need to organize communities and workplaces "which are deliberately structured so as to be participatory, coherent, ecologically sound, and continuously responsive to the needs" of their members. Instead of being unrealistic, this approach—supplemented, of course, by sometimes working through normal institutional channels—is probably the strongest and most reasonable strategy for making change in the real world. For as Gene Sharp notes, "The condition of the society's loci of power will in large degree determine the long-run capacity of the society to control a ruler's power."[11]

Benello's revolutionary decentralist strategy seems well suited to a radical Green movement. Importantly, his strategy parallels the ecological wisdom we have learned from studying the dynamics of natural eco-communities. As political scientist William Ophuls points out, "ecologists have found that the best way of controlling a so-called pest—that is, the way that is both most effective and safest—is not in most cases to attack the pest organism directly, but to modify the community so that the pest is naturally controlled by the network of interdependencies that constitute the community."[12] In this light, radical political education, community and workplace organizing, alternative economic and cultural institutions, local electoral work, nonviolent direct action campaigns, and regional, national, and transnational coordination of grassroots efforts are analogous to what ecologists and organic farmers call integrated pest management. The pests in society, of course, are militarized nation-states and multi-national corporations. The controls are a revitalized and balanced social community at the grassroots level.

The Limits of Benello's Eco-Philosophy

For all of Benello's social insight, the essays in this book are not the last word on creating decentralized, participatory, and ecological societies. Not surprisingly, some oversights and failures of imagination are embedded in Benello's thinking—not the least of which is the fact that Benello, like so many classical anarchist thinkers, was unable to recognize that people politically experience the world through more than their social roles as workers and citizens. Benello's theory highlights class and political authority well, yet neglects the politically relevant dynamics of gender, racial, and cultural conflict.[13] In this short essay, however, I want to focus on perhaps the most limited aspect of Benello's thinking from a radical Green perspective—his anthropocentric view of nature and environmental ethics.

In Dobson's typology, Benello is "dark Green" socially but "light Green" ecologically. For all of Benello's concern for human survival and environmental balance, nowhere in his writings does he evidence any direct moral concern for other forms of life or the biosphere as a whole. Nowhere does he embrace the stance of radical wilderness activist Judi Bari who recently called for the creation of a "society whose goal is to achieve a stable state with nature for the benefit of all species" not just human beings.[14] It would appear from what Benello leaves unsaid that either such thoughts never crossed his mind or that his thoughts along these lines were so embryonic and insufficiently developed that they never entered into his mature political thinking. Thus, while Benello so capably transcended the limits of Marx's social vision, his written work remains trapped within the Marxian view, so dominant on the left, that the natural world is "simply an object for mankind, purely a matter of utility" to be subdued "to human requirements."[15]

Benello's view is different from Marx's mostly in that his eco-philosophy is implicit, and perhaps unconscious, whereas Marx was quite explicit and aware of his own views. Benello's unconscious anthropocentric bias should not come as a particular surprise to us, however. As geographer Bill Lynn has noted, most modern social theory is based on a hidden, assumed-without-comment axiology which recognizes only instrumental value in the natural world and reserves the recognition of intrinsic moral worth to humanity or to some segment of the human species based on class, racial, gender, and political hierarchies.[16] It is a rare modern thinker who significantly breaks out of this paradigmatic view of the world.

Benello was only partially successful in this effort. He certainly never challenged the Wasteland Culture at the deeper axiological level described by Lynn. For all of his talk about appropriate technology, organic agriculture, renewable energy, maximum recycling, and steady-state economics which deservedly mark him as an insightful environmental reformer, Benello never really offered an ecological vision beyond replacing the self-destructive domination of nature with a more prudent and sustainable approach to the exploitation of the natural world for the long-term benefit of the entire human species. In this view, as social ecology pioneer Murray Bookchin notes, "our ethical relationship with nature is neither better nor worse than the success with which we plunder the natural world without harming ourselves."[17]

The social analogy to this approach to humanity's relationship with the rest of the natural world is the reform-minded capitalist of years gone by who attempted to moderate the unrestrained exploitation of the working class under competitive capitalism and supported such social reforms as universal suffrage, collective bargaining, public education, and social security legislation. Like Benello and others who recognize the objective dependency of human beings on the rest of the natural world, these far-seeing capitalists recognized their objective dependence on the working class. They clearly understood that their wealth, power, and prestige was fundamentally dependent on the labor power of the working class and that "sustaining" this subordinate labor power required meeting some of the basic biological/social requirements of workers through paying "the socially necessary wage." They thus urged the other members of the ruling class to stop short of driving the working class to complete immiseration even when it would be in the ruling class' short-term advantage.

Benello, of course, would be among the first to challenge this utilitarian approach to human community as it stops so far short of a moral, communitarian, and non-instrumentalist approach to social relationships. For Benello, the working class deserves much more than prudent manipulation. Indeed, he based his entire social philosophy on the premise that no human being should ever be reduced to merely an instrumental means to another's ends. Benello explicitly argued that all people should be morally respected as intrinsically valuable, as important ends in themselves, with their own interests and goals.

Unfortunately, at least in his writings, Benello never viewed the rest of the natural world through a similar lens of intrinsic value. Benello's work thus falls short of the needed integration of a deep naturalist ethic with a radical decentralist social politics. For this deeper perspective, radical Greens have to turn to other social ecologists than Benello. Murray Bookchin, for example, has written movingly of the urgent need for the Green movement to develop an ecological ethic that recognizes "the balance and integrity of the biosphere as an end in itself" independent of its instrumental value for human society. For Bookchin, "Natural diversity is to be cultivated not only because the more diversified the components that make up an ecosystem, the more stable the ecosystem…[but also because] diversity is desirable for its own sake, a value to be cherished as part of a spiritized notion of the living universe."[18]

Some might argue that this philosophical distinction between Benello and Bookchin is insignificant when it comes to the real world of ecological politics. However, such philosophical differences do yield significant differences in actual political program. Bookchin's more inclusive moral vision, for example, calls on us "to guard and expand wilderness areas and domains for wildlife [as well as to] defend animal species from human depredation."[19] Benello's writings make no such claim on us. In fact, they appear almost completely indifferent to wilderness and wildlife outside of its instrumental value to human beings.

To be sure, a certain amount of wilderness and biodiversity is instrumentally valuable in sustaining human societies. Yet, this does not by itself translate into a call to expand wilderness and protect wild animals from human depredation. As Paul Shepard has noted, "Ecologically, all the creatures in ecosystems are not equally necessary" in maintaining environmental sustainability.[20] Indeed, entire species are expendable if we limit ourselves to this criterion of value. According to Shepard,

> In our present state of knowledge, one cannot show that wolves, bears, tigers, eagles, green sea turtles, orioles, bullfrogs, monarch butterflies, olive baboons, red kangaroos,

bottle-nosed dolphins, or a thousand other big species are really indispensable to their ecosystems...To kill an ecosystem you must burn it up, plow it under, or poison it. Only at the level of its plant life, its microbes and its invertebrate fauna, is the natural system itself vulnerable.[21]

The upshot of Shepard's observation, refracted through an instrumental eco-philosophy like that projected by Benello, is that our society, while clearly needing to break with unrestrained expansion and exploitation at the lower levels of the biotic pyramid, does not need to worry about those wilderness areas or species which have little or no economic or life support value for humans. In this vision, the amount of wilderness beyond that which is necessary to protect the environmental sustainability of human society—or to fulfill the recreational and aesthetic desires of human beings—is the exact amount of wilderness which is available to be developed, and thus destroyed, in the interests of "sustainable development."

The practical distinction between Benello's and Bookchin's perspective should now be clear. A perspective such as Benello's only requires the preservation of *some* of the large remaining wilderness areas around the globe, such as tropical rainforests. It does not encourage us to preserve *all* the remaining large wilderness areas or to *expand* the wild world by carefully restoring large areas of previously "developed" land back to a wilderness condition once again. Only a larger land ethic such as Bookchin's or Bari's justifies this course of action.

Ecologically, Benello's environmental vision—while a significant improvement over the policies and practices of today—seeks only to modify the Wasteland Culture to make it physically nontoxic to human beings; it does not go on to challenge the Wasteland's underlying logic of domination in relation to rest of the natural world. In a world where wilderness will not exist by accident or oversight much longer, radical Greens would be wise to expand the boundaries of our sense of moral community to include the wild world of life with which we share this beautiful, blue-green planet. Had he lived longer, I believe that Benello would probably have come to such a perspective himself. The nonhierarchical logic of his whole worldview, coupled with the explosion of nonanthropocentric eco-philosophies which have emerged in the last decade, would likely have led him to an expanded moral perspective like that outlined here. Regardless of what Benello would have done, however, developing such a perspective is important for Green activists today. Without such an expanded "land ethic," we will be unable to fully envision a fundamental ecological alternative to the Wasteland Culture, let alone bring it to fruition.

Conclusion

Regardless of the ethical limitations I've mentioned here about Benello's nature philosophy, his writings and work articulate a compelling social philosophy, analysis, vision, and strategy of far greater relevance to the Green movement than the limited social goals and conventional political assumptions so deeply embedded in the new survivalism that has come to dominate so much of Green thinking today. While we need to go beyond Benello's limited assumptions about environmental ethics, radical Greens can learn a great deal from his life's work of developing a contemporary decentralist social theory and practice sensitive to the requirements of environmental sustainability.

By critically grappling with his provocative ideas—and building on them—Green activists will be much better prepared to offer a radical social alternative to industrial capitalist society and avoid the limited reformism and cooptation which threatens to weaken their movements worldwide. This is no small contribution to radical Green thought. For this, I salute C. George Benello.

Endnotes

1. Quoted in Andrew Dobson, *Green Political Thought,* (London: Unwin Hyman, 1990), 67.
2. Ibid.
3. André Gorz, *Ecology as Politics,* (Boston: South End Press, 1980), 3.
4. Ibid.
5. Andrew Dobson, 13.
6. Benjamin Barber, *Strong Democracy: Participatory Politics for a New Age,* (Berkeley: University of California Press, 1984), 213.
7. J. Baird Callicott, *In Defense of the Land Ethic: Essays in Environmental Philosophy,* (New York: State University of New York, 1989), 110.
8. For a detailed presentation of Shepard's ideas, see Paul Shepard, *Thinking Animals: Animals & the Development of Human Intelligence,* (New York: Viking, 1978).

9. Gene Sharp, *Social Power and Political Freedom*, (Boston: Porter Sargent, 1980), 26.

10. Ibid., 25.

11. Ibid., 32.

12. William Ophuls, *Ecology and the Politics of Scarcity*, (San Francisco: Freeman, 1977), 22.

13. For a discussion of a radical holistic political philosophy that seeks to integrate race, class, gender, and citizenship perspectives, see Michael Albert *et al.*, *Liberating Theory*, (Boston: South End Press, 1986).

14. Judi Bari, "Expand Earth First!," *Earth First!*, September 22, 1990, 5.

15. Quoted in Murray Bookchin, *Toward an Ecological Society*, (Montréal: Black Rose, 1980), 202.

16. Bill Lynn, "Hidden Axiologies: FitsSimmons' Ethical Assumptions Regarding Nature," (unpublished paper).

17. Steve Chase ed., *Defending the Earth: A Dialogue Between Murray Bookchin and Dave Foreman*, (Boston: South End Press, 1991), 57.

18. Murray Bookchin, *Toward an Ecological Society*, 59.

19. Ibid., 44.

20. Paul Shepard, 247.

21. Ibid.

Chapter 20

The Critic Critiqued

An interview with Harry Boyte

Len Krimerman: Harry, you balked at first when I asked you to contribute a commentary piece to this collection. You said you weren't sure you would be a good commentator on the book because of what you see as some very fundamental differences between your perspective and Benello's. Indeed, when we first talked you distanced yourself not only from Benello but from the New Left and from the Green movement as a whole. While I was frankly surprised by the sharpness of your critique of Benello's work, given your joint concerns with grassroots and workplace democracy, your criticisms struck me as both novel and worth exploring. In particular, they seemed to offer a rare opening for constructive dialogue between two positions equally committed to the expansion and enhancement of democracy, but (on the surface at least) deeply opposed in other respects. Could you spell out your criticisms of Benello's work?

Harry Boyte: In approaching any political or cultural tradition, it is useful to distinguish two very different stances, two opposed modes of communication: that of the prophet and that of the social critic. Someone who operates from the first of these, as did Martin Luther King in his famous "Letter from a Birmingham Jail," stands *within* a tradition and calls people back to its highest shared ideals. As King saw it, freedom for all persons is an American litany, a part of the American Dream; his letter criticizes his country by appealing to *its own principles*. On the other hand, recall the *Port Huron Statement* of SDS: its message expresses the perspective of *outsiders* who are entirely fed up with American society. It condemns not from within but by appealing to abstract principles disconnected from the American tradition, such as those of social equality.

When Benello writes about America as a "wasteland culture" and of the need to radically transform its priorities and organizational forms, his idiom is that of an estranged social critic, and not that of a disappointed, but still connected, prophet. In consequence, his views will remain alien to most Americans; his stance as disconnected critic thus becomes a formula for self-marginalization. In addition, Benello's abstract principles tend to work as pure ideals that mark off saints and sinners, good and evil institutions. This creates major pervasive problems both in how people talk (or fail to talk) with each other and in developing political strategy.

On the first point, the general political language that has grown from the late 1960s social ferment—and not just Benello's—speaks in strongly hortatory terms. From the standpoint of Green politics and other new social movements such as radical feminism and large parts of the peace movement, and even the conservative movement, the public world is theater for a morality play of exhortation and protest, critique or defense of "traditional" values and institutions. Campuses reflect this pattern, with wars between academic traditionalists and those who consider themselves politically correct. On most issues, *every* side uses the language of righteousness and innocence. People have scant experience of a "middle ground" of public life where there is no eternal struggle between saints and sinners, innocence or moral monsters but rather a pragmatic bargaining process between different interests, values, traditions, and ways of looking at the world.

A new democratic movement will have to emerge mostly out of the progressive tradition, since conservatives tend naturally to favor order and stability over the free flow of debate, different perspectives, and popular involvement. But the progressive side of the political spectrum will have to become much more self-reflective about the problems created by the legacy of the 1960s if we are to see much hope for renewed democracy. It will need to understand, for example, that the moralizing which has corrupted politics creates *hierarchies of innocence*. On campuses and in new social movement today, a "preference for the oppressed" means that power depends on the denial of power. There is intense competition to claim the mantle of *most oppressed*, precisely because such a status is the basis for leadership. In consequence, it is in the self-interest of groups to obscure the power resources they do possess.

Secondly, in regards to practical politics: a focus on estranged social criticism leads to a strategic emphasis on alternative institutions outside the compromises of mainstream society. Benello certainly embodied this perspective. Indeed, a great deal of activist political energy from the 1960s has gone into such efforts, from peace encampments to community organizations like ACORN, whose methodology is based on "new leadership" in communities not tied to the existing fabric of churches, unions, small businesses, civic groups like the 4H Clubs, League of Women Voters, etc. Such organizing can generate interesting visions and useful ideas for change. But it can never create a serious foundation for democratic power to transform the large-scale structures and dynamics of the society.

As we've seen, social critic theorists such as Benello rely heavily on pre-established ideologies which dictate priorities if not detailed blueprints. This contrasts very sharply with what I would call a *politics of empowerment*, for which the emphasis always remains squarely on capacity building within the citizenry. Empowerment politics does not try to mobilize people towards pre-decided goals. Instead, it utilizes every struggle, every protest, every community conflict as an opportunity to strengthen character, develop community skills, acquire greater voice and power. Benello's focus on creating the "right" or "best" kind of organization is admittedly different from standard Marxist or top-down ideologies, but it still presupposes that politics is a one-way activity. His position thus lacks a sense of the *interactive process* involved in a strong and vigorous public life: for this, what is required are such political arts as listening, evaluation, and holding people accountable, and, as well, an understanding of political power which enables everyone involved to be subject to continual transformation. In short, for empowerment politics, issues and programs become less crucial than the nature of public interaction itself.

One very practical difficulty with ideologically-oriented politics—whether left, right, or Green—is that its heavy moralization turns people away. Today, unlike the 1960s, what is needed is not the raising of consciousness or the recitation of grievances or problems, but specific and empowering remedies. People need to see what can be done to build and sustain community and public life more broadly, and how to overcome specific obstacles. They don't *mainly* need to be told about the destructive flaws and/or injustices of corporate capitalism, nor about the optimum form of social organization.

Many observers of American society have agreed that public life, the activity of engaged citizens shaping their communities together, is very largely in decay. Today, town meetings and barn raising seem like quaint relics which cannot be revived and have not been replaced. On my view, however, without a vibrant public life there is little hope for a politics of empowerment or for extensive community capacity building. Moreover, there are at least three distinct moments of public life which need to be retrieved. First, the *public as a deliberative, judging, and evaluative body*—one which encourages the expression of and respect for very dissimilar opinions; second, *the public as a problem solver*, relying on itself rather than experts or officials to resolve disputes, cope with crises, create remedies; and last, *the public as an insurgent force*, challenging dominant or exclusionary institutions, holding officials and the entire *polis* accountable.

While Benello may be aware of the need to revive community or public life in these three senses, he does not speak to it directly or in depth. Indeed, at some points he appears to buy into the notion, common enough among the New Left, that "the personal is the political." This slogan has value, highlighting important issues of personal experience and relationship which the classic public/private distinction obscured. But it ignores the fact (analogous to the legal difference between substantive and procedural issues) that while personal issues often appropriately *bring* people into politics or the public world, the principles of effective behavior in public life are different from those in private life. Thus, without clarification, this slogan obscures and may even contribute to the devolution of the political and public world. It confuses such valuable but *personal* dynamics as expressiveness, personal development, and intimacy with *public* activities such as negotiation, holding and being held accountable, and working across radically dissimilar ethnic and cultural boundaries.

LK: I think some of your criticisms may apply fairly to Benello, but aren't you ignoring much of the common ground between the two of you? For example, Benello certainly stressed what you term "specific and empowering remedies" with his emphasis on the need for transitional models in any genuine politics of popular empowerment. Don't you find some common ground here?

HB: Yes, of course. My point is not that there is nothing useful or interesting in Benello's thinking. I agree that his notion of *transitional models* is a fertile one, and one which raises the important question of how and where to cultivate a democratic sensibility. Certainly, as I think he would have agreed, the old environments—labor unions, political parties—are not very reliable; new social inventions are needed that can empower, educate, and encourage people towards democratic change. And this gap exists both at the local level and in regard to connecting local communities to one another.

Benello's later writings, e.g., on Mondragon and on the Italian artisan enterprise networks, contain several accounts of potentially fruitful democracy-building social inventions. As such, they can be useful for a politics of empowerment. They also suggest that he was moving away from a purely ideologically-oriented politics. My point is simply that we need to continue much further along this path than Benello. Benello and I share many goals. We differ mainly in our approaches to fostering empowerment at the grassroots. These differences, however, are not insignificant.

Part VI

Editors' Afterword

Chapter 21

Benello's Enduring Decentralist Legacy

Len Krimerman and Frank Lindenfeld

George Benello wrote and acted within a venerable tradition, one which runs from classic anarchist thinkers like Proudhon, Kropotkin, and Emma Goldman to recent radical community planners such as Lewis Mumford and Paul Goodman, and which plays a key role today in Murray Bookchin's idea of "libertarian municipalism," and in the familiar philosophical pillars of the Green movement. This feisty and persistent tradition combines decentralist and strongly participatory (self-managing) concepts of organization with ecologically responsible notions of technology and community empowerment. And it stresses, as well, the need for resistance to established forms of domination and repression, be these corporate, political, or cultural. Benello not only drew upon this tradition of decentralist ecological insurgence, but made significant and distinctive contributions to it.

Our five critical respondents can be seen as raising two different sorts of objections to Benello's views. On one hand, some of their points represent friendly amendments to or extensions of his perspective. Thus, several constituencies are identified—women, people of color, mainstream American organizations, the eco-sphere itself—whose distinctive needs, strengths, and forms of disempowerment Benello—allegedly, at least—tended to overlook. By including them, so these friendly arguments contend, Benello could provide a deeper and fuller philosophical account of an ecological and democratic community, while at the same time helping to foster the diverse sorts of coalitions needed to initiate the long process of decentralizing.

On the other hand, some of our commentators evidence more basic disagreements with George's decentralist priorities. Jane Mansbridge, for example, while arguing "for decentralizing on all issues to the lowest possible level," maintains that

> on some issues of large-scale ecology, like acid rain, or large-scale economic issues, like redistribution to geographically disadvantaged areas—people need ways of making binding collective decisions at the scale of the modern nation-state or beyond.

And Walda Katz-Fishman contends that, in addition to "grassroots participation and local decision-making," we will need "centralized [economic] planning backed up by workers' state power" to accomplish the transition to "an egalitarian, participatory, and democratic socialist society."

As for the friendly amendments, they would most certainly strengthen Benello's position. Domination and oppression take many forms, and only by recognizing them all—and the unique contributions each now-excluded or exploited constituency can make to the others—can a genuine rainbow of empowerment be woven together. Moreover, their addition is consistent with the spirit of Benello's own position. Though he did not directly examine the implications of his decentralist views for people of color, for women, the biosphere, or for mainstream organizations, wholeness of vision and life was one of his basic themes. In his view, wholeness or integration—of intellectual and manual work, of personal and economic values, of public and private, rural and urban—are "central to the libertarian and anarchist traditions". As a result, he understood those traditions as

> refusing to accept the fact of human domination *wherever it is experienced.* Rather than seeing it as a necessary step in human evolution, to be transcended when the final revolution establishes the classless society, they've continuously

opposed all forms of domination, *whether it be of the state, the industrial system, or the family.*

As for the less-than-friendly, pro-centralist, critiques, they require much more extensive discussion. In order to assess their force, what is required is a closer look at Benello's own form of decentralism; in particular, at the distinctive ideas he contributed to the ecological anarchist tradition. These seem to us to be three-fold:

1. *The psycho-social dialectic of both domination and liberation.*

2. *The strategic primacy of real life transitional models.*

3. *The indispensability of worklife transformation and democratization.*

In what follows, our aim is to clarify these three distinctive elements in Benello's insurgent eco-decentralism. In their light, we argue, the force of centralist objections like those of Walda Katz-Fishman and Jane Mansbridge is substantially diminished. Moreover, other standard complaints with anarchist reconstruction—e.g., that it is alien to mainstream political life or otherwise doomed to marginality (see here, the interview with Harry Boyte)—can also be effectively countered. Finally, these three Benello theses should permit us to identify what is of enduring— and also of very timely—value in his perspective. To bring this out, we will examine the implications of that perspective for understanding and combatting the quintessential *fin de siecle* social problem—worldwide American militarism. We will do this, in part, by comparing and contrasting Benello's proposals here with other recent calls for building a "pro-democracy peace movement."

The Psycho-Social Dialectic

Decentralists and anarchists have on the whole ignored an obvious question: "If self-management and local control are so desirable, why is there so little of, or desire for, them?" "Why are their opposites so pervasive?" Benello's first distinctive thesis attempts to fill this gap. In his view, "the crisis of our times is as much one of consciousnesss as it is of social forms." Amplifying this thought, he contended:

Any movement for social change with enduring value must be capable of confronting the basic psycho-social contradiction of society. It must come up with answers capable of integrating subjectivity and objectivity, the individual and the social. This is the essence of liberation.

What he has in mind here surfaces throughout his writings, appearing most explicitly in "Wasteland Culture," and "The Utopian Urge." In these pieces, he exposes a symbiosis between "psychic scarcity" or "affective deprivation", on one hand, and centralized hierarchical organization on the other. Each of these fosters and sustains the other. Psychic deprivation obtains when one lacks not "material goods, but...the requisite of shared living—family, working partners, intimate friends, face-to-face associations." Beyond this, it obtains when people are treated not as whole persons, but as specialized and fragmented personnel. Thus, in contemporary, corporate society:

Work is specialized, and jobs are narrowly defined according to a set of procedures. As a result, there is little chance for an integration of purposes and functions, and less chance still for an overall integration of work with the *other* spheres of life.

In short, we have psychic scarcity when both "the deep psychic need for wholeness" as well as any real bonds with "widening spheres of commitment and concern" are frustrated. The result of this frustration, according to Benello's psycho-social dialectic, is a self which seeks satisfaction at a regressed level, an "authoritarian personality" who sees the world, in Maslow's words, "as made up of two kinds of persons: those he can dominate and those who dominate him." Benello's account of the genesis of disempowerment (and of disempowering centralized institutions) is stated most explicitly in "The Utopian Urge":

The power orientation is thus a personality system created in part by [psychic] deprivation. Where natural forms of face-to-face association have broken down, seeking after power becomes an alternative means to security and a sense of the self. Where natural human functions cannot be fulfilled, power becomes an end in itself. From this comes the mega-lomania which results in an institutional order Lewis Mumford characterized as the "mega-machine"—a mass form of social organization based on coercion and the bribery of external rewards.

This account goes further than merely explaining the prevalence of anti-democratic forms of social life. In addition, it begins to identify ways of *breaking out* of the psycho-social circle. What is needed for this, Benello asserts, is to "integrate subjectivity and objectivity," to confront directly both psychic scarcity and the lack of wholeness on one hand, and, on the other, degenerate forms of social life. Put negatively, what is needed goes well beyond eliminating current oppressions or even the dismantling of our current mega-machine. Nor will individual acts of protest or rebellion make much of a difference. For each of these works too exclusively—and too *reactively*—on only one horn of the psycho-social contradiction. To break free of it, the creation of a new and different form of sociality is required, one that provides cohesion and concrete commitments while at the same time nurturing individual integrity and fuller self-realization. As Benello notes:

> Not only must organizations be built to human scale, but instead of the narrow-scope organizations that are the present style, we must create [ones] capable of embodying the major spheres of human activity in an integrated fashion.

The Primacy of Practical Models

All this may be well and good, but how do we develop these new forms of primary association or community? How can "seeds of liberation", even "psycho-social" ones, take root in a wasteland culture dead set on destroying them? In responding to this question—another of those conveniently overlooked by most decentralists—Benello appealed to what he early on referred to as "paradigms":

> In a one-dimensional society, pervaded by its monolithic assumptions, the importance of paradigms is great....To create paradigms that represent serious structural change, it is imperative that [they] be significant alternatives to existing institutions, capable of equaling or surpassing them in quality of output.

Almost two decades later in discussing Mondragon, the remarkable Basque cooperative network, this notion becomes that of "an effective working model."

> Mondragon represents something that works, and that in turn constitutes a statement about human nature. If a picture is worth a thousand words, an effective working model is worth at least a thousand pictures.

The point of emphasizing such models is to remind us that our first (and second, and third…) attempts to reconstruct social life need not be perfect pre-figurations of an decentralized ecological society. Instead, we can rely—and build—upon *imperfect, but transitional,* efforts that are replicable, expandable, and which clearly demonstrate that ordinary people are neither powerless nor incompetent. How we can know which sorts of models to favor—or which alternative paths are truly transitional—is a cogent and thorny question and one that George did not explicitly address. But the examples he selects appear to meet such criteria as the following:

1. they involve many thousands of people, rather than only a few dozen or hundred, e.g., as gathered in a single intentional community;

2. they have lasted, or seem able to last, over at least two generations;

3. they can be widely replicated, in spirit, if not in detail;

4. they encompass not one but rather many different spheres of life, e.g., housing as well as work, politics as well as child-rearing;

5. they are capable of evolving democratically, e.g., through widening access to, and intensifying, their face-to-face participatory culture;

6. In addition to fulfilling democratic and ecological criteria, they work—in the sense of delivering the goods—as well as or better than established top-down organizations;

7. They challenge presuppositions—about human nature or the possible forms of social life—central to established institutions, thus tending to undermine those institutions.

There is an important implication to be drawn from this emphasis on practical or working models: i.e., *that in devising strategies, practice has precedence over theory.* Theoretical analyses can certainly aid in identifying or clarifying our general goals—wholeness, participatory organization, and ecological sustainability. Moreover, it can suggest strategies that might be worth some consideration, such as nuclear free zones and libertarian municipalities. But what has already survived the test of time, coped long and well against the current enemies of liberation without compromise, provides the firmest basis for practical action. For such survivor working models represent the only clearly viable competitors to the existing mega-machine. As George put it in discussing the value of Mondragon:

> the burden of proof is on the theorist. The problem with capitalism and, more generally, with coercive industrial systems of whatever persuasion, is not that they don't work; they do deliver the goods, but in the process grind up human beings. The only answer to this is to prove that a better system also works; theory alone simply will not do. And, if we wish to claim that something better than Mondragon needs to be built, it is incumbent on us to do it.

On the Indispensability of Worklife Transformation

For Benello (especially if we understand the central place in his thought of "wholeness"), projects of many different sorts can and should reinforce the "central participatory vision": "cooperative schools, day care centers, community unions, newspapers, radio stations…" But for numerous reasons, he felt that a movement to create participatory democracy "must sooner or later confront the workplace." By this he did not mean that such a movement should be restricted to the "production" sector, nor that those in democratized workplaces should have a greater voice in overall planning than, say, those engaged in community media or in child-rearing, and so forth. His rationale, once again, was not theoretical, but practical and time-bound:

> A movement seeking to organize from the ground up to achieve full participation will have the greatest impact when it creates effective productive organizations; it is here that social organization confronts most fully the existing technology. The productive enterprise is the core institution in an advanced industrial society, and hence if it can be self-administering and participative, this will take the ground out from under the supporters of the present authoritarian system.

In addition to this "greatest-impact-today" rationale, George had other reasons for viewing workplace reconstruction as crucial. First, such a focus—as Mondragon illustrates so fully—would provide sources of capital essential for additional reconstruction, both of work and of other spheres of life. Secondly, if we are really to "deliver the goods" and meet people's legitimate material needs at least as well as corporate capitalism, control over economic production is obviously essential. Finally, is there a better arena than the workplace for most people in contemporary society to gain confidence and competence in participatory community life? No doubt work takes up too much of many peoples' lives, yet it continues to touch us all, more so than almost any other shared activity. It can thus provide a comparatively unique common learning experience in face-to-face problem resolution and in the give-and-take of mutual respect and shared empowerment.

The Costs—and Expendability—of Centralism

How can Benello's distinctive contributions to decentralism help strengthen it against centralist critics? Most important, they bring out sharply the *ongoing* and *enormously tragic costs* of centralized organization: those resulting from the downward psycho-social spiral of powerlessness, acquiescence to remote authority, and domination. As Benello put it, some thirty years ago:

> As long as our sense of powerlessness continues to be fed by our massive and depersonalized institutions, we will continue to organize for war…we will find warfare a vicarious substitute for our own lack of responsibility and integrity.

Thus, for us to build a society capable of achieving peace, we will need "pervasive decentralization and dispersion of power." In this light, centralization can no longer be seen as a neutral phenomenon—sometimes used for good, sometimes for evil. On the contrary, like a loaded and cocked weapon, or better, like a brutalizing and dispiriting whip, it is bound to have destructive impact. Centralists, in short, have much to answer for.

But perhaps centralization, though a major source of evil, is unavoidable, a necessary (and perhaps redeemable) evil? This appears to be the view of both Walda Katz-Fishman and Jane Mansbridge, though their notions of what exactly is necessary, and why it is, are quite divergent. Katz-Fishman contends that there is no way, short of centralized economic planning, to eliminate capitalism's endemic sexual and racial exploitation and hence that "the authority of a workers' state" is required for "the transition to an egalitarian, participatory, and democratic socialist" society. For Mansbridge, representative but nationally (or even internationally?) centralized institutions wielding coercive collective power are essential, given that (a) what is done locally often has very wide-spread impact, e.g., in the building or obstruction of public roads, the use or abuse of basic natural resources, or the spread or prevention of life-threatening pollution; (b) irreconcilable conflicts of interest are bound to arise in any polity, regardless of its size; and (c) small face-to-face groups, however beneficial for individual growth and whole person relationships, are unable to cope effectively with extralocal problems or to exert much influence on regional, national, or international policy.

In response to these pro-centralist rationales—and to the many others which construct evils or crises with which decentralist communities allegedly cannot cope—we would make two sorts of replies.[1] In the first place, they are based very largely on bald conjecture. There is really no firm evidence in place, for example, that widespread decentralist approaches emphasizing local community self-reliance and worker-owned enterprises could not effectively depose corporate capitalism. Indeed, we have argued elsewhere that the emerging grassroots workplace democracy movement, in the USA and elsewhere, "displays historically novel features that not only set it apart from prior worker cooperative activity but enable it to seriously challenge corporate capitalism."[2] Moreover, in the light of such durable and democratic intermediate-sized alternatives as Mondragon, the (speculative) assumption that *only* centralized and nation-sized institutions can keep order or settle conflicts of interest is at least problematic. More specifically, this assumption appears to ignore crucial distinctions between *coordination, coercion,* and *centralized nation-state power.* Because decentralists like Benello disavow the latter, it does not follow that they leave no room for coordination between localities, for planning on regional or even global levels, or for the setting of policy on issues that affect wide ranges of communities and peoples.

Communites of whatever size can voluntarily come together, without a centralized authority, to establish generally binding toxic waste management or acid rain policies—much as the rail systems in many different European countries (one of Kropotkin's favorite examples) have voluntarily agreed to cooperate for over a century. Nor do *all* forms of "coercion" or "power" require permanent nation-states for their exercise. The withdrawal of rights from an uncompliant or destructive member in a voluntary association of producers or communities can be a powerful disincentive, as can such measures as economic boycotts or refusal of needed services. Where necessary, temporary problem-solving or conflict-settling task forces can be set up, through delegation or referendum, to design large-scaled plans to deal with problems like border disputes, ecological hazards, economic disparities, mafioso or vigilante gangs. Such temporary bodies would have sharply delimited powers and life-spans, and, in contrast to centralized authorities, would go out of business when they had fulfilled their temporary functions. No doubt, this will become untidy or time-consuming upon occasion, but this is a small price to pay for breaking the psycho-social habits of disempowerment and domination, obedience and militarism.[3]

Which brings us to our second response to pro-centralist arguments, i.e., that they run afoul of the psycho-social dialectic. They ignore, pre-empt, and impair the capacity for local self-reliance, for genuine community, for personal integration and wholeness. They condone the centralized collection of tax revenues and their use in building up military machines rather than for local community needs and empowerment. Thus, even those centralists, like Katz-Fishman and Mansbridge, who claim to be advocates of (limited) decentralism must therefore recognize that they are playing with very deadly fire: there are no greater evils today that those produced by nation-against-nation warfare. As Mansbridge herself concedes, "both in nations and in simpler societies, the larger the society, the more likely it is to go to war." Whatever the (mainly conjectural) costs of decentralizing, they hardly compare with this all-too-real cost of failing to decentralize.

Perhaps there are some forms of national or state power which promote an increase of local self-reliance, ecological sustainability, and community empowerment, which diminish their own stock of concentrated authority and resources by transferring them to regional, municipal, or neighborhood associations. Such "self-eliminating" or "decentralist-nurturing" centralization, in principle at least, is imaginable, and should be distinguished from the usual form which arrogates revenues and sovereignty to itself. However, neither Mansbridge nor Katz-Fishman make this sort of distinction, and hence they cannot show how the life-threatening dangers of traditional centralization can be minimized, much less avoided.

But isn't decentralism, especially in the context of today's multi-national corporations and giant nation-states, a "recipe for marginality"? This complaint is also a familiar one, and is echoed in Harry Boyte's criticism of Benello's views as being "alien to most Americans" and by much of Mansbridge's analysis as well. The response George would have made to this line of argument is not difficult to imagine; it would be based on his distinctive decentralist theses. First of all, as we have seen, the psycho-social dialectic is precisely an effort to explain why decentralist associations have historically been "marginal" and how centralist institutions can be displaced, e.g., by appealing to needs (for wholeness and empowering community) sabotaged by the latter. Secondly, the primacy of imperfect transitional models is based, in part, on their capacity to appeal to increasingly large segments of mainstream folks, and this in turn is spawned by their proven ability to both "deliver the goods" and nurture fuller human growth. Given these features, Benello's decentralizing models can separate themselves from any tendency towards self-marginalization. Finally, the arena for transformation on which Benello placed the most emphasis is the workplace, and, with Mondragon, the industrial, medium- to large-sized, workplace. On his view, this is where efforts to decentralize and democratize would have the greatest impact. But nothing could be more "mainstream" than the industrial workplace, whether it fabricates electronic products, sells and services group insurance, or manufactures stoves and refrigerators.

Indeed, recent events in this country, as well as others, have confirmed the mainstream appeal of work-connected ideas very much like those of Benello. Several powerful labor unions have endorsed worker ownership, when union-based and democratically structured, as a strategically sound vehicle; this includes the United Steelworkers of America (USWA) and the Amalgamated Clothing and Textile Workers Union (ACTWU). The former has now established an employee ownership department in its national office and has assisted the take-over, by its locals, of some fifteen large steel plants in the United States.[4] Furthermore, the national AFL-CIO has created the Employee Partnership Fund to provide workers with needed capital to buy out, and take control over, their own firms. In brief, worker ownership—of a sort similar to that in Mondragon but with roots in established labor unions—has become part of a mainstream agenda for change. And this should caution us against viewing Benello's form of decentralism as dead-ended in self-marginalization.

The Continuing Benello Legacy

George Benello's distinctive form of decentralism, we have argued, strengthens that tradition against pro-centralist arguments. It reveals the intolerably high costs and pervasive damage—both psychically and socially—of centralized approaches. Moreover, it explains why such costs, e.g., the propensity for and acceptance of patriotic militarism, are not incidental, but can be traced to an underlying and regressive psycho-social dynamic, which only participatory and decentralized associations can hope to avoid. Furthermore, his position provides hope and a strategy for displacing centralized authority, through transitional models focused in large part around the transformation of work. With this sort of emphasis, decentralism would no longer speak only to the already converted but would have the potential to meet widespread needs and gain mainstream support and credibility.

But what does all of this mean for activists and radicals today? To address this question, we will compare Benello's perspective with one of more recent vintage. Both provide proposals—and apparently similar ones—for coping with what is perhaps the most pressing issue of our decade: American militarism. In the October 8, 1990 issue of *The Nation,* Randy Kehler, formerly a national coordinator of the Nuclear Weapons Freeze Campaign, develops a case for a new kind of peace movement: one which focuses not on reacting to this outbreak or that crisis, but on creating "fire-resistant structures for the future." To do this, Kehler claims, we must examine what a "dynamic, self-sustaining *peace* system looks like." To do so, he maintains, will "broaden the traditional definition of peace to include questions of economic justice, ecology and technology, politics and culture."[5] Moreover, he continues, a critical element in any such "robust peace system" is "democracy," by which he means "a politics of human dignity and equality that affords all citizens an equal opportunity to shape decisions that affect their lives."[4] It is, on his view, the lack of democracy that has kept the peace movement from achieving its goal of avoiding war. In short, to be anti-war means to be "pro-democracy."

So far, so good. Up to this point, Benello and Kehler would be pretty much in agreement—both stressing the need for "structural change" in order to prevent future wars, and for "fundamental reform of our system of political democracy." The contrasts between them begin to appear when we consider the specific strategic steps advocated by Kehler, what he sees as the agenda for a "broad-based...citizens' pro-democracy movement." For this appears to consist solely of "reforms designed to make the political process serve the public's interest before those of the corporate elite", e.g., such reforms as (1) financing public elections entirely with public rather than private sources of funding and (2) requiring TV stations to ensure free and equal broadcast access to all eligible candidates. In short, Kehler's program for building democracy boils down to reforming the electoral process, so that those without much wealth have "equal political opportunity."

From Benello's decentralist perspective, however, the project of building a movement for peace or democracy around such reforms as these is fundamentally flawed. Not that the reforms themselves are suspect—a society with them in place would certainly be to that extent more justly egalitarian than what we have today. On the other hand, they make no real contact with what Benello viewed as the underlying sources of war and militarism; they would "democratize", but only at a great distance, leaving the great bulk of power in the hands of remote representatives, albeit ones more fairly elected. Put another way, Kehler's electoral reforms do not offer a way out of the psycho-social dialectic nor do they diminish the psychic scarcity to which Benello attributed the strong hold of authoritarian and war-centered forms of social life. On the contrary, a program with these reforms as its center-piece appears to assume that simply changing—or, better, simply prom-ising to change—electoral procedures will *by itself* draw people away from long-standing and culturally reinforced habits of powerlessness, isolation, and acceptance of domination.

For Benello, however, to offset and dissipate these habits will require a great deal more: the creation of intensified participatory com-munities, a heightened sense of integrated and full selfhood, viable organizations that provide needed services, products, and worklives that compare well with those offered by mainstream and undemocratic institutions. Lacking this sort of energizing and alienation-combatting potency, how would "a diverse, multi-racial movement" be likely to take root on the soil of electoral reforms? These reforms, after all, promise only distant and very indirect sorts of benefits. Perhaps if they were somehow enacted, there might then be greater political equality, and maybe this might in turn allow for better laws about "affordable hous-ing," "health care as a universal right," or military spending. Such a scenario is no doubt *possible*. But laws are only laws, and getting them enforced is quite another matter from getting them enacted, as the civil rights and feminist movements can well testify. And such conjectural gains will hardly appeal to or animate those convinced that they are largely excluded from social or political influence.

Yes, peace does require democracy, but building democracy re-quires that we identify and confront the sources of undemocratic behavior, the vicious cycle that fuels our current inegalitarian and authoritarian structures. In his 1964 article, "Genuine Peace Requires Real Democracy," in *Liberation* magazine, George put the point in this striking way:

> To counter the power of the present elites on the one hand and the alienation of the citizen and worker on the other, a combination of organization and insurgency must create new centers of power based on new models of decision-making, where human beings confront each other directly and responsibly. Insurgency will be necessary at the point that these new groupings seek to be more than simply one more voluntary organization and claim their say within the whole. From this can arise a new set of priorities based on a new kind of moral commitment, sufficient to defuse the war system.

Carrying the Light Behind

Benello's decentralist perspective may thus be indispensable for liberating the energies required to create what Kehler called a "dynamic peace system." For Benello's form of eco-decentralism combines a psycho-social explanation for why centralization and militarism have been so prevalent with practical transitional models for resisting their influence and for developing an empowered citizenry. Without this sort of approach, those who would make any fundamental change of a democratic or progressive sort are bound to come up short: instead of enthusiasm and hope, they would encounter hostility, indifference, despair, and cynicism from those disempowered by the mega-machine.

This is not of course to say that Benello's contributions to decentralism provide the final word on any of these issues. They do represent, as we have argued, a significant step beyond most other decentralist positions and they do raise deep and very troubling questions for those who would simply reform, rather than resist and replace, centralized arrangements. Still, Benello's views may need to be supplemented in at least two ways.

First, as Steve Chase cogently points out in his commentary, George's decentralist perspective appears, in some respects at least, to implicitly accept the domination of non-human nature by human beings. While George was an advocate of planet-friendly approaches to development and technology, his writings do tend to overlook those energies and insights informed by a nonanthropocentric ecological ethic. Combining Benello's strong concern for a sustainable, just, and decentralized human community with a fuller and more explicit concern for the "wild world" could only strengthen Green politics. This synthesis would avoid both human domination of the natural world and so-called radical ecology concerns for non-human nature which ignore the needs of disempowered humans. It could explore the strategic common ground of those for whom *both* human and non-human life are precious and irreplaceable. In this way, lighter and darker shades of Green could work together in a fashion pointed to, but not completely realized, in George's own work.

Secondly, Benello may not have fully explained or appreciated the remarkably durable appeal of centralized organizations. Some of these no doubt are maintained primarily by some combination of physical force and mental manipulation. Some may fill a void created by psychic scarcity or by the absence of a rich and empowering community life. But others command forms of loyalty that do not seem to arise entirely from fear of coercion, from cultural brainwashing or reinforcement, or from the suppression of higher needs for self-directed commitment and concern. Loyalty to one's country or culture and to its centralized institutions, may in part arise from quite different and more positive sources, e.g., the desire to give appreciation to and receive it from those one has ties with, to be of service to a larger community which has helped to form and make a place for one, to be connected with what has existed long before one's birth and will persist beyond one's own death. Benello appealed to the psycho-social dialectic in order to *begin* making sense of the seemingly perennial appeal of centralist and war-prone institutions. But that dialectic assumes that little if anything desirable is at the base of that appeal—and this assumption, accepted by him uncritically, seems to us questionable. For example, the ability of large-scale, albeit hierarchical, institutions to maintain secure and stable social orders and to provide traditions which survive our own individual deaths may be an element in why they remain abiding objects of loyalty. In this light, centralization may have some positive functions and the task of supplanting it may require, in William James' sense, something like "moral equivalents"—decentralist ways of achieving the same desired and worthwhile ends now served, though with horrendous costs, by centralization.

Nonetheless, at the very least, George Benello can be said to have initiated the exploration of centralization's longevity and the sources of its appeal. He raised the right questions, even if we need to go beyond some of his answers. Here is how Steve Dawson and David Ellerman, drawing on Dante, portrayed George's groundbreaking efforts to help initiate a worker ownership movement in this country:

> You did as one who walks at night,
> Carrying the light behind,
> With no help to yourself,
> But illuminating those who follow behind...[6]

The same could be said of George Benello's pioneering intellectual contribution to the ongoing and increasingly relevant decentralist tradition in radical social and ecological thought.

Endnotes

1. In addition to some of our commentators' arguments, many others have been trotted out to persuade people that centralization is indispensable. These all have much the same form, depicting monstrous evils or disasters to which, allegedly, decentralized communities are especially prone. Examples of these arguments include:

> 1) vicious or insane persons who, instead of following ordinary rules of civility, murder, pillage, or otherwise invasively interfere with their fellows;
> 2) irresponsible people whose carelessness causes injury to others, as in accidental fires or auto accidents;
> 3) brutal and tightly organized mafia-like groups who rely on violence and threats to compel others to accept their domination;
> 4) ruthless governments such as that of Saddam Hussein (or George Bush) who use despotism (or bureaucracy and manipulation) to build up their own armies and then invade other countries;
> 5) ordinary folks who live in regions favored by abundant natural resources, but who are unwilling to share with those in regions less fortunate.

Our reply to these stock and stale objections to decentralism would parallel our response to the points raised by Mansbridge and Katz-Fishman, whose objections are not grounded in fact or history, but in speculation. The problem with all of these objections is that they overlook intermediate-sized decentralist options as well as inter-community forms of coordination not based on nation-state and permanent forms of hierarchy.

2. Len Krimerman and Frank Lindenfeld, "Contemporary Workplace Democracy in the United States: Taking Stock of an Emerging Movement," in *Socialism and Democracy,* September, 1990 (#11), 109-139. See also our forthcoming book, *When Workers Decide: Workplace Democracy Takes Root in America,* (Philadelphia: New Society Publishers, 1991).

3. In her essay in this volume, Jane Mansbridge definitely appears to be moving in this direction.

4. Indeed, as this book goes to press, another steel buyout, giving 450 workers 77% of their company, has just been concluded in Ansonia, Connecticut.

5. Randy Kehler, "Antiwar Means Pro-Democracy," in *The Nation,* October, 8, 1990, 382.

6. This quotation from Dante's *Purgatorio XXII* appears at the conclusion of Dawson's and Ellerman's "Remembrance and Appreciation" of George Benello in *Changing Work,* Winter, 1988, C3.

Bibliography

Works by C. George Benello

Books

1971. C. George Benello and Dimitrios I. Roussopoulos (eds), *The Case for Participatory Democracy,* (New York: Viking).

1985. C. George Benello and Walda Katz Fishman (eds), *Readings in Humanist Sociology,* (New York: General Hall).

Articles in Books

1969. "Participatory Democracy and the Dilemma of Change," in Priscilla Long (ed), *The New Left: A Collection of Essays,* (Boston: Porter Sargent). Reprinted in part in *Current Magazine,* No. 138, March, 1972.

1971. "Organization, Conflict, and Free Association," in Benello and Roussopoulos, *The Case for Participatory Democracy.*

1971. "Group Organization and Socio-political Structure," in Benello and Roussopoulos, *The Case for Participatory Democracy.*

1972. "Social Animation among Anglophile Groups in Quebec," in F. Lesemann and M. Thiend (eds), *Animations Sociales au Quebec,* (Ecole de Service Sociale, Universite de Montreal).

1977. "Organizational Functions and Structure," in *Democracy in the Workplace: Readings on the Implementation of Self Management in America, A Resource Manual.* Published by Strongforce, Inc., under NIMH Training Grant, No. 1T21MH14002.

1978. "Economic Democracy and the Future: The Unfinished Task,"in Clement Bezold (ed), *Anticipatory Democracy: People in the Politics of the Future,* (New York: Random House).

1979. "Technology and Power: the Scope and Limits of La Technique as a Mode of Understanding Modernity," in Clifford G. Christians and Jay M. Van Hook (eds) *Jacques Ellul: Interpretative Essays,* (Champaign: University of Illinois Press).

1981. "Workplace Democratization," published by the Project on Work and Democracy, Hampshire College. Reprinted in Ward Morehouse (ed), *Building Sus-*

tainable Communities: Tools and Concepts For Self Reliant Economic Change, (New York: Bootstrap Press, 1989).

1983. "Economic Behavior and Self Management: Some Governing Principles," in Ward Morehouse (ed), *Handbook of Tools for Community Economic Change,* (New York: Intermediate Technology Development Group of North America). Reprinted in Morehouse (ed), *Building Sustainable Communities.*

1984. "Worker Management and the American Labor Movement," in Frank Lindenfeld and Joyce Rothschild-Whitt (eds), *Workplace Democracy and Social Change,* (Boston: Porter Sargent).

1989. "Worker-Managed Enterprises: Legal Shells, Structures, and Financing," in Morehouse (ed), *Building Sustainable Communities.*

1989. "Community Financing and Resource Optimization," in Morehouse (ed), *Building Sustainable Communities.*

Magazine and Journal Articles

1957. "A Foreigner Looks at Japan," *Japan Digest,* May. Reprinted in Japanese in *Kokusai Bunka Shinkokai* (Journal of International Culture), August, 1957.

1964. "Morality, Politics, and Peace," *War/Peace Report,* November. Reprinted in the *St. Louis Post-Dispatch,* December 15, 1964 and in the *Vancouver Sun,* December 14, 1964.

1965. "Non Violence: the Gorilla and the Saint," *Liberation,* Vol. X, No. 9, December.

1966. "Thinking about a College," *Manas,* Vol. XIX, August 24.

1966. "Pacifism and Pop Mythology," *Peace News,* No. 1592, December 30.

1967. "Wasteland Culture: Notes on Structures and Restructuring for Social Change," *Our Generation,* Vol. 5, No. 2, Fall. Reprinted in Gerald F. McGuigan (ed), *Student Protest,* (Toronto: Metheun, 1968); in *Anarchy,* No. 88, June, 1968; and in Hans Peter Dreitzel (ed), *Recent Sociology,* (New York: Macmillan, 1969).

1967. "Politics, Resistance, and Marxism," *Our Generation,* Vol. 5, No. 4.

1968. "Some Questions on the New Truth: Notes on Progressivism," *The Goddard Journal,* Vol. II, No. 1, November.

1969. "The Failure of Imagination," (with Peter Katodotis) *Our Generation,* Vol. 7, No. 4.

1970. "On Meta-Planning," (extracts) *Le Carre Bleu,* No. 3.

1973. "A Future History, " Prize essay for a Symposium on Cultural Alternatives, sponsored by the American Anthropological Association. Published in the *Proceedings of the 9th International Congress on Anthropological and Ethnological Sciences,* (New York: Mouton). Reprinted in American Anthropological

Association, *Experimental Symposium on Cultural Futuristics,* Office for Applied Social Science and the Future, Minneapolis, University of Minnesota, 1973.

1974. "Anarchism and Marxism: A Confrontation of Traditions," *Our Generation,* Vol. 10, No. 1. Reprinted in Howard Ehrlich et al. (eds), *Reinventing Anarchy* (London: Routledge, Kegan and Paul, 1979).

1975. "The Utopian Urge," *Liberation,* Vol. 19, No. 5, May. Reprinted in Gary Coates and Jack Smith (eds), *In Search of Symbiotic Community.*

1975. "Les Perspectives du Control Ouvrier aux Etats-Unis," *Autogestion et Socialism,* No. 32, November. Reprinted in English as "Worker Control in the United States: the Prospects," in *Self-Management in North America: Thought, Research and Practice,* (Program on Participation and Labor Managed Systems, No. 11, Cornell University, 1975).

1978. "Self-Management: the Paradigm and the Possibilities," *Humanity and Society,* Vol. 2, No. 2.

1979. "Self-Management in the U.S.: The Movement for Economic Self Determination and Workers Rights," *ALSA Forum,* Vol. 4, No. 2, Fall.

1980. "Toward a Grounded Theory of Humanist Organization," *Humanity and Society,* Vol. 4, No. 2.

1982. "The Experience of Developing Worker Management," *Clinical Sociology Review,* Vol. 1.

1983. "Anarchism and the Technological Imperative," *Black Rose,* Vol. II, Spring.

1986-7. "The Challenge of Mondragon," *Black Rose,* Winter. Reprinted in Benello memorial issue of *Changing Work,* No. 7, Winter 1988.

1988. "Political Education for Worker-Management," *Changing Work,* No. 7, Winter.

1988. "Peace Presupposes Democratic Participation—and Insurgency," *Changing Work,* No. 7, Winter.

1988. "Do You Know Where Your Tax Money Is?" *Changing Work,* No. 7, Winter.

1988. "Putting the Reins on Technology: Towards Full Scale Workplace Democracy," *Changing Work,* No. 7, Winter.

1988. "Growing a Local Economy: Self Financing and Democratic Development," *Changing Work,* No.7, Winter.

Book Reviews and Review Essays

1966. "Man in an Imperfect Democracy," review essay on *Democracy and Nonviolence* by Ralph Templin in *Peace News,* No. 1592, London, December 30.

1966. *The Technological Society,* by Jacques Ellul. Reviewed in *Our Generation,* Vol 4, No. 4.

1967. *Big School, Small School: High School Size and Student Behavior,* by Roger G. Barker and Paul V. Gump. Reviewed in *Our Generation,* Vol. 5, No. 1.

1968. *Social Policies for America in the Seventies,* edited by Robert Theobold. Reviewed in *Our Generation,* Vol. 6, No. 4.

1969. *The Pursuit of Loneliness,* by Phillip Slater. Reviewed in *Our Generation,* Vol. 7, no. 3.

1981. *Economic Democracy: The Challenge of the 80's,* by Martin Carnoy and Derek Shearer. Reviewed in *Humanity and Society,* Vol. 5, No. 2.

1982. Review Essay on Jane Mansbridge, *Beyond Adversary Democracy* and Kirkpatrick Sale, *Human Scale,* in *Our Generation,* Vol. 15, No. 2, Summer.

1987. *The Evolution of Cooperation,* by Robert Axelrod. Reviewed in *Our Generation,* Vol. 18, No 2, Spring/Summer.

References and Selected Bibliography

Adorno, Theodore *et al., The Authoritarian Personality,* (New York: Harper, 1950).

Allport, Floyd H., *Structuring of Events,"Psychological Review,* 1961, 281-303.

Arendt, Hannah, *Origins of Totalitarianism,* (Cleveland: Meridian Books, 1966).

Arendt, Hannah, *On Revolution,* (New York: Penguin Books, 1977).

Argyris, Chris and David A. Schon, *Theory and Practice: Increasing Professional Effectiveness,* (Washington, D.C.: Jossey Bass, 1974).

Argyris, Chris, *Personality and Organization: The Conflict Between the System and the Individual,* (New York: Harper, 1957).

Aronowitz, Stanley, *False Promises: The Shaping of the American Working Class Consciousness,* (New York: Seabury Press, 1974).

Ashbee, Charles R., *Craftsmanship in a Competitive Industry,* (New York: Garland Publishers, 1977).

Balbus, Isaac D., *Marxism and Domination,* (Princeton: Princeton University Press, 1982).

Barber, Benjamin R., *Strong Democracy: Participatory Politics for a New Age,* (Berkeley: University of California Press, 1984).

Barker, Roger G. and Paul V. Gump, *Big School, Small School: High School Size and Student Behavior,* (Palo Alto: Stanford University Press, 1964).

Bell, Daniel, *The End of Ideology: On the Exhaustion of Political Ideas in the Fifties,* (Glencoe: Free Press, 1960).

Bell, Daniel, "The Subversion of Collective Bargaining," in Gerry G. Hunnius *et al.* (eds), *Workers' Control: A Reader on Labor and Social Change,* (New York: Vintage, 1973).

Berger, Peter and Thomas Luckman, *The Social Construction of Reality,* (New York: Anchor, 1967).

Bernstein, Paul, 1974. "Worker-owned Plywood Co-ops in the Northwest," *Working Papers for a New Society,* Summer.

Bernstein, Paul, *Workplace Democratization: Its Internal Dynamics,* (Kent: Kent State University Press, 1976).

Blauner, Robert, *Alienation and Freedom: The Factory Worker and His Industry,* (Chicago: University of Chicago Press, 1964).

Blumberg, Paul, *Industrial Democracy: The Sociology of Participation,* (New York: Schocken, 1973).

Bookchin, Murray, *Post Scarcity Anarchism,* (Berkeley: Ramparts, 1971).

Bookchin, Murray, *The Limits of the City,* (Montréal: Black Rose, 1986).

Bookchin, Murray, *Towards an Ecological Society,* (Montréal: Black Rose, 1980).

Bookchin, Murray, *The Modern Crisis,* (Philadelphia: New Society Publishers, 1986).

Bookchin, Murray, *Remaking Society: Pathways to a Green Future,* (Boston: South End Press, 1990).

Borsodi, Ralph, *Prosperity and Security,* (New York: Harper and Row, 1939).

Borsodi, Ralph, *Seventeen Problems of Man and Society,* (Anand, India: Charotar Book Stall, 1968).

Borsodi, Ralph, *This Ugly Civilization,* (Philadelphia: Porcupine Press, 1975). Reprint of 1929 edition.

Boulding, Kenneth, *The Image: Knowledge in Life and Society,* (Ann Arbor: University of Michigan Press, 1961).

Boulding, Kenneth, *The Organizational Revolution: A Study in the Ethics of Economic Organization,* (Chicago: Quadrangle, 1968).

Bourne, Randolph, *War and The Intellectuals,* (New York: Harper and Row, 1964).

Boyte, Harry, *Common Wealth,* (New York: Free Press, 1989).

Boyte, Harry, *Community Is Possible,* (New York: Harper & Row, 1984).

Boyte, Harry, *The Backyard Revolution,* (Philadelphia: Temple, 1980).

Braverman, Harry, *Labor and Monopoly Capital: The Degradation of Work in the Twentieth Century,* (New York: Monthly Review, 1974).

Brecher, Jeremy, *Strike,* (Boston: South End Press, 1972).

Brecher, Jeremy and Tim Costello, *Building Bridges,* (New York: Monthly Review Press, 1990).

Brown, Norman O., *Life Against Death,* (Middletown: Wesleyan University Press, 1959).

Burnheim, John, *Is Democracy Possible? The Alternative to Electoral Politics,* (Berkeley, CA: University of California Press, 1985).

Burns, Thomas, Lars Erik Karlsson, and Velijko Rus (eds), *Work and Power,* (Beverly Hills: Sage, 1979).

Callicott, J. Baird, *In Defense of the Land Ethic,* (New York: State University of New York, 1989).

Campbell, Alistair *et al., Worker Owners: The Mondragon Achievement,* (London: The Anglo-German Foundation, 1977).

Capouya, Emile and Keitha Tompkins (eds), *The Essential Kropotkin,* (New York: Liveright, 1975).

Carnoy, Martin and Derek Shearer, *Economic Democracy: The Challenge of the 1980s,* (White Plains: Sharpe, 1980).

Case, John and Rosemary C.R. Taylor, *Co-ops, Communes, and Collectives,* (New York: Pantheon, 1979).

Chase, Steve (ed), *Defending the Earth: A Dialogue Between Murray Bookchin and Dave Foreman,* (Boston: South End Press, 1991).

Coates, Gary (ed), *Resettling America: Energy, Ecology, and Community,* (Andover: Brick House, 1981).

Cole, George D. H., *Guild Socialism Restated,* (New Brunswick: Transaction, 1980). Reprint of 1920 edition.

Comfort, Alex, *Authority and Delinquency in the Modern State,* (London: Routledge and Kegan Paul, 1950).

Cooley, Charles H., *Human Nature and the Social Order,* (New York: Schocken, 1964).

Cronin, Thomas E., *Direct Democracy: The Politics of Initiative, Referendum and Recall,* (Cambridge: Harvard University Press, 1989).

Dahl, Robert A., *After the Revolution? Authority in a Good Society,* (New Haven: Yale University Press, 1970).

Dahl, Robert A. with Edward R. Tufte, *Size and Democracy,* (Palo Alto: Stanford University Press, 1973).

Dahl, Robert A., 1977. "On Removing Certain Impediments to Democracy in the United States," *Political Quarterly,* 92, pp. 1-20.

De Tocqueville, Alexis, 1960. *Democracy in America,* (New York: Vintage, 1960). Originally printed 1835-1840.

Diamond, Stanley, *In Search of The Primitive,* (New Brunswick: Transaction, 1974).

Djilas, Milovan, *The New Class,* (New York: Praeger, 1957).

Dobson, Andrew, *Green Political Thought,* (London: Unwin Hyman, 1990).

Dolgoff, Sam (ed), *Bakunin on Anarchism,* (Quebec: Black Rose, 1980).

Domhoff, G. William, *The Higher Circles,* (New York: Vintage, 1971).

Dunn, William N, "Self-management and the Crisis of Public Organization in Advanced Industrial Society," paper given at the Third International Conference on Self-management. (Washington, D.C.: The American University, June 1976).

Elliot, T.S., *The Wasteland,* (New York: Harper, 1946).

Ellerman, David, *On the Legal Structure of Workers' Cooperatives: An Overview,* (Cambridge: The Industrial Cooperative Association, 1978).

Ellsberg, Daniel, Introduction to E. F. Thompson and Don Smith (eds)., *Protest and Survive,* (New York: Monthly Review, 1981).

Engels, Friederich, *Socialism: Utopian and Scientific,* (New York: Pathfinder, 1972).

Espinosa, Juan G., and Andrew Zimbalist, *Economic Democracy: Workers' Participation in Chilean Industry, 1970-1973,* . Updated Student Edition. (New York: Basic, 1981).

Etzioni, Amitai, 1972. "Basic Human Needs, Alienation, and Inauthenticity" in John Glass and John Staude (eds). *Humanistic Society: Today's Challenge to Sociology,* (Santa Monica: Goodyear, 1972).

Follett, Mary Parker, *The New State: Group Organization the Solution of Popular Government,* (Magnolia, MA: Peter Smith, 1965). Reprint of 1919 publication.

Freire, Paulo, *Pedagogy of The Oppressed,* (New York: Seabury, 1974).

Freud, Sigmund, *Civilization and its Discontents,* (New York: Norton, 1961).

American Friends Service Committee, *Speak Truth to Power,* (Philadelphia: AFSC, 1962).

Fromm, Erich, *Marx's Concept of Man,* (New York: Continuum, 1989).

Fromm, Erich and Michael Maccoby, *Social Character in a Mexican Village,* (Englewood Cliffs: Prentice Hall, 1970).

Fromm, Erich, *The Sane Society,* (New York: Holt, Rinehart, Winston, 1955).

Fromm, Erich, *Escape From Freedom,* (New York: Rinehart, 1941).

Garson, G. David, "Self-management and the Public Sector." Paper given at the Second International Conference on Self-management. (Ithaca: Cornell University, June 1975).

Goodman, Paul, *Growing Up Absurd: Problems of Youth in the Organized Society,* (New York: Vintage, 1960).

Goodman, Paul (ed), *Seeds of Liberation,* (New York: George Braziller, 1962).

Goodman, Paul, *People or Personnel: Decentralizing the Mixed System,* (New York: Random House, 1965).

Gorz, André, *Strategy for Labor,* (Boston: Beacon Press, 1967).

Gorz, André (ed), *The Division of Labor,* (Atlantic Highlands, NJ: Humanities Press, 1976).

Gorz, André, "Workers' Control is More Than Just That," in Frank Lindenfeld and Joyce Rothschild-Whitt (eds), *Workplace Democracy and Social Change,* (Boston: Porter Sargent, 1982).

Gorz, André, *Ecology as Politics,* (Boston: South End Press, 1980).

Gramsci, Antonio, *Selections from the Prison Notebooks,* (New York: International Publishers, 1971).

Gutierrez-Johnson, Ana and William F. Whyte, "The Mondragon System of Worker Production Cooperatives," in Frank Lindenfeld and Joyce Rothschild-Whitt (eds), *Workplace Democracy and Social Change,* (Boston: Porter Sargent, 1982).

Habermas, Jurgen, *Legitimation Crisis,* (Boston: Beacon Press, 1975).

Habermas, Jurgen, *Theory and Practice,* (Boston: Beacon Press, 1973).

Hackman, Richard J. and Greg Oldham, *Work Redesign,* (Reading: Addison Wesley, 1980).

Hampden-Turner, Charles, *Radical Man,* (New York: Anchor, 1971).

Henderson, Hazel, *Creating Alternative Futures: The End of Economics,* (New York: Berkeley Windhover, 1978).

Hobbes, Thomas, *Leviathan,* (New York: Dutton, 1950).

Holleb, Gordon P. and Walter H. Abrams, *Alternatives in Community Health,* (Boston: Beacon Press, 1975).

Homans, George C., *The Human Group,* (New York: Harcourt Brace, 1950).

Hunnius, Gerry G., David Garson, and John Case (eds), *Workers' Control: A Reader on Labor and Social Change,* (New York: Vintage Books, 1973).

Illich, Ivan, *Tools for Conviviality,* (New York: Harper and Row, 1973).

Illich, Ivan, *Deschooling Society,* (New York: Harper and Row, 1971).

Kohr, Leopold, *The Breakdown of Nations,* (New York: E.P. Dutton, 1978). Reprint of 1957 edition with foreword by Kirkpatrick Sale.

Kohr, Leopold, *The Overdeveloped Nations,* (New York: Schocken, 1978).

Kolakowski, Leszek, *Main Currents of Marxism: Its Rise, Growth, and Dissolution,* (New York: Oxford University Press, 1972).

Krimerman, Len and Frank Lindenfeld (eds), *When Workers Decide: Workplace Democracy Takes Root in America,* (Philadelphia: New Society Publishers, 1991).

Kropotkin, Peter, *Fields, Factories, and Workshops,* (New York: Harper and Row, 1975).

Lefebvre, Henri, *Everyday Life In the Modern World,* (New York: Harper and Row, 1971).

Lenin, Vladimir I., *The State and Revolution,* (New York: S. French, 1977).

Lewin, Kurt, "Group Decision and Social Change," in Theodore M. Newcomb and Eugene L. Hartley (eds). *Readings in Social Psychology,* (New York: Henry Holt, 1947).

Lindenfeld, Frank and Joyce Rothschild-Whitt (eds), *Workplace Democracy and Social Change,* (Boston: Porter Sargent, 1982).

Lodge, George, *The New American Ideology,* (New York: Alfred Knopf, 1975).

Lukacs, George, *History and Class Consciousness,* (Cambridge: MIT Press, 1971). Originally published in 1922.

Lukes, Steven, *Power: A Radical View,* (London: Macmillan, 1974).

Macdonald, Dwight, *The Root is Man,* (Alhambra, CA: Cunningham Press, 1953).

Macpherson, C.B., *The Life and Times of Liberal Democracy,* (Oxford: Oxford University Press, 1977).

Mansbridge, Jane, *Beyond Adversary Democracy,* (Chicago: University of Chicago Press, 1980).

Mansbridge, Jane, *Beyond Self-Interest,* (Chicago: University of Chicago Press, 1990).

Mansbridge, Jane, "Measuring the Effects of Direct Democracy," paper presented at the annual meeting of the International Political Science Association. (Paris, July 1985).

Mansbridge, Jane, *Why We Lost the ERA,* (Chicago: University of Chicago Press, 1986).

Marcuse, Herbert, *Eros and Civilization,* (New York: Random House, 1955).

Marcuse, Herbert, *One Dimensional Man,* (Boston: Beacon Press, 1964).

Marx, Karl, *Economic and Philosophical Manuscripts,* (New York: McGraw-Hill, 1956).

Marx, Karl and Friederich Engels, *Communist Manifesto,* (New York: Modern Library, 1959).

Maslow, Abraham H., *Eupsychian Management: A Journal,* (Homewood: R. D Irwin, 1965).

Maslow, Abraham H., *Toward a Psychology of Being,* (Princeton: Van Nostrand, 1962).

Mills, C. Wright, *The Power Elite,* (New York: Oxford University Press, 1959).

Morehouse, Ward (ed), *Building Sustainable Communities: Tools and Concepts For Self Reliant Economic Change,* (New York: Bootstrap Press, 1989).

Mumford, Lewis, *Technics and Civilization,* (New York: Harcourt Brace, 1934).

Mumford, Lewis, *The Condition of Man,* (New York: Harper and Row, 1973). Reprint of 1944 edition with new preface by the author.

Neill, A. S., *Summerhill,* (New York: Hart, 1960).

Nisbet, Robert A., *Community and Power,* (New York: Oxford University Press, 1962).

Offe, Claus and Helmut Wiesenthal, "Two Logics of Collective Action: Theoretical Notes on Social Class and Organizational Form," in Maurice Zeitlin (ed), *Political Power and Social Theory, vol. 1,* (Greenwich: JAI Press, 1980).

Ophuls, William, *Ecology and the Politics of Scarcity,* (San Francisco: Freeman, 1977).

Pannekoek, Anton, "Workers' Councils" in Root and Branch Collective (eds), *Root and Branch,* (Greenwich: Fawcett, 1975).

Pareto, Vilfredo, *Mind and Society: A Treatise on General Sociology,* (New York: Dover, 1963).

Pateman, Carol, *Participation and Democratic Theory,* (Cambridge: Cambridge University Press, 1970).

Rawls, John, *A Theory of Justice,* (Cambridge: Harvard University Press, 1971).

Reich, Wilhelm, *The Mass Psychology of Fascism,* (New York: Farrar Straus, 1970).

Reich, Wilhelm, *Character Analysis,* (New York: Farrar Straus and Giroux, 1974).

Riesman, David with Nathan Glazer and Reuel Denney, *The Lonely Crowd,* (New Haven: Yale University Press, 1973).

Sale, Kirkpatrick, *Human Scale,* (New York: Coward McCann and Geoghegan, 1980).

Schumacher, Ernest F., *Small is Beautiful: Economics as if People Mattered,* (New York: Harper Colophon, 1975). Introduction by Theodore Roszak.

Sharp, Gene, *Social Power and Political Freedom,* (Boston: Porter Sargent, 1980).

Shepard, Paul, *Thinking Animals,* (New York: Viking, 1978).

Stein, Maurice, *Eclipse of Community: An Interpretation,* (Princeton: Princeton University Press, 1972).

Stone, Katherine, "The Origin of the Job Structure in the Steel Industry," in Root and Branch Collective (eds), *Root and Branch,* (Greenwich: Fawcett, 1975).

Tipps, Dean and Lee Webb, *State and Local Tax Revolt: New Directions for the 80s,* (Washington D.C.: Center for Policy Alternatives, 1980).

Vanek, Jaroslav, *The Participatory Economy,* (Ithaca, NY: Cornell University Press, 1971).

Vanek, Jaroslav, *The Labor Managed Economy: Some Fundamental Considerations on Financing and the Form of Ownership Under Labor Management,* (Ithaca: Cornell University Press, 1977).

Veblen, Thorstein, *The Instinct of Workmanship,* (New York: W.W. Norton, 1964). Reprint of 1914 publication.

Verba, Sidney and Norman H. Nie, *Political Participation in America,* (New York: Harper and Row, 1961).

Walzer, Michael, *Spheres of Justice,* (New York: Basic, 1974).

Ward, Benjamin, "The Firm in Illyria: Market Syndicalism," *American Economic Review,* 48, 1958.

Webb, Sidney and Beatrice Webb, "Constitution of the Socialist Commonwealth of Great Britain," in Ken Coates and Tony Topham (eds)., *Workers' Control,* (London: Panther Books, 1970). Reprint of the Webbs' 1920 publication.

Weber, Max, *Economy and Society: An Outline of Interpretive Sociology,* (New York: Bedminster, 1968).

Wolff, Robert Paul, *In Defense of Anarchism,* (New York: Harper and Row, 1970).

Index

About South End Press

South End Press is a nonprofit, collectively-run book publisher with over 150 titles in print. Since our founding in 1977, we have tried to meet the needs of readers who are exploring, or are already committed to, the politics of fundamental social change.

Our goal is to publish books that encourage critical thinking and constructive action on the key political, cultural, social, economic, and ecological issues shaping life in the United States and in the world. In this way, we hope to give expression to a wide diversity of democratic social movements and to provide an alternative to the products of corporate publishing.

If you would like a free catalog of South End Press books or information about our membership program—which offers two free books and a 40% discount on all titles—please write us at South End Press, 116 Saint Botolph Street, Boston, MA 02115.

Other Books of Interest Available From South End Press

Looking Forward:
Participatory Economics For The Twenty First Century
by Michael Albert and Robin Hahnel

Remaking Society:
Pathways to a Green Future
by Murray Bookchin

The Politics of Human Services:
A Radical Alternative to the Welfare State
by Steven Wineman

The Imagination of the New Left
by George Katsiaficas